THE CANADIAN ENCYCLOPEDIC DIGEST
FUNDAMENTALS OF ONTARIO
REAL PROPERTY LAW

J. Leanne Andree, B.A., LL.B.

Originally published as Volume 28, Title 123 of
The Canadian Encyclopedic Digest (Ontario), Third Edition

THOMSON

™

CARSWELL

National Library of Canada has Catalogued this publication as follows:

Andree, J. Leanne
The Canadian encyclopedic digest Fundamentals of Ontario real property law / J. Leanne Andree.

Being title 123 from volume 28 of the Canadian encyclopedic digest (Ontario) Third edition.

Includes bibliographical references and index.
ISBN 0-459-24104-4

1. Real property--Ontario--Digests.
I. Carswell Company
II. Title.
III. Title: Fundamentals of Ontario real property law.

KEO236.A76 2003   346.71304'3'02638   C2003-904432-7
KF570.A86 2003

∞ The paper used in this publication meets the minimum requirements of the American National Standard for Information Sciences – Permanence of Paper for Printed Library Materials. ANSI Z39.48-1984.

FOREWORD

Property is one of those essential topics. It is found in the first year curriculum in every law school in Canada, and among law students it has gained the reputation - whether justified or not - of being among the most difficult subjects encountered during one's legal education.

It may be challenging, but it is also engaging. The law of property as understood in Canada is a multi-faceted subject; it is a vein of law that is both deep and rich. However, to mine the depths one needs effective tools. This collection of principles and authorities provides for students an accessible treatment of basic concepts. Most of the topics addressed are to be found in the study of property in first year. Beyond this, it furnishes a foundation for research. Indeed, despite the central place of property doctrine in the law, there are few research resources that provide the kind of ordered and detailed treatment of the case law and statutory refinements as that found in Fundamentals of Ontario Real Property Law.

Property law might appear at first glance to be a static set of obscure principles, seemingly irrelevant to today's needs. Such a description is thoroughly misguided. In Fundamentals of Ontario Real Property Law, one sees ancient principles articulated in early Canadian decisions set side-by-side with modern adaptations. The property law described here is dynamic and evolving; it is not an ossified relic. Moreover, real property is, to borrow from Gray and Simes, about real people. It is not an assortment of abstract concepts with negligible practical import (see K.J. Gray and P. Simes, *Real Property and Real People* (1981)).

I commend the publishers at Carswell for making this handy research tool and helpful study aid available as a student edition.

Bruce Ziff
University of Alberta

August 5, 2003

iii

C.E.D. Editorial Board

FUNDAMENTALS OF ONTARIO REAL PROPERTY LAW

prepared by

J. Leanne Andree, B.A., LL.B.

updated by the legal editorial staff of Carswell

Table of Cases

All references are to paragraph numbers.

FUNDAMENTALS OF ONTARIO REAL PROPERTY LAW

Table of Statutes

All references are to paragraph numbers.

Table of Rules

All references are to paragraph numbers.

I Interests in Land

1. TENURE

§1   All land in Ontario is held of the Crown in free and common soccage.[1]

1. Constitutional Act, 1791, See R.S.C. 1985, App. II, No. 3, s. 43; **see also** Act respecting Real Property, R.S.O. 1897, c. 330 [NC/NR]; Property and Civil Rights Act, R.S.O. 1990, c. P.29 (in all matters of controversy relative to property and civil rights, resort to be had to laws of England as at October 15, 1792, except as since repealed, altered, varied, modified or affected by any legislation valid in Ontario).

2. POSSESSORY AND PROPRIETARY INTEREST IN AIR SPACE

§2   Although air and space are not susceptible to ownership,[1] some proprietary rights have been exerted over air space. For example, where an advertising sign on an adjoining building projects into the air space over a lessee's premises, the lessee may be entitled to an injunction requiring the sign to be removed.[2]

1. *Lacroix v. R.*, [1954] Ex. C.R. 69.

2. *Kelsen v. Imperial Tobacco Co. of Great Britain & Ireland Ltd.*, [1957] 2 Q.B. 334.

3. MERGER

§3   As a general rule, a lesser estate is merged or extinguished by the acquisition of a higher or greater estate.[1] This remains true although the greater estate was created or acquired with intent to defraud creditors.[2] But the question is one of intention.[3]

1. *Wigle v. Merrick* (1858), 8 U.C.C.P. 307; *Dayle v. Robertson* (1860), 19 U.C.Q.B. 411.

2. *Doe d. McPherson v. Hunter* (1847), 4 U.C.Q.B. 449.

3. *Union Bank of Canada v. Makepeace* (1918), 44 O.L.R. 202 (C.A.); **see also** *Heney v. Low* (1862), 9 Gr. 265; *May Brothers Farms Ltd. v. R.*, [1992] 3 F.C. 389 (C.A.); affirming on other grounds [1991] 1 F.C. 681 (T.D.) (plaintiff seeking declaration that purchase of fee simple resulting in merger of that interest with prior profit à prendre held by plaintiff in respect of land; trial judge holding there being no merger by operation of law, and dismissing application; merger occurring only if that being intention of parties; intention of parties determined by examining deeds).

4.　FIXTURES AS PART OF REAL PROPERTY

(a)　General

§4　To determine whether an article is a fixture or a chattel, the court must consider the degree of annexation; the relationship of the parties interested in the land and the addition; the nature of the property added; and the purpose served and the object of annexation.[1]

> 1.　*Reynolds v. Ashby & Son*, [1904] A.C. 466 at 474 (H.L.); **see also** *Stack v. T. Eaton Co.* (1902), 4 O.L.R. 335 (C.A.); *Ross Cromarty Developments Inc. v. Arthur Bell Holdings Ltd.* (1993), 85 B.C.L.R. (2d) 77 (C.A.) (purchasers dumping sand onto property prior to completion of sale; sand constituting chattel); *Boxrud v. R.* (1996), 12 R.P.R. (3d) 163 (main offices and swimming pool of resort affixed permanently and constituting fixtures; prefabricated rental cottages, docks and wharf designed to be removable and constituting chattels).

§5　Once a chattel is attached to the realty in such a way as to become a fixture, then it is land and no longer a chattel.[1]

> 1.　*Hoppe v. Manners* (1931), 66 O.L.R. 587 (C.A.); **see also** Federal Real Property Act, S.C. 1991, c. 50, s. 2("federal real property"), ("real property") (real property including buildings, structures, improvements and other fixtures on, above or below surface of land); *North West Trust Co. v. Rezyn Developments Inc.*, [1991] 6 W.W.R. 359 (B.C.C.A.) (bowling lanes and associated equipment in recreation centre constituting fixtures); *Bank of Nova Scotia v. Mitz* (1979), 27 O.R. (2d) 250 (C.A.) (barn affixed to ground for purpose of owner making better use of land; no circumstances altering prima facie character of barn as fixture; barn becoming part of realty; horse stalls losing character of chattels); *Pezzack v. Irving Bank Canada* (1989), 69 O.R. (2d) 536 (H.C.) (equipment being fixtures, as could be removed without serious injury to realty); *Alberta Agricultural Development Corp. v. Pierog* (1991), 1 Alta. L.R. (3d) 72 (C.A.) (movable skid granaries qualifying as chattels); Landlord and Tenant.

(b)　Effect of Agreement

§6　A party can agree to affix a chattel to the soil of another party so that it becomes part of the other party's freehold, on the terms that the affixing party may retake possession upon the happening of certain events.[1] However, there is no authority for the contention that, by reason of an agreement between the parties, a de facto fixture can become a chattel or is not a fixture when the land to which it is affixed is purchased for value and without notice.[2]

> 1.　*Hobson v. Gorringe*, [1897] 1 Ch. 182; **see also** *Credit Valley Cable TV/FM Ltd. v. Peel Condominium Corp. No. 95* (1980), 27 O.R. (2d) 433 (H.C.) (TV cable installed in walls of building; agreement providing that cable to remain property of installing company; agreement not registered on title but building owners having notice; cable remaining chattel).
>
> 2.　*Miles v. Ankatell* (1898), 25 O.A.R. 458; **see also** *Brazeau v. Wilson* (1916), 36 O.L.R. 396 (C.A.); *Oldershaw v. Garner* (1876), 38 U.C.Q.B. 37; *Pezzack v. Irving Bank Canada* (1989), 69 O.R. (2d) 536 (H.C.) (equipment not trade fixtures, because installed primarily to enhance building and not owner's business).

§7   Chattels incapable of being affixed to the freehold cannot be made fixtures by any form of words.[1]

> 1.   *Agricultural Development Board v. Ricard* (1927), 32 O.W.N. 140 (H.C.) (mortgagee not entitled to injunction to prevent removal of cattle, implements, furniture, etc. from mortgaged premises); **see also** *Credit Valley Cable TV/FM Ltd. v. Peel Condominium Corp. No. 95* (1980), 27 O.R. (2d) 433 (H.C.) (TV cable installed in walls of building; cable readily removed with minimal injury to building; cable remaining chattel).

(c) Buildings as Fixtures

§8   Regarding the question of annexation to the land, a wooden building erected for use as a ship and afterwards used as a dwelling-house, even though it is attached to the land only by its own weight, is viewed differently than is a piece of machinery or other weighty article constructed as a distinct chattel.[1]

> 1.   *Miles v. Ankatell* (1898), 25 O.A.R. 458.

§9   The term "buildings" in a contract for sale and purchase of buildings has been held to include the foundations.[1]

> 1.   *M.J. O'Brien Ltd. v. Freedman* (1923), 54 O.L.R. 455 (C.A.); *Brantford Electric & Power Co. v. Draper* (1896), 28 O.R. 40 (Div. Ct.); affirmed, 24 O.A.R. 301; **see also** Federal Real Property Act, S.C. 1991, c. 50, s. 2("federal real property"), ("real property") (real property including buildings, structures, improvements and other fixtures on, above or below surface of land); *Phillips v. Grand River Farmers' Mutual Fire Insurance Co.* (1881), 46 U.C.Q.B. 334.

II   Estate in Fee Simple

1. WORDS IN CONVEYANCE SUFFICIENT TO
CREATE FEE SIMPLE

(a) General

§10   At common law, it was essential that a grant be to the grantee "and his heirs" in order to convey a fee simple to a natural person. If the technical words of limitation"and his heirs" were not used in the operative clause of the conveyance, the grantee obtained only a life estate.[1] However, by statute, in all conveyances made after July 1, 1886, it is not necessary to use the word "heirs" in the limitation of an estate in fee simple, but it is sufficient to use the words"in fee simple" or such other words as sufficiently indicate that the conveyance is intended to create a fee simple.[2]

> 1. *Re Airey* (1921), 21 O.W.N. 190 (H.C.); **see also** *Re Davison's Settlement*, [1913] 2 Ch. 498 (conveyance to person and "his heir" operating to convey life estate only; at common law, in order to convey fee simple to corporation sole, essential to use words"and his successors" in operative clause of conveyance); *Gold v. Rowe* (1913), 23 O.W.R. 794 (H.C.) (transfer to "A in fee simple" passing life interest); *Jack v. Lyons* (1879), 19 N.B.R. 336 (C.A.) (transfer to A "forever" passing life interest); *Millard v. Gregoire* (1913), 11 D.L.R. 539 (C.A.).
>
> 2. Conveyancing and Law of Property Act, R.S.O. 1990, c. C.34, s. 5(1), (2), (5).

§11   Where no words of limitation are used, the conveyance passes a fee simple (or the largest estate held by the grantor) unless a contrary intention appears from the conveyance.[1] Where a conveyance executed after July 1, 1886 contains no words of limitation, and the words in "fee simple" are not used, the effect of the conveyance is to pass all the interest of the grantor.[2] To convey a fee simple it is not necessary to use the word "grant" in the operative clause; the word"transfer" is adequate.[3]

> 1. Conveyancing and Law of Property Act, R.S.O. 1990, c. C.34, s. 5(3), (4); **see also** Federal Real Property Act, S.C. 1991, c. 50, s.C. 1991, c. 50, s. 9 (fee simple or equivalent estate in property conveyed although no words of limitation used in instrument, providing that Her Majesty having power to grant such estate in property and no contrary intention expressed in instrument); *Armstrong v. Brown*, [1952] O.W.N. 55 (C.A.).
>
> 2. *Re Airey* (1921), 21 O.W.N. 190 (H.C.); *Chandler v. Gibson* (1901), 2 O.L.R. 442 (C.A.); **see also** *Bayliss v. Balfe* (1917), 38 O.L.R. 437 (H.C.).
>
> 3. *Re Airey* (1921), 21 O.W.N. 190 (H.C.).

§12   "Fee" refers to an interest involving an absolute right of disposal.[1]

> 1. *Dean v. Coyle*, [1973] 3 O.R. 185 (Co. Ct.); **see also** *Taylor, Re* (1916), 36 O.L.R. 116 (C.A.) (words "in fee" not necessarily meaning in fee simple).

§13   A conveyance of land by way of mortgage to the mortgagee, omitting the word "heirs", is effective to convey a life estate only and not the fee simple.[1]

   1.   *Millard v. Gregoire* (1913), 11 D.L.R. 539 (C.A.).

§14   A limitation in a conveyance or will which before May 27, 1956 would have created an estate tail is now to be construed as an estate in fee simple or the greatest estate that the grantor or testator has had in the land.[1]

   1.   Conveyancing and Law of Property Act, R.S.O. 1990, c. C.34, s. 4.

(b) Inconsistency Between Habendum and Operative Clause

§15   The office of the habendum is properly to determine what estate or interest is granted by the deed,[1] though this may be and sometimes is done in the premises, in which case the habendum may lessen, enlarge, explain or qualify but not totally contradict or be repugnant to the estate granted in the premises.[2]

   1.   See Deeds and Documents (as to interpretation of repugnant provisions in a deed).

   2.   *Gold v. Row* (1913), 4 O.W.N. 642 (H.C.); **see also** *Spencer v. Registrar of Titles*, [1906] A.C. 503 (P.C. [Aus.]) (habendum cannot retract gift in premises; however, it may construe and explain sense in which words in premises should be taken).

§16   Where land is granted to a person solely in fee simple by the operative clause, and the habendum purports to limit the estate to the person and his or her spouse, the habendum is repugnant to the operative clause and the spouse takes no interest.[1]

   1.   *Langlois v. Lesperance* (1892), 22 O.R. 682 (H.C.).

§17   Where a grantee is given a life estate by an operative clause, a habendum which purports to give the grantee a fee simple is repugnant and the grantee obtains only a life estate.[1] Similarly, where an estate in fee simple is given to a grantee by an operative clause, such an estate cannot be cut down by an inconsistent habendum.[2] Although it is reasonable to construe grants in light of the manifest intention of the party executing, which is to be gathered from the whole of the instrument, it is the general rule that a deed is to be construed most strongly against the grantor, and that when the grantor has by the premises in the deed plainly granted an estate to the grantee and his or her heirs, the grantor cannot retract that disposition by using the words in the habendum utterly inconsistent with the grant of such an estate. If, by the operative clause of the conveyance, lot A is granted and the habendum is of lots A and B, the conveyance will not operate to pass lot B to the grantee.[3]

1. *Purcell v. Tully* (1906), 12 O.L.R. 5 (C.A.).

2. *Doe d. Meyers v. Marsh* (1852), 9 U.C.Q.B. 242.

3. *Doe d. Wood v. Fox* (1846), 3 U.C.Q.B. 134.

§18 Words used in a recital will not prevail over the operative part of a deed which clearly shows the granting of a fee simple on condition subsequent; hence, to create a fee simple determinable, the words "so long as" would have to appear immediately after the granting clause and the usual form of habendum.[1]

1. *Re McKellar*, [1972] 3 O.R. 16 (H.C.); affirmed [1973] 3 O.R. 178n (C.A.).

§19 Where the operative clause of a deed of assignment transfers the indenture only, and the habendum is of the estate in the indenture, the estate passes to the assignee.[1]

1. *Doe d. Wood v. Fox* (1846), 3 U.C.Q.B. 134.

§20 Trusts and uses may be created by the habendum, and it is not necessary to name the cestui que use or cestui que trust in the operative clause.[1]

1. *Spencer v. Registrar of Titles*, [1906] A.C. 503 (P.C. [Aus.]); **see also** *Bayliss v. Balfe* (1917), 38 O.L.R. 437 (H.C.) (property granted to man and his heirs, with habendum to use of grantor until marriage and thereafter to use of intended wife and her heirs; after solemnization of marriage, wife acquiring estate in fee simple).

§21 A habendum is not an essential part of a deed, and the granting or operative part of a deed is sufficient of itself to pass the estate created.[1]

1. *Dunlap v. Dunlap* (1883), 6 O.R. 141; reversed on other grounds, 10 O.A.R. 670; **see also** Short Forms of Conveyances Act, R.S.O. 1980, c. 472 [NC/NR], Sched. A; **see** Deeds and Documents (as to other essential elements of valid deed of grant, such as parties, execution, sealing and delivery).

2. WORDS IN WILL SUFFICIENT TO CREATE FEE SIMPLE

§22 At common law, a devise[1] to a person without any words of limitation gave the devisee an estate for life only.[2] But it is now provided by statute that where any real estate is devised to any person without words of limitation, such devise is construed to pass the whole estate which the testator had power to dispose of by will, unless a contrary intention appears by the will.[3] Where no words of limitation are used, but the executors are directed to sell the property after the death of two devisees, a contrary intention appears on the face of the will and the devisees take life estates only.[4] If land is devised to one "and his heirs but not to their assigns", the devisee takes a fee simple.[5] If a devisee under a will is given an estate in fee simple, that estate cannot be cut down by any subsequent repugnant expression of intention in the will.[6]

1. See §98-105 (as to creation of estates in fee simple by operation of rule in *Shelley's Case* (1581), 1 Co. Rep. 93); Wills (as to rules of construction applicable to wills); Devolution of Estates (as to descent of estate in fee simple).

2. *Doe d. Ford v. Bell* (1850), 6 U.C.Q.B. 527; *Dumble v. Johnson* (1866), 17 U.C.C.P. 9; *Hamilton v. Dennis* (1866), 12 Gr. 325.

3. Succession Law Reform Act, R.S.O. 1990, c. S.26, s. 26; **see also** *Re Armstrong* (1918), 15 O.W.N. 148 (H.C.) (devisee given fee simple); *Re Grafton* (1924), 25 O.W.N. 666 (H.C.); varied on other ground, 26 O.W.N. 262 (Div. Ct.) (testator devising residence to daughter for her own use; daughter obtaining fee simple by force of Wills Act, s. 30); *Re Hammond* (1920), 18 O.W.N. 253 (H.C.); *Re Langevin* (1921), 20 O.W.N. 384 (C.A.); *Chandler v. Gibson* (1901), 2 O.L.R. 442 (C.A.) (remainder to "lawful children" to be read as remainder to "lawful children and their heirs"); *McIsaac v. Beaton* (1905), 38 N.S.R. 60 (C.A.); affirmed (1905), 37 S.C.R. 143 (testator devising land to wife "to be disposed by her amongst my children"; wife holding absolute estate in fee simple; reference to children not cutting down estate).

4. *Re Virtue* (1922), 22 O.W.N. 482 (H.C.).

5. *Traynor v. Keith* (1888), 15 O.R. 469 (Ch.); **see also** *Ahearn v. Ahearn* (1894), 1 N.B. Eq. 53 (S.C.) (only life estate created if word "heirs" not used).

6. *Re Cathcart* (1915), 8 O.W.N. 572 (H.C.); *Re Miller* (1914), 6 O.W.N. 665 (H.C.); *Re Laundry* (1924), 26 O.W.N. 475 (H.C.); *Re Doran* (1924), 25 O.W.N. 665 (H.C.); *Re Lake* (1924), 26 O.W.N. 98 (H.C.); *Re Walker* (1925), 56 O.L.R. 517 (C.A.); *Re Loveless* (1929), 36 O.W.N. 340 (H.C.).

§23   A conveyance by way of mortgage to the mortgagee which omits the word "heirs" is effective to convey a life estate only, and not the fee simple.[1]

1. *Millard v. Gregoire* (1913), 11 D.L.R. 539 (C.A.).

§24   If a testator devises an estate in fee simple, intending the devisee to have all the rights incident to ownership, and attempts to add a gift over by way of executory devise defeating or abridging the estate in fee simple by altering the course of its devolution, which alteration is to take effect at the moment of devolution, such a gift over is bad and no effect can be given to it.[1]

1. *Re Walker* (1925), 56 O.L.R. 517 (C.A.); *Re Moore* (1925), 57 O.L.R. 530; *Re Scott* (1925), 58 O.L.R. 138 (C.A.); *Re Hornell*, [1945] O.R. 58 (C.A.); **but see** *Comiskey v. Bowring-Hanbury*, [1905] A.C. 84 (P.C.).

§25   If a testator seised of an estate in fee simple devises the estate to A absolutely, and to be divided equally among A's children in the event of A's death, then A, if alive at the date of the death of the testator, takes an estate in fee simple in the land.[1] Where land is devised to a person "or his heirs", it will be read as a devise to the person "and his heirs", and the devisee will take a fee simple.[2]

1. *Walker v. Drew* (1892), 22 O.R. 332 (H.C.); **see also** *Re Lake* (1924), 26 O.W.N. 98 (H.C.); *Re Urry* (1929), 35 O.W.N. 281 (Div. Ct.) (if immediate gift to A, with gift over in case of A's death, or any similar expression implying death to be contingent event, gift over taking effect only in event A dying before testator); *Re Hornell*, [1945] O.R. 58 (C.A.) (testator leaving whole of estate to wife, with stipulation that on death of wife remainder to go to their daughter; testator's intention interpreted as wishing wife to have estate absolutely; wife's interest not cut down to life estate merely); *McIsaac v. Beaton* (1905), 38 N.S.R. 60 (C.A.); affirmed (1905), 37 S.C.R. 143 (testator devising all property to spouse, to be divided among children as spouse judging most beneficial; absolute estate in fee simple not cut down by reference to children).

2. *Wright v. Fowler* (1916), 10 O.W.N. 299 (H.C.) (applying language of Eve J. in *Re Clerke*, [1915] 2 Ch. 301; **but see** *Re Whitehead*, [1920] 1 Ch. 298 (in devise to A "or his heirs", words used as words of substitution, not of limitation; A not taking fee simple).

§26   An absolute devise of the rents and profits or of the income from land confers an estate in fee simple upon the devisee; a devise of the rents and profits for life confers a life estate upon the devisee.[1] But a devise not of all the rents and profits but only of certain occasional income derived from pasturage or other casual sources does not confer a fee simple on the devisee.[2]

1. *Brennan v. Munro* (1841), 6 O.S. 92; *Moore v. Power* (1858), 8 U.C.C.P. 109; *Vair v. Doyle* (1922), 23 O.W.N. 407 (H.C.); *Re Thomas* (1901), 2 O.L.R. 660 (Ch.); *McKenzie v. McKenzie* (1924), 56 O.L.R. 247 (H.C.).

2. *McKenzie v. McKenzie* (1924), 56 O.L.R. 247 (H.C.), per Riddell J.

3. ESTATES BY ESTOPPEL

§27   An interest in land is created by estoppel when the grantor has no legal estate or interest in land at the time of the grant, and although the grantee's title by estoppel is good not as against the world but only as against the grantor (who is estopped by his or her own deed as against him or herself), it has all the elements of a real title. Where the grantor subsequently obtains a legal title to such land, the legal estate or interest is said to feed the estoppel, and the original grant then takes effect in interest and not by estoppel, but the grantor is estopped from saying he or she had no interest at the time of the grant. Thus, by operation of law, the grantee's estate by estoppel, valid only against the grantor, becomes an interest valid against the rest of the world, without the necessity for the grantee to obtain a further or supplementary grant from the grantor, or without any further documentation.[1]

1. *Re Certain Titles to Land in Ontario*, [1973] 2 O.R. 613 (C.A.); *Niagara-on-the-Lake (Town) v. Gross Estate* (1991), 4 M.P.L.R. (2d) 54 (Gen. Div.); affirmed (1993), 13 M.P.L.R. (2d) 11 (C.A.); leave to appeal to S.C.C. refused (1993), 18 M.P.L.R. (2d) 100n (S.C.C.); **see also** Estoppel.

4. RIGHT TO EVERYTHING IN, ON OR OVER THE LAND

§28   There may be a severance of the mines and minerals from the ownership of the surface. The mines and minerals so severed are a separate tenement capable of being held for the same estates as other hereditaments. A separate estate in fee simple may be held in mines and minerals in, on or under land, apart from the ownership of the surface.[1]

1. *Algoma Ore Properties v. Smith*, [1953] O.R. 634 (C.A.); **see also** Mines and Minerals.

III   Estate in Fee Tail

1. FATE OF ESTATE IN FEE TAIL

§29   At common law, to create a fee tail[1] in favour of a natural person, it was essential to grant the property to the grantee"and heirs of his body". It was essential to use the technical word of limitation "heirs" accompanied by some other phrase such as "of his or her body" or "of his or her flesh", indicating that heirs were to include only the direct lineal descendants of the grantee, and not all heirs both lineal and collateral. Eventually, it was legislated that in all conveyances made after July 1, 1886,[2] it was no longer necessary to use the words "heirs of the body" in the limitation of an estate in fee tail, or to use the words "heirs male of the body" or "heirs female of the body" in the limitation of an estate in tail male or in tail female. It was sufficient to use the words "in tail", "in tail male" or "in tail female", according to the limitation intended, or to use any other words sufficiently indicating the limitation intended.

1.   Estate in fee tail was a statutory estate created by De Donis Conditionalibus (1285), 13 Edw. I, c. 1, which became part of Ontario's real property law by the introduction of English law into Upper Canada as of October 15, 1792 [see Property and Civil Rights Act, R.S.O. 1990, c. P.29]. De Donis Conditionalibus was re-enacted as s. 1 of R.S.O. 1897, c. 330, and was repealed by S.O. 1956, c. 76, s. 1; **see also** Estates Tail Act, R.S.O. 1950, c. 117, which was repealed by S.O. 1956, c. 19.

2.   Conveyancing and Law of Property Act, R.S.O. 1950, c. 68, s. 4. For the subsequent historical development of these provisions, see S.O. 1956, c. 10, and R.S.O. 1960, c. 66, ss. 4 and 5.

§30   In the present day, a limitation in a conveyance or will which before May 27, 1956 would have created an estate tail must be construed as an estate in fee simple or the greatest estate that the grantor or testator had in the land.[1]

1.   Conveyancing and Law of Property Act, R.S.O. 1990, c. C.34, s. 4; **see also** Pt. II Estate in Fee Simple (§§10-28).

2. COMMON LAW

§31   Prima facie, "issue" means heirs of the body. Consequently, unless the context of the will made it clear that"issue" was not used in its prima facie sense, a devise to A and A's issue conferred an estate in fee tail upon A.[1] Where land was devised to a devisee "and to his heirs lawfully begotten", the devisee took an estate in fee tail.[2] If an estate for life was devised to A, with remainder to the heirs of the body of A, then by the operation of the rule of law known as the rule in *Shelley's Case*, A took a fee tail.[3]

1.   *Roddy v. Fitzgerald* (1858), 6 H.L. Cas. 823.

11

2. *Ray v. Gould* (1857), 15 U.C.Q.B. 131.

3. *See Also* §§98-105 (rule in *Shelley's Case*).

§32   Where real estate was devised over in default of heirs of the first devisee, and the ulterior devisee stood related to the prior devisee so as to be in the course of descent from him or her, whether in the lineal or collateral line and however remote, as the prior devisee in that case could not die without heirs while the devisee over existed, the word "heirs" was construed to mean "heirs of the body". Accordingly, the estate of the first devisee, by the effect of the devise over, was restricted to an estate tail, and the estate of the devisee over became a remainder expectant on that estate.[1]

> 1. *Re McDonald* (1903), 6 O.L.R. 478 at 479 (C.A.); *Colliton v. Landergan* (1888), 15 O.R. 471 (Ch.); *Doe d. Anderson v. Fairfield* (1848), 3 U.C.Q.B. 140; *Iler v. Elliot* (1872), 32 U.C.Q.B. 434; **see also** *Re Thompson*, [1936] O.R. 8 (C.A.) (devise to testator's son with proviso that if son "dies without leaving an heir", estate tail in son created).

§33   If land was devised to A and the heirs of A's body, an estate in fee tail was thereby created, and any power given to A to vary the proportions to be taken by his or her heirs in tail did not affect the quality of the estate.[1] Similarly, where a fee tail was created by a devisee to A and the heirs of A's body, a modification of the estate given to the heirs, however plainly inconsistent with an estate of inheritance, could not be given.[2]

> 1. *Fleming v. McDougall* (1880), 27 Gr. 459; **see also** *Jordan v. Adams* (1861), 9 C.B.N.S. 483 (once donor using term "heirs" or "heirs of the body" as following on estate of freehold, no inference or declaration of intention, however explicit, having effect); *Trust & Loan Co. v. Fraser* (1871), 18 Gr. 19 (where testator devising property to A and to heirs of A's body with power to appoint to any one as such heirs, A taking estate in fee tail; mortgages executed by A taking precedence over claims of children under power of appointment which A afterwards executing in their favour); *Fetherston v. Fetherston* (1835), 6 E.R. 1363 at 1366 (H.L.) (applying only where testator using words "heirs" or "heirs of the body" in their technical sense and not in some other sense).
>
> 2. *Re Cleator* (1885), 10 O.R. 326 (C.A.).

§34   By the rule of construction known as the rule in *Wild's Case*, if A devised his or her lands to B and B's children or to B and B's issue, and B had no issue at the date of the will, B would take an estate in fee tail.[1] But if B did have issue at the date of the will, then, under such a devise, the words "children" or "issue" were considered as words of purchase conferring an interest upon the children, and not as words of limitation denoting the kind of estate to be taken by B.[2] However, if there was a devise by A to B for life and on B's death to the children of B, then even if at the date of the will B had no children, any children would take by way of remainder and B would take merely a life estate.[3]

1. *Wild's Case*, 77 E.R. 277; *Peterborough Real Estate Co. v. Patterson* (1888), 15 O.A.R. 751 (first branch of rule in *Wild's Case*); *Byng v. Byng* (1862), 10 H.L. Cas. 171; **see also** *Grant v. Fuller* (1902), 33 S.C.R. 34; *Re Haig* (1924), 57 O.L.R. 129 (C.A.); *Re Beckstead* (1928), 62 O.L.R. 690 (C.A.).

2. *Peterborough Real Estate Co. v. Patterson* (1888), 15 O.A.R. 751 (second branch of rule in *Wild's Case*).

3. *Peterborough Real Estate Co. v. Patterson* (1888), 15 O.A.R. 751 (third branch of rule in *Wild's Case*).

§35 The rules enunciated in *Wild's Case* are rules of construction and are always subject to a contrary expression of intention.[1]

1. *Byng v. Byng* (1862), 10 H.L. Cas. 171; **see also** *Peterborough Real Estate Co. v. Patterson* (1888), 15 O.A.R. 751 (devise to A and to A's wife, B, and"to their children and children's children for ever . . . Provided always that A and B shall not be at liberty . . . or dispose of [said lot] as it is my will that the same may be entailed for the benefit of their children"; held that A and B taking life estates); *Grant v. Fuller* (1902), 33 S.C.R. 34 (land devised to A for life "and to her children if any at her death"; A having no children at date of will; A taking life estate because"the gift to the children was not 'immediate', and the word 'children' cannot be construed as a word of limitation"; *Re Haig* combined application of rule in *Shelley's Case* and first branch of rule in *Wild's Case*; land devised to A for life, remainder on death to sons and daughters; A at date of will having no children; A taking estate in fee tail; words "sons and daughters" read as words of limitation); *Sweet v. Platt* (1886), 12 O.R. 229; *Young v. Denike* (1901), 2 O.L.R. 723 (Ch.); *Chandler v. Gibson* (1901), 2 O.L.R. 442 (C.A.); *Sharon v. Stuart* (1906), 12 O.L.R. 605 (K.B.); *McPhail v. McIntosh* (1887), 14 O.R. 312 (C.A.), *Jeffrey v. Scott* (1879), 27 Gr. 314; *Re Robertson* (1916), 10 O.W.N. 365 (H.C.); *Purcell v. Tully* (1906), 12 O.L.R. 5 (C.A.); *Stuart v. Taylor* (1914), 33 O.L.R. 20 (C.A.); **but see** *Re Beckstead* (1928), 62 O.L.R. 690 (C.A.) (decision in *Haig* confined to particular facts before court; appellate division failing to consider third branch of rule in *Wild's Case*; by devise to A for life, remainder "to his first and each subsequent son successively according to seniority", A obtaining life estate).

§36 A devise of land in the words "all of which shall be and is hereby entailed on my said son and his heirs forever" was held by two judges of the Ontario Court of Appeal to confer an estate in fee tail upon the son.[1] A devise to A for life with a remainder in tail made to A's first and other sons successively according to priority of birth conferred upon A not an estate in fee tail but only a life estate.[2]

1. *Culbertson v. McCullough* (1900), 27 O.A.R. 459.

2. *Riddell v. McIntosh* (1885), 9 O.R. 606 (Ch.).

IV   Life Estates

1. CREATION OF LIFE ESTATE

(a) Words in Conveyance Sufficient to Create Life Estate

§37   At common law, if no words of limitation were used in a deed, the deed operated to pass only a life estate.[1] However, conveyances made after July 1, 1886 without words of limitation pass all the estate, right, title, interest, claim and demand that the conveying parties have in, to or on the property conveyed or expressed or intended so to be, or that they have power to convey in, to or on the same.[2]

1. *Re Airey* (1921), 21 O.W.N. 190 (H.C.).

2. Conveyancing and Law of Property Act, R.S.O. 1990, c. C.34, s. 5(3), (5).

(b) Words in Will Sufficient to Create Life Estate

§38   At common law, although the intention to pass a fee simple might appear from other clear expressions in the will, a devise to A simply, without any words of limitation, passes to A a life estate only.[1] But since, by the Succession Law Reform Act,[2] a devise to A simply, without words of limitation, is to be construed so as to pass the whole estate of the testator unless a contrary intention appears, if a testator wishes to devise a life estate, he or she must use some restrictive words indicative of an intention to devise only a life estate.[3]

1. *Doe d. Ford v. Bell* (1850), 6 U.C.Q.B. 527; *Dumble v. Johnson* (1866), 17 U.C.C.P. 9; *Hamilton v. Dennis* (1886), 12 Gr. 325.

2. Succession Law Reform Act, R.S.O. 1990, c. S.26, s. 26.

3. *Re Virtue* (1922), 22 O.W.N. 482 (H.C.) (although no words of limitation used by testator, only life estate passing, as there being direction to executors to sell property on death of devisee); see also *Doe d. Keeler v. Collins* (1850), 7 U.C.Q.B. 519 (property devised to wife "to be at her will and disposal during her life", with subsequent direction as to disposition after her death; wife taking life estate only); *Burgess v. Burrows* (1871), 21 U.C.C.P. 426; *Wilson v. Graham* (1866), 12 O.R. 469 (C.A.); *Re Nelson* (1914), 7 O.W.N. 250 (H.C.); affirmed, 7 O.W.N. 425 (C.A.).

§39   A gift to A, with a direction that at A's death"the residue" or "whatever remains" of the property will go to B, may give A a life interest only, while somewhat similar words may give A an absolute interest, or a life interest with a power of appointment or disposition.[1] Some courts have refused to apply a rigid, technical attitude to the construction of this type of bequest. They look not so much to the institutions chosen by the testator in expressing his or her intention, but rather allow the construction which most closely reflects the testator's true intention.[2] The problem is one of construction, and it is the task of the court to define the intention of the testator through the language he or she has used in the will, in light of the facts and circumstances known to the testator.[3]

1. *Re Cutter* (1916), 37 O.L.R. 42; *Re Walker* (1925), 56 O.L.R. 517 (C.A.); *Re Hornell*, [1944] O.W.N. 664; affirmed [1945] O.R. 58 (testator leaving whole of estate to wife, remainder to daughter on death of wife; testator's intention interpreted as passing life estate); *Montreal Trust Co. v. Tutty*, [1950] 4 D.L.R. 523 (N.S.C.A.); **see also** *Royal Trust Co. v. Freedman* (1973), 41 D.L.R. (3d) 122 (Man. Q.B.); *Montreal Trust Co. v. Klein* (1971), 20 D.L.R. (3d) 487 (Man. C.A.); affirmed (1973), 38 D.L.R. (3d) 320 (S.C.C.).

2. *Montreal Trust Co. v. Tutty*, [1950] 4 D.L.R. 523 (N.S.C.A.) (testatrix leaving residue of estate to husband "to have and to own until his death and then to pass whatever is left of my estate to my nephew"; court refusing to find that effect of will being to make absolute gift of estate to husband and that words attempting to reduce absolute effect of gift being repugnant and void; husband taking life interest only, with power nevertheless to encroach upon principal).

3. *Re Cutter* (1916), 37 O.L.R. 42 (apparent absolute gift by testator to sister cut down to life estate); *Re Hornell*, [1945] O.R. 58 (C.A.); *Montreal Trust Co. v. Tutty*, [1950] 4 D.L.R. 523 (N.S.C.A.); **see also** *Re Walker* (1925), 56 O.L.R. 517 (C.A.) (absolute gift to widow of testator not cut down by direction that on widow's death "any portion . . . undisposed of by her" to go over; latter clause being repugnant to absolute gift); *Aspden v. Seddon* (1874), 10 Ch. App. 396n; on appeal 10 Ch. App. 394 (duty of judge being to construe instrument at hand, and not to refer to construction put by another judge upon instrument perhaps similar but not same).

§40   It is the task of the court to ascertain whether the dominant intention of the testator was to give the devisee a life estate merely, or to give him or her an absolute interest, with all the rights incidental to such an absolute interest. If the court is of the opinion that the latter is the dominant intention of the testator, any subordinate expression of intention purporting to cut down the absolute interest must be rejected as repugnant.[1]

1. *Re Loveless* (1929), 36 O.W.N. 340 (H.C.); *Re Walker* (1925), 56 O.L.R. 517 (C.A.); *Re Lake* (1924), 26 O.W.N. 98 (H.C.); *Re Doran* (1924), 25 O.W.N. 665 (H.C.); *Re Laundry* (1924), 26 O.W.N. 475 (H.C.); *Re Miller* (1914), 6 O.W.N. 665 (H.C.); *Re Cathcart* (1915), 8 O.W.N. 572 (H.C.); *Re Hodgkins* (1918), 14 O.W.N. 105 (H.C.); *Re McClennan* (1925), 58 O.L.R. 24 (C.A.); *Re Scott* (1925), 58 O.L.R. 138 (C.A.).

§41   A testator may, in addition to giving the devisee a mere life estate, also give him or her a power of sale or power of encroachment which may be exercised at any time during the currency of the life estate.[1]

1. *Re Gouinlock* (1915), 8 O.W.N. 561 (H.C.) (question whether testator having given this additional power being "altogether a matter of construction"); *Re Walker* (1925), 56 O.L.R. 517 (C.A.); *Montreal Trust Co. v. Tutty*, [1950] 4 D.L.R. 523 (N.S.C.A.); **see also** *Re Richer* (1919), 46 O.L.R. 367 (C.A.) (testator giving wife "the free use of all my estate, both real and personal, for her lifetime. After [her] decease the balance of my said estate that will remain unspent, if any, I give, devise, and

bequeath to my four children"; widow taking life estate without any power of sale or encroachment; one spends money, not land, and word "unspent" being inappropriate to land); *Re Scott* (1925), 58 O.L.R. 138 (C.A.).; *Re Van de Bogart* (1927), 32 O.W.N. 182 (H.C.); *Re Wallace* (1926), 29 O.W.N. 323 (H.C.); affirmed, 30 O.W.N. 264 (C.A.); *Re McCaffrey* (1927), 32 O.W.N. 97 (H.C.).

§42   In addition to giving a devisee a mere life estate, a testator may also give a power to appoint the remainder, either generally or to a class.[1]

1.   *Wolfe v. Holland* (1912), 3 O.W.N. 900 (Ch.); *Henderson v. Henderson* (1922), 52 O.L.R. 440 (H.C.); **see also** Pt. VI Remainders.

§43   A devise of the profits of land to A for life will give A a life estate.[1] A direction in a will that the testator's wife "shall be allowed to live on the said property during the term of her natural life" gives the wife a life estate.[2] But where a farm is conveyed to A subject to the use by B of a bedroom for as long as B remains resident on the farm, B takes no estate under the deed.[3] Where property is devised to A for life, A being unmarried at the date of the will, remainder to his wife for life, remainder to their children and their heirs, A, now a widower, may marry again and his second wife will be entitled to a life estate.[4]

1.   *Vair v. Doyle* (1922), 23 O.W.N. 407 (H.C.); *Brennan v. Munro* (1841), 6 O.S. 92; *Fulton v. Cummings* (1874), 34 U.C.Q.B. 331; *Manning's Case* (1609), 77 E.R. 618.

2.   *Fulton v. Cummings* (1874), 34 U.C.Q.B. 331; *Bartels v. Bartels* (1877), 42 U.C.Q.B. 22 (testator devising property to A in fee simple subject to condition "that my daughters shall have at all times a privilege of living on the homestead and maintained out of the proceeds of the said estate during their natural lives"; daughters taking life estate); *Smith v. Smith* (1889), 18 O.R. 205 (C.A.) (devise to testator's widow "of one bedroom and one parlor of her own choice in the dwelling house"; life estate in such rooms as widow should select); *Judge v. Splann* (1892), 22 O.R. 409 (H.C.) (direction that testator's daughter "shall remain and live on said place as long as she remains unmarried"; daughter given life estate so long as remaining unmarried); *Re McDonald* (1919), 46 O.L.R. 358 (C.A.); *Shaw v. Shaw* (1920), 17 O.W.N. 458 (Div. Ct.) (widow of testator given right to reside in house during widowhood obtaining life estate while widow); **see also** *Scouler v. Scouler* (1858), 8 U.C.C.P. 9 (direction in will, that testator's mother and daughter should have lien or claim on lands as home during their natural lives, conferring joint life estate on them).

3.   *Wilkinson v. Wilson* (1894), 26 O.R. 213 (C.A.) (so long as B remaining on farm, B entitled to use of room; such entitlement constituting charge on land); *Lapointe v. Cyr* (1950), 29 M.P.R. 54 (N.B.S.C.) (right to live on and use lands at will conferring life estate); **but see** *Powell v. Powell* (1988), 90 A.R. 291 (Q.B.); *Moore v. Royal Trust Co.*, [1956] S.C.R. 880 [B.C.].

4.   *Sharon v. Stuart* (1906), 12 O.L.R. 605 (K.B.) (by virtue of third branch of rule in *Wild's Case*, children taking by purchase remainder in fee simple; devise to children being gift to class; as period of distribution postponed until death of prior life tenants, class comprising all children coming into existence before period of distribution).

17

2. RIGHTS AND LIABILITIES OF TENANT FOR LIFE

(a) Obligations and Rights

§44   Certain persons, unless the settlement contains an express declaration that it is not lawful for them to do so, may, under certain conditions and without application to the court, demise the settled estate or any part thereof for any term not exceeding 21 years, to take effect in possession at or within one year next after the making thereof. Additional powers in respect to a demise by such persons are also provided.[1]

> 1. Settled Estates Act, R.S.O. 1990, c. S.7, s. 32 [am. 1997, c. 24, s. 221(2)]; **see also** §155 Settled estates.

§45   A special trusteeship arises by operation of law upon the creation of a life tenancy which does not need to be deduced from uncertain terms in the will. Fiduciary obligations of the tenant for life to the remaindermen arise. The tenant is a trustee in the sense that he or she cannot injure or dispose of the property to the detriment of the rights of the remainderman, or acquire an outstanding title for his or her own benefit, but differs from the trustee of a pure trust in that he or she may use the property for his of her exclusive benefit and take the income and profits.[1]

> 1. *Perry v. Perry*, [1918] 2 W.W.R. 485 (Man. C.A.); affirming [1917] 3 W.W.R. 315 (K.B.).

(b) Liability for Waste

§46   A tenant for life is impeachable for waste and is liable in damages to the person injured.[1] The Superior Court of Justice may grant an interlocutory injunction or mandatory order where it appears to a judge of the court to be just or convenient to do so.[2]

> 1. Conveyancing and Law of Property Act, R.S.O. 1990, c. C.34, s. 31.
>
> 2. Courts of Justice Act, R.S.O. 1990, c. C.43, s. 101(1) [am. 1994, c. 12, s. 40; 1996, c. 25, s. 9(17)]; **see also** Rules of Civil Procedure, R.R.O. 1990, Reg. 194, RR. 40, 41.

§47   A plaintiff claiming an injunction for waste must specify the acts complained of as waste, as a general charge of waste is not sufficient to sustain an application for an injunction.[1] An act is not waste unless it is injurious to the inheritance, either by diminishing the value of or increasing the burden on it, or by impairing the evidence of title.[2]

> 1. *Sanders v. Christie* (1850), 1 Gr. 137; **see also** *Raven v. Lovelass* (1865), 11 Gr. 435 (injunction to restrain waste continued at hearing; waste not exceeding $20; court refusing to order accounting, leaving amount of waste to be dealt with in action for mesne profits).
>
> 2. *Holderness v. Lang* (1886), 11 O.R. 1 at 17; *McPherson v. Giles* (1919), 45 O.L.R. 441 (H.C.).

§48   A tenant for life who cuts timber for the purpose of clearing land and bringing it under cultivation is not guilty of waste. A tenant for life does not commit waste if he or she cuts down timber on wild land for the sole purpose of bringing the land into cultivation, provided that the inheritance is not damaged and the cutting is done in accordance with the rules of good husbandry.[1]

> 1. *Drake v. Wigle* (1874), 24 U.C.C.P. 405; *Weller v. Burnham* (1853), 11 U.C.Q.B. 90; *Whitesell v. Reece* (1903), 5 O.L.R. 352 (C.A.); **see also** *Currie v. Currie* (1910), 20 O.L.R. 375 (H.C.) (tenant liable for waste where timber not cut in ordinary course of clearing land for cultivation).

§49   Whether the act of cutting a tree in any particular case is waste depends on whether the act is consistent with what a prudent farmer would do upon his her own land, having regard to the land as an inheritance, and whether such action would diminish the value of the land as an estate.[1] A tenant for life who removes stones which impede full use of the land for agriculture is not guilty of waste.[2]

> 1. *Lewis v. Godson* (1888), 15 O.R. 252 (C.A.); *Saunders v. Breakie* (1884), 5 O.R. 603 (Ch.); *Campbell v. Shields* (1879), 44 U.C.Q.B. 449 (covenant by lessee not to cut timber except for lessee's use or for purposes of improvement; whether tapping maple trees for sugar having effect of injuring trees being question of fact for jury; if so found, covenant broken); *Humble v. Fullarton* (1958), 41 M.P.R. 164 (N.B.S.C.); affirmed (1958), (*sub nom.* Fullarton v. Humble) 42 M.P.R. 118 (C.A.).
>
> 2. *Lewis v. Godson* (1888), 15 O.R. 252 (C.A.); *Toronto Harbour Commissioners v. Royal Canadian Yacht Club* (1913), 29 O.L.R. 391 (H.C.).

§50   A tenant for life who cuts timber or removes stones for the purpose of sale is guilty of waste.[1] But a tenant for life who cuts timber or removes stones for the purpose of agricultural improvement and then sells the timber or stones is not guilty of waste.[2]

> 1. *Lewis v. Godson* (1888), 15 O.R. 252 at 254 (C.A.); *Currie v. Currie* (1910), 20 O.L.R. 375 (H.C.).
>
> 2. *Lewis v. Godson* (1888), 15 O.R. 252 (C.A.) (no sale being waste if first act not waste).

§51   An act complained of as waste must be one that results in injury to the inheritance. "Waste" is a spoil or destruction in houses, gardens, trees or other corporeal hereditaments to the disherison of the person in remainder or reversion, or to the prejudice of the heir or reversioner.[1]

> 1. *Drake v. Wigle* (1874), 24 U.C.C.P. 405.

§52   "Waste" is a flexible term which varies with local and other circumstances; its essence is injury to the reversion.[1]

1. *Drake v. Wigle* (1874), 24 U.C.C.P. 405.

§53   Cutting down timber for use in the repair of an estate is not waste.[1]

1. *Hixon v. Reaveley* (1904), 9 O.L.R. 6 (Ch.).

§54   Although cutting down timber without any intention of repairs, but for sale generally, is waste, nevertheless, if the cutting down and sale are originally for the purpose of repair and the sale is an economical mode of making the repairs and is for the benefit of all concerned, and if the proceeds are bona fide applied for that purpose in pursuit of the original intention, such cutting down and sale is not waste.[1]

1. *Hixon v. Reaveley* (1904), 9 O.L.R. 6 (Ch.); *Lewis v. Godson* (1888), 15 O.R. 252 (C.A.).

§55   A life tenant is liable for wilful or commissive waste but not for permissive waste.[1] An estate for life without impeachment of waste will not confer upon the tenant for life any legal right to commit waste of the description known as equitable waste unless an intention to confer such right expressly appears by the instrument creating the estate.[2]

1. *Monro v. Toronto Railway* (1904), 9 O.L.R. 299 (C.A.); *Zimmerman v. O'Reilly* (1868), 14 Gr. 646; *Patterson v. Central Canada Loan & Savings Co.* (1898), 29 O.R. 134 (C.A.) (remainderman seeking to make life tenant liable for spread of noxious weeds from natural causes; life tenant not liable for permissive waste; Noxious Weeds Act [now Weed Control Act, R.S.O. 1990, c. W.5] not rendering life tenant liable qua life tenant to remainderman, although some direct remedy against occupant possibly existing under statute); *Currie v. Currie* (1910), 20 O.L.R. 375 (C.A.); *Morris v. Cairncross* (1907), 14 O.L.R. 544 (C.A.) (tenant for years responsible for permissive waste).

2. Conveyancing and Law of Property Act, R.S.O. 1990, c. C.34, s. 30.

§56   Where a testator's intention requires that an estate devised in terms larger than a mere life estate be cut down to a life estate in order to give effect to other, conflicting dispositions of the same property, such life estate will be considered as unimpeachable for waste. But where a testator devises a life estate only, with a direction that the property will be under the control of the life tenant, such direction does not change or enlarge the usual character of the life estate, and the life tenant is liable for waste.[1]

1. *Clow v. Clow* (1883), 4 O.R. 355 (Ch.).

(c) Right to Possession

§**57** Where a property is devised to trustees in trust for A for life, remainder over, the court in dealing with such equitable estates has a discretion as to giving possession to the life tenant.[1]

1. *Re Cunningham* (1917), 12 O.W.N. 268 (H.C.); *Orford v. Orford* (1884), 6 O.R. 6 (Ch.).

(d) Right as to Management and Control of Property

§**58** Where the intention of the testator is clear that the management and control of the testator's property are to rest with the executors, the life tenant is not entitled to management and control.[1]

1. *Whiteside v. Miller* (1868), 14 Gr. 393; *Orford v. Orford* (1884), 6 O.R. 6 (Ch.); *Hefferman v. Taylor* (1886), 15 O.R. 670 (H.C.); *Re Cunningham* (1917), 12 O.W.N. 268 (H.C.).

(e) Responsibility for Payment of Taxes

§**59** As between remainderman and life tenant, the interest of the life tenant is chargeable with the payment of all annual taxes imposed on the land.[1]

1. *Biscoe v. Van Bearle* (1858), 6 Gr. 438; *Gray v. Hatch* (1871), 18 Gr. 72; *Re Cunningham* (1917), 12 O.W.N. 268 (H.C.); *Mayo v. Leitovski*, [1928] 1 W.W.R. 700 (Man. K.B.); **see also** *Re McDonald* (1919), 46 O.L.R. 358 (C.A.) (determinable life estate subject, so long as existing, to ordinary incidents of life estate; life tenant not entitled to occupy land without paying taxes thereon).

§**60** A life tenant cannot collect the rents from productive portions of lands and refuse to pay the taxes on unproductive portions.[1] The person entitled to possession is the person to pay the taxes chargeable yearly on the property, and the funds out of which the taxes are ordinarily payable are the rents of the lands.[2]

1. *Re Denison* (1893), 24 O.R. 197; *Re May* (1914), 6 O.W.N. 29 (H.C.).

2. *Re Denison* (1893), 24 O.R. 197.

(f) Responsibility for Repairs

§**61** As between life tenant and remainderman, repairs necessary to overcome dilapidation are properly charged against the interest of the remainderman.[1]

1. *Patterson v. Central Canada Loan & Savings Co.* (1898), 29 O.R. 134 (C.A.); *Currie v. Currie* (1910), 20 O.L.R. 375 (H.C.); *Re Cunningham* (1917), 12 O.W.N. 268 (H.C.); *Re Elliot* (1917), 41 O.L.R. 276 (C.A.); *Re Vair* (1923), 54 O.L.R. 497 (H.C.); *Re Andrews*, [1952] O.W.N. 163.

§62   Although it may be in the interest of a tenant for life to keep the buildings in a habitable condition, the tenant for life cannot charge that expense against the remainderman, nor can he or she be punishable for waste when repairs are not made. A tenant for life is not bound to repair fences if there is no suitable material on the property.[1]

  1. *Patterson v. Central Canada Loan & Savings Co.* (1898), 29 O.R. 134 (C.A.).

(g) Responsibility for Payment of Insurance Premiums

§63   As between life tenant and remainderman, the interest of the life tenant is not to be charged with the payment of premiums on a fire insurance policy.[1]

  1. *Re Betty*, [1899] 1 Ch. 821; *Re Cunningham* (1917), 12 O.W.N. 268 (H.C.).

(h) Responsibility for Payment of Encumbrances

§64   A life tenant is responsible for interest due on a a mortgage debt.[1]

  1. *Re Morrison Estate* (1922), 16 Sask. L.R. 7 (K.B.).

§65   As between remainderman and life tenant, while the life tenant is bound to pay the interest on a mortgage, the remainderman is responsible for payment of the principal.[1] Prima facie, a tenant for life who pays the principal on a mortgage does so for his or her own benefit and not to exonerate the estate, and in the absence of any contrary intention on the part of the life tenant, he or she will be entitled to be subrogated to the position of the mortgagee.[2]

  1. *Biscoe v. Van Bearle* (1858), 6 Gr. 438; *Reid v. Reid* (1881), 29 Gr. 372 (rule applying to dower interest taken by widow); *Carrick v. Smith* (1874), 34 U.C.Q.B. 389.

  2. *Macklem v. Cummings* (1859), 7 Gr. 318; *Carrick v. Smith* (1874), 34 U.C.Q.B. 389; **see also** *Burrell v. Earl of Egremont* (1844), 49 E.R. 1043 (if life tenant paying off charge on inheritance, then prima facie entitled to that charge for own benefit; but may exonerate estate; in absence of evidence, presumption being that life tenant paying charge for own benefit, not for benefit of persons entitled in remainder); *Leitch v. Leitch* (1901), 2 O.L.R. 233 (C.A.).

§66   Where a life tenant makes payments on an annuity secured by a mortgage on property, the payments of the annuity must be treated partly as interest which the tenant for life must pay, and partly as principal for which the tenant has a charge on the inheritance, in the proportion which the value of the life estate bears to the value of the reversion.[1]

  1. *Whitesell v. Reece* (1903), 5 O.L.R. 352 (C.A.).

V   Estates Upon Conditions

1. CONDITIONS PRECEDENT OR SUBSEQUENT

§67   A condition is a qualification or restriction, annexed to a conveyance of lands, which provides that in case a particular event does or does not happen, or in case the grantor or grantee does or omits to do a particular act, an estate will commence, be enlarged, or be defeated[1]

> 1. *McIntosh v. Samo* (1875), 24 U.C.C.P. 625 (condition being clause of restraint in deed, or bridle annexed and joined to estate, staying and suspending same and making it uncertain whether it to take effect or not); **see also** *Ally v. Harding Addison Properties Ltd.* (1990), 14 R.P.R. (2d) 244 (Ont. Gen. Div.) (provision for registration within 270 days being condition precedent and not able to be unilaterally waived by any party; no indication in clause implying strictly for vendor's benefit; in any event, registration out of vendor's control and depending entirely upon will of third party municipality); *Riordan v. Chan* (1991), 16 R.P.R. (2d) 283 (Ont. Gen. Div.) (right of way clause not true condition precedent, but more in nature of representation coupled with promise; to that end, vendor having taken all reasonable steps and utilizing best efforts in obtaining right of way; vendor not breaching agreement).

§68   The intent that a gift is to take effect or continue only upon the happening of some named event must be clear in order for the language used in an instrument to constitute a condition.[1]

> 1. *McKinnon v. Lundy* (1893), 24 O.R. 132 at 137; varied (1894), 21 O.A.R. 560; reversed (1895), 24 S.C.R. 650; *Hamilton v. McKellar* (1878), 26 Gr. 110; *Re Deller* (1903), 6 O.L.R. 711 (H.C.).

§69   A condition attached to a devise of real property may be a condition precedent to a certain date and a condition subsequent thereafter. No particular words are necessary to render a condition subsequent or precedent.[1]

> 1. *Jordan v. Dunn* (1887), 13 O.R. 267 (H.C.); affirmed (1888), 15 O.A.R. 744; **see also** *McKinnon v. Lundy* (1893), 24 O.R. 132 at 137; varied (1894), 21 O.A.R. 560; reversed (1895), 24 S.C.R. 650 (whether condition being precedent or subsequent being matter of construction dependent upon testator's intention as manifested by will); *Doe d. McGillis v. McGillivray* (1852), 9 U.C.Q.B. 9 (conditions must be construed liberally according to intention of grantors; in will, such intent must especially be regarded); *Turner v. Turner* (1902), 4 O.L.R. 578 (H.C.).

§70   A condition subsequent is one which may operate to defeat an estate granted to and vested in the owner. Where the condition requires something to be done that requires time, the tendency is in favour of construing it as a condition subsequent.[1]

> 1. *Lundy v. Maloney* (1861), 11 U.C.C.P. 143; *Re McKellar*, [1972] 3 O.R. 16 (H.C.); affirmed [1973] 3 O.R. 178n (C.A.) (grant subject to condition that lands granted to grantee only so long as grantee continuing to occupy and use for railway purposes; held to be grant, fee simple, on condition subsequent); *Re Essex Roman Catholic*

Separate School Board (1977), 17 O.R. (2d) 307 (H.C.) (deed containing covenant that property be used for school purposes only, and reserving to grantor and heirs preference to buy at current price should property cease to be used for purposes intended, creating fee simple subject to condition subsequent).

§71   A condition, contained in a devise, as to the retention and not the acquisition of the land devised is a condition subsequent.[1] A remainder subject to a condition subsequent is a vested remainder.[2]

1. *Re Ross* (1904), 7 O.L.R. 493 (K.B.).

2. *Lundy v. Maloney* (1861), 11 U.C.C.P. 143.

2. DEFEASIBLE AND DETERMINABLE LIMITATIONS

§72   Conditions subsequent may take either the form of a conditional limitation or the form of a pure condition, strictly so called at common law.[1]

1. *Re Melville* (1886), 11 O.R. 626 (Ch.); *McIntosh v. Samo* (1875), 24 U.C.C.P. 625; *Doe d. Henniker v. Watt* (1828), 108 E.R. 1057.

§73   A determinable limitation operates to determine the estate by the intrinsic force of the limitation, and on the event prescribed, the estate terminates automatically.[1] An estate subject to a determinable limitation terminates automatically, without entry, on breach of the determinable limitation.[2]

1. *Re Melville* (1886), 11 O.R. 626 (Ch.); **see also** *North Gower (Township) Public School Board v. Todd*, [1968] 1 O.R. 63 (C.A.) (clause providing land conveyed to school board to revert to grantor if no longer used for purpose for which granted; held to be condition subsequent in that it being superadded condition upon grant of fee simple, rather than integral part of limitation of estate granted); *Re Tilbury West Public School Board v. Hastie*, [1966] 2 O.R. 20 (H.C.); varied [1966] 2 O.R. 511 (H.C.) (determinable fee with right to reverter created); *Fitzmaurice v. Monck (Township) School Trustees*, [1949] O.W.N. 786 (H.C.).

2. *McKinnon v. Lundy* (1893), 24 O.R. 132 at 137; varied (1894), 21 O.A.R. 560; reversed (1895), 24 S.C.R. 650.

§74   A pure common law condition operates by reserving a right of re-entry to the grantor and his or her heirs, and in the event prescribed, the estate of the grantee becomes defeasible by entry; but until entry is actually made, the estate of the grantee continues. The right of entry for breach of a pure condition may be reserved in a conveyance at common law only to the grantor and his or her heirs and to no other person.[1]

1. *Re Melville* (1886), 11 O.R. 626 (Ch.).

§75 Subject to the application of the rule against perpetuities, a pure condition may be reserved upon a conveyance in fee simple which leaves no reversion in the grantor.[1]

1. *Re Melville* (1886), 11 O.R. 626 (Ch.) (conveyance to municipal council in fee simple, subject to condition that if council should ever erect any building other than school on land, grantor and heirs could re-enter and avoid estate; condition attached to fee simple valid; no objection taken to condition on ground of violation of rule against perpetuities); **but see** *Matheson v. Mitchell (Town)* (1919), 46 O.L.R. 546 (C.A.) (rule against perpetuities applying to rights of entry for condition broken; condition subsequent, attached to conveyance in fee simple to municipal corporation, providing that if at any time land not used for park purposes, grantor and heirs could enter; condition void as offending rule against perpetuities); *North Gower (Township) Public School Board v. Todd*, [1968] 1 O.R. 63 (C.A.) (condition subsequent offending rule against perpetuities); *Missionary Church, Canada East v. Nottawasaga (Township)* (1980), 32 O.R. (2d) 88 (H.C.) (land conveyed to municipality on condition that it be used for road purposes only; condition being condition subsequent and therefore void as offending rule against perpetuities; municipality taking fee simple absolute); **see also** Perpetuities and Accumulations.

§76 Before breach of a condition subsequent by the grantee, the grantor has a mere possibility and not a reversion, whereas after breach, the grantor has a right of entry for a broken condition.[1]

1. *Re Melville* (1886), 11 O.R. 626 (Ch.); **see also** Succession Law Reform Act, R.S.O. 1990, c. S.26, s. 2; Estates Administration Act, R.S.O. 1990, c. E.22, s. 2.

3. REPUGNANCY

§77 Where property is given absolutely, a condition cannot be annexed to the gift inconsistent with its absolute character; and where a devise in fee simple is made upon condition that the estate will be shorn of some of its necessary incidents, such as that the devisee will not take the profits, or that the devisee will not have the power to alienate, either generally or for a specified time, such conditions are void because they are repugnant to the estate created.[1]

1. *Blackburn v. McCallum* (1903), 33 S.C.R. 65; *Mildmay's Case* (1605), 77 E.R. 331; *Portington's Case* (1613), 77 E.R. 976.

§78 Whether or not a condition restrains alienation is a matter of substance, not form.[1]

1. *Re Macleay* (1875), L.R. 20 Eq. 186.

§79 A condition attached to a devise in fee simple, that if the devisee dies intestate, there will be an executory devise over, is void as repugnant to the estate devised. Similarly, a condition attached to a devise in fee simple, that if the devisee alienates or refrains from alienating, there will be an executory devise over, is void on grounds of repugnancy.[1]

1. *Kerr v. Leishman* (1860), 8 Gr. 435; *Re Babcock* (1862), 9 Gr. 427; *Re McIntyre* (1919), 16 O.W.N. 260 (H.C.); *Re Walker* (1925), 56 O.L.R. 517 (C.A.).

§80   A condition attached to a devise or grant of lands in fee simple which is in absolute restraint of alienation is void as repugnant, because the power of alienation is an inseparable incident of an estate in fee simple.[1]

1. *Blackburn v. McCallum* (1903), 33 S.C.R. 65; *Re Casner* (1883), 6 O.R. 282 (Ch.); *Watson v. Woods* (1887), 14 O.R. 48 (H.C.); *Heddlestone v. Heddlestone* (1888), 15 O.R. 280 (H.C.); *Shanacy v. Quinlan* (1897), 29 O.R. 372 (H.C.); *Thomas v. Shannon* (1898), 30 O.R. 49; *Hutt v. Hutt* (1911), 24 O.L.R. 574 (C.A.); *Paul v. Paul* (1921), 50 O.L.R. 211 (C.A.); **see also** *Re Malcolm*, [1947] O.W.N. 871 (H.C.) (absolute devise containing provision that property not to be sold or mortgaged; condition invalid).

§81   Although a condition must be limited so as to operate within the perpetuity period, a condition in restraint of alienation which otherwise is absolute is not rendered valid by a limitation as to time.[1] However, a condition in restraint of alienation which is partial, in the sense that alienation is prohibited only to a certain, particular class, is valid, provided that the class is not so large that in effect a prohibition of alienation to the class amounts to an absolute restraint on alienation.[2] A condition which forbids disposition of land to the whole world except one person is an absolute restraint on alienation and is void.[3]

1. *Blackburn v. McCallum* (1903), 33 S.C.R. 65 (period being 25 years from death of testator); *Re Rosher* (1884), 26 Ch. D. 801 (period being during life of testator's widow); see *Hutt v. Hutt* (1911), 24 O.L.R. 574 (C.A.) (Court of Appeal pointing out that earlier Ontario cases upholding validity of restraint on alienation limited as to time must be considered as overruled by S.C.C. decision in *Blackburn v. McCallum*); *Matheson v. Mitchell (Town)* (1919), 46 O.L.R. 546 (C.A.); **see also** *Earls v. McAlpine* (1881), 6 O.A.R. 145, *Pennyman v. McGrogan* (1868), 18 U.C.C.P. 132; *Smith v. Faught* (1881), 45 U.C.Q.B. 484; *Gallinger v. Farlinger* (1857), 6 U.C.C.P. 512; *Chisholm v. London & Western Trusts Co.* (1897), 28 O.R. 347 (H.C.); *Paul v. Paul* (1921), 50 O.L.R. 211 (C.A.); *Huron & Erie Mortgage Corp. v. Coghill* (1918), 13 O.W.N. 442 (H.C.); *Re Newcastle (Town) Zoning By-law 89-103* (1991), 27 O.M.B.R. 123 (condition imposed on consent for severance of land, precluding subject property from being sold for ten years, illegal as being restraint on alienation; such condition not authorized under Planning Act or any other statute); **see** Perpetuities and Accumulations.

2. *Blackburn v. McCallum* (1903), 33 S.C.R. 65; *Doe d. Gill v. Pearson* (1805), 102 E.R. 1253; *Re Macleay* (1875), L.R. 20 Eq. 186; **see also** *Heddlestone v. Heddlestone* (1888), 15 O.R. 280 (H.C.) (condition against disposing of property except by will to lawful heirs of devisee held void as being absolute restraint); *Re Tuck Estate* (1905), 10 O.L.R. 309 (H.C.); **but see** *Rogerson v. Campbell* (1905), 10 O.L.R. 748 (H.C.) (condition against disposition except to children or grandchildren of testator held valid; devisee left with "comparatively large class" among whom property could be disposed of); *Lane v. Beacham* (1912), 4 O.W.N. 243 (H.C.).

3. *Re Buckley* (1910), 1 O.W.N. 427 (H.C.) (testator devising land to two grandchildren, with "power of disposing of the right, title and interest of the one to the

other, but to no other person whomsoever"; restraint void); *Re Metcalfe* (1925), 27 O.W.N. 438 (H.C.); *Re Dowsett* (1926), 31 O.W.N. 353 (H.C.) (condition in will that "should my . . . wife . . . decide to sell the real estate she shall sell the same to my brother . . . for the sum of $2,200"; restraint void).

§82 A restraint on alienation that is partial in the sense that it forbids certain modes of disposition, e.g., selling and mortgaging, while permitting other modes, e.g., leasing and devising, is valid.[1]

1. *Smith v. Faught* (1881), 45 U.C.Q.B. 484; *Re Winstanley* (1884), 6 O.R. 315 (C.A.) (condition restraining disposition except by will held valid); *Re Northcote* (1889), 18 O.R. 107 (H.C.) (condition against selling or mortgaging estate in fee simple during lifetime of devisee held valid); *Meyers v. Hamilton Provident & Loan Co.* (1890), 19 O.R. 358 (C.A.) (condition against selling held valid); *Re Casner* (1883), 6 O.R. 282 (Ch.) (condition against conveying or disposing of lands in any manner whatsoever held void); *Heddlestone v. Heddlestone* (1888), 15 O.R. 280 (H.C.) (condition against disposing by sale, mortgage or otherwise except by will to lawful heirs held void as absolute restraint on alienation); *Shanacy v. Quinlan* (1897), 29 O.R. 372 (H.C.) (condition against selling or mortgaging held void as absolute restraint on alienation); *Thomas v. Shannon* (1898), 30 O.R. 49 (condition that the devisees will "have no power to make sale or mortgage any of the lands . . . but to go to their heirs and successors" held void as absolute restraint on alienation); *Re Buckley* (1910), 1 O.W.N. 427 (H.C.); *Blackburn v. McCallum* (1903), 33 S.C.R. 65 (absolute restraint limited only as to time held void); *Martin v. Dagneau* (1906), 11 O.L.R. 349 (H.C.) (condition against selling or mortgaging held valid; *Blackburn v. McCallum*, distinguished); *Re Corbit* (1905), 5 O.W.R. 239 (H.C.) (condition against sale valid); *Re Porter* (1907), 13 O.L.R. 399 (C.A.) (condition against mortgaging or selling valid); *Re Dalton* (1921), 20 O.W.N. 344 (H.C.); *Huron & Erie Mortgage Corp. v. Coghill* (1918), 13 O.W.N. 442 (H.C.) (condition against leasing, mortgaging or deeding lands until devisee reaching age 60 void).

§83 A condition, attached to a devise in fee simple, prohibiting all modes of alienation by the devisee without consent of some other named person is void.[1] Similarly, a condition in a deed to the effect that no conveyance or lease of certain lands would be valid without the written consent of the vendor was held void.[2]

1. *McRae v. McRae* (1898), 30 O.R. 54 (C.A.); **see also** *Rutherford v. Rispin* (1926), 59 O.L.R. 506 (H.C.) (members of unincorporated fishing club purchasing land for club purposes; club regulation forbidding disposition of interest in land by member without consent of fellow members held void and ineffective as being in restraint of alienation).

2. *Pardee v. Humberstone Summer Resort Co. of Ontario*, [1933] O.R. 580 (H.C.).

§84 A restrictive covenant containing a clause requiring any construction on the affected land to be carried out by a designated builder is void because it creates a substantial restraint on alienation.[1]

1. *Fuji Builders Ltd. v. Tresoor*, [1984] 5 W.W.R. 80 (Man. Q.B.).

4. CONDITIONS VOID ON GROUNDS OF PUBLIC POLICY

§85   Conditions in general restraint upon marriage are prima facie void on grounds of public policy.[1] But a condition, attached to a gift, which provides that in the event of marriage the property will go over is not void if the condition was inserted to make more adequate provision for the objects of the testator's bounty, and not for the purpose of discouraging marriage.[2]

> 1. *Re Deller* (1903), 6 O.L.R. 711 (H.C.) (principle applying equally to men and women); *Allen v. Jackson* (1875), 1 Ch. D. 399; **see also** *Re Cutter* (1916), 37 O.L.R. 42.
>
> 2. *Re McBain* (1915), 8 O.W.N. 330 (H.C.); *Jones v. Jones* (1876), 1 Q.B.D. 279 ("looking at the object of this will, and the fact that the testator probably thought that his property was not more than enough for these women to live upon together, his direction that the one who married should lose her share cannot be said to be opposed to public policy").

§86   Conditions in restraint of a second marriage are not void on grounds of public policy, whether attached to a gift by a husband to his wife, or by a wife to her husband, or by a stranger to either husband or wife.[1]

> 1. *Cowan v. Allen* (1896), 26 S.C.R. 292 (gift by will to widow "as long as she remains unmarried"); *Re Deller* (1903), 6 O.L.R. 711 (H.C.); *Allen v. Jackson* (1875), 1 Ch. D. 399.

§87   Conditions in partial restraint of marriage which prohibit marriage to a certain person or to persons or to a class of persons are prima facie valid.[1] But a condition in restraint of marriage which, although in partial terms, would or might from its nature lead in practice to a probable prohibition of marriage is void.[2]

> 1. *Re Bathe*, [1925] Ch. 377 (conditions, contained in codicils to will, forbidding marriage to three named ladies held valid); *Perrin v. Lyon* (1807), 103 E.R. 538 (condition against marriage with any person born in Scotland or born of Scottish parents held valid); *Jenner v. Turner* (1880), 16 Ch. D. 188 (condition against marrying a domestic servant held to be valid).
>
> 2. *Re Lanyon*, [1927] 2 Ch. 264.

§88   A condition, attached to a bequest of personalty, that the donee marry with the consent of the executor or some other person, without any gift over, is void as being merely in terrorem. This rule is applicable also to realty when the gifts of realty and personalty are mixed or massed together in one bequest.[1]

> 1. *Re Hamilton* (1910), 1 O.L.R. 10 (H.C.).

§89   A condition that requires a married woman to disregard her matrimonial obligations is void as offending public policy.[1]

1. *Re Nurse* (1921), 20 O.W.N. 428 (H.C.) (testator devising and bequeathing all property to married woman, subject to condition that if woman consorted with her husband, executors could withhold part of property; condition void).

§90 A condition attached to a gift to an infant, by the infant's grandfather, that the infant should forfeit his interest if he were to go to live with his father, was held to be void.[1] But a condition attached to a devise by a father to his infant son, that the infant must live with a guardian named in the will and not with his mother, was held to be valid.[2]

1. *Clarke v. Darraugh* (1884), 5 O.R. 140 (H.C.).

2. *Davis v. McCaffrey* (1874), 21 Gr. 554.

5. CONDITIONS VOID BECAUSE OF UNCERTAINTY

§91 Where a vested estate is to be defeated by a condition on a contingency that is to happen afterward, that condition must be such that the court can see from the beginning, precisely and distinctly, what event was the one upon which the preceding vested estate was to determine; otherwise the condition is void for uncertainty.[1] A condition attached to a devise of realty, that the devisee abstain from intoxicating liquors and card playing and that he be kind and obedient to his mother, is not invalid because of uncertainty or on grounds of public policy.[2]

1. *Re Ross* (1904), 7 O.L.R. 493 (K.B.) (condition that devisee"comes to live and reside on the land" void for uncertainty); *Clavering v. Ellison* (1859), 11 E.R. 282 (condition that if devisees "educated abroad, or not in the Protestant religion", gift should fail; void for uncertainty); *Re Lanyon*, [1927] 2 Ch. 264 (condition that donee "does not marry a relation by blood" held void for uncertainty).

2. *Jordan v. Dunn* (1887), 13 O.R. 267 (H.C.); affirmed (1888), 15 O.A.R. 744; **see also** *Re Fox* (1884), 8 O.R. 489 (C.A.) (condition attached to devise, that devisee remain sober for five years, held valid); *Pew v. Lefferty* (1869), 16 Gr. 408 (condition that legatee continue to be steady boy and remain in some respectable family valid).

6. CONDITIONS VOID BECAUSE OF IMPOSSIBILITY

§92 A condition, annexed to a conveyance or a devise of land, which, in its creation, is impossible to perform, is void.[1]

1. *McKinnon v. Lundy* (1893), 24 O.R. 132 (H.C.); varied (1894), 21 O.A.R. 560; reversed (1895), 24 S.C.R. 650; (condition subsequent attached to devise, that devisee pay off mortgage; testator himself having paid off mortgage in his lifetime, thus rendering condition impossible of performance by devisee).

7. EFFECT OF VOID CONDITIONS

§93   A void condition precedent renders the conveyance or devise void, whereas a void condition subsequent renders the conveyance or devise absolute.[1] If a devise is made upon several conditions, one of which is void, the others, although good by themselves but being coupled with the void one, will also be rejected.[2]

1. *McKinnon v. Lundy* (1893), 24 O.R. 132; varied (1894), 21 O.A.R. 560; reversed (1895), 24 S.C.R. 650; *Jordan v. Dunn* (1887), 13 O.R. 267 at 281, 282 (H.C.); affirmed (1888), 15 O.A.R. 744.

2. *Re Babcock* (1862), 9 Gr. 427.

VI   Remainders

1. VESTED AND CONTINGENT REMAINDERS

§94   A remainder is vested in interest if the person entitled thereto will obtain possession upon the happening of no other contingency than the natural expiration of the prior estate.[1] A remainder which is subject to a condition subsequent is a vested remainder.[2]

> 1. *Lundy v. Maloney* (1861), 11 U.C.C.P. 143; **see also** *Re Badgerow* (1930), 39 O.W.N. 74 (H.C.).
>
> 2. *Lundy v. Maloney* (1861), 11 U.C.C.P. 143.

§95   Unless the estates are limited by way of use, a remainder in fee simple cannot, by a conveyance, be created to take effect after a prior estate in fee simple.[1] At common law, a contingent remainder could not take effect if the prior estate of freehold came to an end by forfeiture, surrender or merger before the contingent remainder became vested; but, by statute, every contingent remainder will be capable of taking effect notwithstanding the determination by forfeiture, surrender or merger of any preceding estate of freehold.[2]

> 1. *Re Chauvin* (1920), 18 O.W.N. 178 (H.C.); **see also** *Bayliss v. Balfe* (1917), 38 O.L.R. 437 (H.C.) (if conveyance operating by way of use, fee simple after prior fee simple valid).
>
> 2. Conveyancing and Law of Property Act, R.S.O. 1990, c. C.34, s. 35; *Re Crow* (1984), 48 O.R. (2d) 36 (H.C.) (remainder being legal contingent remainder, as rule in *Purefoy v. Rogers* (1671), 85 E.R. 1181 (K.B.) applying; rule applicable where, at date gift created, limitation capable of vesting before termination of estate and therefore capable of complying with common law rules as to legal remainders; gift over thus creating contingent remainder infringing common law rule requiring vesting during continuance of estate or at moment of termination).

§96   A contingent remainder may be disposed of by deed inter vivos or by will.[1]

> 1. Conveyancing and Law of Property Act, R.S.O. 1990, c. C.34, s. 10; Succession Law Reform Act, R.S.O. 1990, c. S.26, s. 2.

§97   At common law, the rule against perpetuities was applicable to contingent remainders, and hence, unless such a remainder vested, if it vested at all, within a life or lives plus 21 years, it was void.[1] A contingent remainder limited to the unborn issue of an unborn person, after a prior life estate to that unborn person, was void.[2] Thus, where land devised to A, an unmarried man, for life, remainder to his wife for life, remainder to their children in fee simple, the remainder to the children was void as offending the rule against perpetuities.[3] The rule against perpetuities has since been modified by statute.[4]

1. *Re Ashforth*, [1905] 1 Ch. 535; **see also** *Re Prong*, [1966] 2 O.R. 470 (H.C.) (special statutory power exempting operation of rule against perpetuities); *Kitchener (City) v. Weinblatt*, [1966] 2 O.R. 740 (C.A.); affirmed [1969] S.C.R. 157 (covenant to reconvey creating equitable interest in land not contrary to rule against perpetuities); *Tilbury West Public School Board v. Hastie*, [1966] 2 O.R. 20 (H.C.).

2. *Stuart v. Taylor* (1914), 33 O.L.R. 20 (C.A.); *Whitby v. Mitchell* (1890), 44 Ch. D. 85; *Re Nash*, [1910] 1 Ch. 1; *Re Park's Settlement*, [1914] 1 Ch. 595; *Re Bullock's Will Trusts*, [1915] 1 Ch. 493 (rule in *Whitby v. Mitchell* applying only to contingent remainders).

3. *Stuart v. Taylor* (1914), 33 O.L.R. 20 (C.A.); *Re Park's Settlement*, [1914] 1 Ch. 595; **but see** *Re Bullock's Will Trusts*, [1915] 1 Ch. 493.

4. Perpetuities Act, R.S.O. 1990, c. P.9; **see** Perpetuities and Accumulations; **see also** Morris and Leach, The Rule Against Perpetuities, 1956.

2. THE RULE IN *SHELLEY'S CASE*

(a) Statement and Nature of Rule

§**98**   The rule in *Shelley's Case*[1] is that if a grant or devise is made to a person for life, with a remainder, either immediately following that estate or after other, intermediate remainders, to the heirs or the heirs of the body of that person, the word "heirs" is taken as a word of limitation and not of purchase, and the remainder vests in the ancestor as if limited to him or her and to his or her heirs.[2]

1. *Shelley's Case* (1581), 76 E.R. 199; *Van Grutten v. Foxwell*, [1897] A.C. 658 (H.L.).

2. *Shelley's Case* (1581), 76 E.R. 199; *Re Kendrew* (1918), 43 O.L.R. 185 (C.A.); *Van Grutten v. Foxwell*, [1897] A.C. 658 (H.L.).

§**99**   The rule in *Shelley's Case* is a rule of law, and not a rule laid down for the purpose of giving effect to a grantor's or testator's expressed or presumed intention.[1] Wherever the court comes to the conclusion that the gift over includes the whole line of heirs, general or special, the rule immediately applies, and an estate of inheritance is executed in the ancestor or tenant for life, even though the testator has expressly declared that the ancestor will take for life and no longer, or has endeavoured to graft upon the words of gift to the heirs, or heirs of the body, additions, conditions or limitations which are repugnant to an estate of inheritance and are such as the law cannot give effect to. The rule is not one of construction, and indeed usually overrides and defeats the expressed intention of the testator.[2] The rule in *Shelley's Case* is a rule of tenure, which is not only independent of but generally operates to subvert the intention; so that no words, however positive, negativing the continuance of the ancestor's estate beyond the period of its primary express limitation would exclude the rule. In like manner, a declaration that the heirs shall take as purchasers is equally inoperative.[3]

1. *Tunis v. Passmore* (1872), 32 U.C.Q.B. 419.

2. *Van Grutten v. Foxwell*, [1897] A.C. 658 (H.L.).

3. *Romanes v. Smith* (1880), 8 P.R. 323 (Ont. Ch.); *King v. Evans* (1895), 24 S.C.R. 356; *Re Casner* (1884), 6 O.R. 282 (Ch.) (testator devising land to A and A's heirs and assigns and stating a distinct wish that A should have only a life estate with no power of disposition; held that, by rule in *Shelley's Case*, A acquiring fee simple, and that condition restraining alienation void for repugnancy); *Re Nicholson* (1928), 34 O.W.N. 111 (H.C.).

§100 The basis for the application of the rule must exist, and always the question is present whether the language of the gift after the life estate, properly construed, is such as to embrace the whole line of heirs or heirs of the body or issue; and this question must be determined apart from the rule, according to the ordinary principles of construction.[1] The testator may conceivably show by the context that he or she has used the words "heirs" or"heirs of the body" or "issue" in some limited or restricted sense of his or her own which is not the legal meaning of the words; for example, the words may have been used in the sense of children or as designating some individual person who would be heir of the body at the time of the death of the tenant for life or at some other particular time. If the court is judicially satisfied that the words are so used, the premises for the application of the rule in *Shelley's Case* are wanting and the rule is foreign to the case.[2]

1. *Van Grutten v. Foxwell*, [1897] A.C. 658 (H.L.) (question in every case must be whether expression requiring exposition, be it "heirs" or "heirs of the body" or any other expression which may have like meaning, being used as designation of particular individual or class of objects or as including whole line of succession capable of inheriting).

2. *Van Grutten v. Foxwell*, [1897] A.C. 658 (H.L.); **see also** *Re Tuck Estate* (1905), 10 O.L.R. 309 (H.C.); *King v. Evans* (1895), 24 S.C.R. 356 (application of rule in *Shelley's Case* depending on question whether"heirs" being designation of some particular person, or included successively all who might pretend to inheritable blood).

§101 Where the words of a gift make it plain that the subsequent gift does not include the whole inheritable issue of the person who is given an estate for life, the rule in *Shelley's Case* does not apply.[1]

1. *Re Badgerow*, [1940] O.W.N. 109 (H.C.); **but see** *Re Armstrong*, [1943] O.W.N. 43 (rule applying).

§102 The rule in *Shelley's Case* applies both to wills and deeds and to the creation of both legal and equitable interests.[1] The application of the rule is not affected by the fact that the estate devised to the ancestor is without impeachment for waste.[2]

1. *Van Grutten v. Foxwell*, [1897] A.C. 658 (H.L.)*Romanes v. Smith* (1880), 8 P.R. 323 (Ont. Ch.); *Re Hooper* (1914), 7 O.W.N. 104 (H.C.).

2. *Tunis v. Passmore* (1872), 32 U.C.Q.B. 419; *Re Hawkins* (1920), 19 O.W.N. 18 (H.C.).

§103   In considering the application of the rule, it is immaterial whether the testator has used the expression "on the determination of the life estate" or "on the determination of that estate" or "on the determination of the life" or "on the death of the tenant for life".   The rule is applicable only if the limitation of the estate to the ancestor and the limitation to the heir of the ancestor are contained in the same instrument.[1]

1. *Tunis v. Passmore* (1872), 32 U.C.Q.B. 419.

§104   If the required elements for the application of the rule in *Shelley's Case* are present, the existence of a power of appointment in the ancestor, which the ancestor is under no obligation to exercise, does not prevent the operation of the rule.[1]

1. *Re Hawkins* (1920), 19 O.W.N. 18 (H.C.); *Re Hooper* (1914), 7 O.W.N. 104 (H.C.).

§105   The rule in *Shelley's Case* is incompatible with the Torrens system.[1]

1. *Re Budd* (1958), 24 W.W.R. 383 (Alta. T.D.); *Smith v. MacLaren*, [1945] 1 W.W.R. 722 (B.C.S.C.); **see also** Conveyancing and Law of Property Act, R.S.O. 1990, c. C.34, s. 4.

(b) Gift to "Heirs" or "Heirs of the Body" of Ancestor

§106   If land is conveyed to A for life, remainder to A's heirs "and their heirs and assigns forever", the addition of words of limitation to the gift limited to the heirs of the ancestor does not affect the operation of the rule, and by the conveyance, A acquires an estate in fee simple.[1]

1. *Brown v. O'Dwyer* (1874), 35 U.C.Q.B. 354.

§107   The use of distributive words such as "share and share alike" or "equally to be divided among them", added to "heirs" or "heirs of the body", does not take a case out of the operation of the rule in *Shelley's Case*.[1] Where lands are devised to A for life, remainder "to her heirs, executors, and administrators and assigns", and there is no intention on the testator's part to give the executors or administrators any beneficial interest, A will acquire a fee simple by operation of the rule in *Shelley's Case*.[2]

1. *Van Grutten v. Foxwell*, [1897] A.C. 658 (H.L.); *Re McTavish* (1923), 25 O.W.N. 362 (C.A.); **see also** Conveyancing and Law of Property Act, R.S.O. 1990, c. C.34.

2. *Re Hays* (1917), 13 O.W.N. 25 (H.C.).

§108   The word "heir" may be used by a testator in a will as a collective term for "heirs" or"heirs of the body"; hence, if a testator uses the word"heir" in a devise to A for life and on A's death to his or her heir, A will, by operation of the rule in *Shelley's Case*, take a fee simple or a fee tail.[1] If a testator clearly is using the word "heirs" in a non-technical sense as meaning child or children, the rule in *Shelley's Case* does not apply.[2]

1. *Grant v. Squires* (1901), 2 O.L.R. 131 (Ch.); **see also** *Re Davison's Settlement*, [1913] 2 Ch. 498 ("heir" in singular in deed cannot be construed as "heirs of the body"; grant to A for life and on A's death to A's heir conferring upon A a life estate only, as premises for application of rule in *Shelley's Case* lacking); *Silcocks v. Silcocks*, [1916] 2 Ch. 161 (testator devising land to A for life and "on his death to his male heir forever"; testator using "male heir" as collective term for "male heirs of his body"; A, by operation of rule in *Shelley's Case*, acquiring estate in fee tail male).

2. *Smith v. Ready* (1927), 60 O.L.R. 617 (C.A.); *Smith v. Smith* (1885), 8 O.R. 677 (Ch.) (testator devising property"to my son J.S. for the term of his natural life . . . but if my said son J.S. should leave a lawful heir or heirs then said lands shall be equally divided among them at the death of their father"; testator interpreting first words "lawful heir or heirs" to mean child or children, by declaring that farm to be divided among them at father's death).

§109   A devise of "rents" by will is equivalent to a devise of an estate; thus, where a testator directs that A is to receive the rents from a lot for life, and that on A's decease the rents shall be invested for the heirs of A, A takes an estate in fee simple.[1]

1. *Re Thomas* (1901), 2 O.L.R. 660 (Ch.).

(c) Gift to "Issue" of Ancestor

§110   The word "issue" is prima facie a word not of purchase but of limitation, equivalent to heirs of the body; but it will be interpreted as meaning children when the context, as a matter of construction, calls for such interpretation.[1]

1. *Roddy v. Fitzgerald* (1857), 10 E.R. 1518; *Shaw v. Thomas* (1872), 19 Gr. 489; *King v. Evans* (1895), 24 S.C.R. 356 (expression "heirs of the body" may be read as children if testator sufficiently expressing intention that such be done;"issue" being more flexible expression than "heirs of the body" and more readily diverted by force of context or superadded limitations from its prima facie meaning; **see also** *Re Taylor* (1916), 36 O.L.R. 116 (C.A.) (testator using word"issue" but clearly indicating its use in sense of children and not as meaning "heirs of the body"; rule in *Shelley's Case* not applying); *Montreuil v. Walker* (1911), 3 O.W.N. 166 (Ch.); *Re Russell* (1915), 8 O.W.N. 248 (H.C.) ("issue" used by testator as meaning children; rule in *Shelley's Case* not applicable); *Watson v. Phillips* (1910), 2 O.W.N. 261 (C.A.) ("issue" used in

normal sense as equivalent to "heirs of the body"; and rule in *Shelley's Case* applying to give ancestor estate in fee tail); *Re Davidson* (1926), 59 O.L.R. 643 (C.A.) ("issue" appearing in will must be given technical meaning of"descendants" unless expression can be found on face of will of intention that word meaning child or children).

§111   Where there is a gift to A for life and after A's death to the issue of A and their heirs, the addition of those words of limitation to the word "issue" will not convert"issue" into a word of purchase, and A will take an estate in fee tail.[1] If there is a gift to A for life and after A's death to the issue of A "to hold in fee simple","issue" will be given its secondary meaning as equivalent to children and will not be considered a word of limitation.[2]

1. *Parker v. Clarke* (1855), 43 E.R. 1169 (L.C.); *King v. Evans* (1895), 24 S.C.R. 356; **but see** *Re Addison* (1920), 19 O.W.N. 142 (under devise to A for life, remainder "to his lawful issue and to their heirs and assigns forever"; A acquiring life estate only, with gift over to A's children in fee simple).

2. *King v. Evans* (1895), 24 S.C.R. 356; **see also** *Re Taylor* (1916), 36 O.L.R. 116 (C.A.).

(d) Gift to "Children" of Ancestor

§112   Prima facie the rule does not apply where, after a life estate, there is a gift to the children of the life tenant; but if the testator uses the word "children" as equivalent to"heirs" or "heirs of the body", or as importing the whole line of succession capable of inheriting, the rule does apply. "Children" in its normal and natural meaning refers only to immediate offspring and should be so interpreted unless there is something in the context to indicate that the testator used the word in a broader sense.[1] If there is a gift to A for life, remainder on the death of A to A's children, with words of division or inheritance annexed to the gift to the children, the children take as purchasers and the rule in *Shelley's Case* does not apply.[2]

1. *Grant v. Fuller* (1902), 33 S.C.R. 34 (devise to D for life "and to her children if any at her death"; D taking life estate only); *Chandler v. Gibson* (1901), 2 O.L.R. 442 (C.A.) (devise to M for life "and then to go to his children, if he has any, but should he have no issue then to be equally divided among all my grandsons"; M taking life estate only; "in default of issue" or expressions of similar import following devise to children in fee simple meaning "in default of children"); *Re Walters* (1922), 22 O.W.N. 305 (H.C.); *Re Simpson*, [1928] S.C.R. 329 (lands devised to A for life "and after her death to her children in equal shares per stirpes"; rule in *Shelley's Case* not applying; precise question being whether"to her children in equal shares per stirpes" being words of designation or of limitation; whether these words "include the whole line of succession capable of inheriting"; prima facie, "children", in such a context, denoting persons of first degree of descent and therefore being word of designation); *Peterborough Real Estate Co. v. Patterson* (1888), 15 O.A.R. 751; *Re Anderson* (1911), 2 O.W.N. 923; *Re Haig* (1924), 57 O.L.R. 129 (C.A.); *Re Beckstead* (1928), 62 O.L.R. 690 (C.A.); *Sweet v. Platt* (1886), 12 O.R. 229; *Young v. Denike* (1901), 2 O.L.R. 723 (Ch.); *Sharon v. Stuart* (1906), 12 O.L.R. 605 (K.B.); **see also** Child and Family Services Act, R.S.O. 1990, c. C.11, s. 158(4) (as to whether bequest to

"children" would benefit adopted children); *Re Hughes*, [1944] O.R. 407 (H.C.); *Baldwin v. Mooney*, [1929] S.C.R. 306; **see also** Wills.

2. *Bowen v. Lewis* (1884), 9 App. Cas. 890; *Thompson v. Robbins* (1917), 11 O.W.N. 344 (H.C.); *Re Simpson*, [1928] S.C.R. 329; *Re Robertson* (1916), 10 O.W.N. 365 (H.C.).

(e) Gift to "Descendants"
of Ancestor or to Those Entitled on Intestacy of Ancestor

§113 The normal meaning of "descendants" is equivalent to "heirs of the body"; and if a testator uses"descendants" in its normal meaning and devises land to A for life, remainder to the descendants of A, A formerly acquired an estate in fee tail.[1] If there is a gift to A for life, remainder to such persons as would be entitled to A's interest if it were absolute and if A were to die intestate, the rule in *Shelley's Case* operates to confer upon A an estate in fee simple.[2]

1. *Re Sutherland* (1911), 19 O.W.R. 702 (Ch.).

2. *Re Hooper* (1914), 7 O.W.N. 104 (H.C.).

(f) Gift to "Sons and Daughters"
or to "Family" of Ancestor

§114 The rule in *Shelley's Case* does not apply to a devise to A for life, remainder to the sons and daughters of A, unless the testator has most clearly indicated that he or she used the words "sons and daughters" in an unusual sense as embracing the whole line of descendants capable of inheriting.[1] If a testator uses the word "family" in its ordinary meaning of "children", and devises land to A for life, remainder to the family of A, the rule in *Shelley's Case* does not apply and A acquires merely a life estate with remainder in fee to the children of A.[2]

1. *Re Chandler* (1889), 18 O.R. 105 (Ch.); **see also** *Re Simpson*, [1928] S.C.R. 329 (whatever may be said about"children", would require very demonstrative context, having force and value of interpretation clause, to impart to"sons and daughters" meaning embracing whole line of descendants capable of inheriting).

2. *McKinnon v. Spence* (1909), 20 O.L.R. 57 (C.A.); **see also** *Re Quebec* (1929), 37 O.W.N. 271 (H.C.) (in absence of manifest intention to contrary, gift to "family" of specified person will be construed to mean children of such person, and does not include the parent).

(g) Estate Limited to Ancestor and Estate
Limited to Heirs

§115 If the estate taken by the person to whom the lands are granted or devised for a life estate is not of the same quality as the estate limited to the "heirs" or "heirs of the body" of that person, i.e., if the one is legal and the other equitable, the rule in *Shelley's Case* has no application.[1]

1. *Re McAllister* (1911), 25 O.L.R. 17 (C.A.); *Van Grutten v. Foxwell*, [1897] A.C. 658 (H.L.); *Romanes v. Smith* (1880), 8 P.R. 323 (Ont. Ch.) (lands devised to T to hold in trust for A for life and on A's death in trust to convey to A's heirs when youngest reaching age 21; rule in *Shelley's Case* not applying; A acquiring legal estate by operation of Statute of Uses, whereas interest of heirs of A purely equitable; had active duties been imposed upon trustee during A's lifetime, Statute of Uses would not have operated to execute use, and legal title would have remained in trustee; had that been true, then both A and heirs would have had equitable interests and rule in *Shelley's Case* would have operated to give A equitable fee simple); *Re Fanning*, [1934] O.W.N. 397 (C.A.) (estates of ancestor and descendant both held to be equitable; rule in *Shelley's Case* applying).

VII   Interests in Land Arising by Operation of Statute of Uses

§116   If lands are devised or conveyed to T in trust for or to the use of or for the benefit of C, and no active duties are imposed upon T, then C, by force of the Statute of Uses,[1] acquires a legal estate in the land.[2]

> 1.   By the introduction of English law into Upper Canada as of October 15, 1792 [see Property and Civil Rights Act, R.S.O. 1990, c. P.29], the Statute of Uses (1536), 27 Hen. VIII, c. 10, became part of the real property law of Ontario. Re-enacted by R.S.O. 1897, c. 331 [NC/NR], the Statute of Uses in effect enacts that persons who prior to the statute had merely an equitable interest by way of use have thereafter the legal seisin.
>
> 2.   *Fair v. McCrow* (1871), 31 U.C.Q.B. 599 (devise to A "in trust for the sole benefit of" B); *Williams v. Waters* (1845), 153 E.R. 434; *Romanes v. Smith* (1880), 8 P.R. 323 (Ont. Ch.); *Tunis v. Passmore* (1872), 32 U.C.Q.B. 419; *Hall v. Urquhart* (1928), 35 O.W.N. 201 (H.C.); **see also** Federal Real Property Act, S.C. 1991, c. 50, s.C. 1991, c. 50, s. 13 (no person acquiring any federal real property by virtue of provincial Act); *Barker v. Greenwood* (1838), 150 E.R. 1494 (where words "in trust to permit and suffer A.B. to take the rents and profits" used, use is divested out of trustees and executed in party; purposes of trust not requiring that legal estate remain in them).

§117   Where land is conveyed by the grantor to T and T's heirs until T's intended marriage, and thereafter to the uses of the intended spouse and such spouse's heirs for his or her own sole and separate use and benefit forever, the spouse, on marriage, acquires a legal fee simple.[1]

> 1.   *Bayliss v. Balfe* (1917), 38 O.L.R. 437 (H.C.).

§118   If an instrument imposes active duties upon the trustee, or if the progress of the trust requires that the trustee retain legal title, the Statute of Uses does not apply and the person for whose benefit the trustee is to hold the land acquires an equitable interest only.[1] Where an estate is given to trustees to receive rents and pay them to the beneficiary, the trustees take the legal estate to enable them to perform the trust; but if the estate is given to them to permit another to receive the rents, the beneficial devisee, and not the trustee, takes the legal estate.[2] Where an estate is limited to the trustee to permit a tenant for life to receive the rents during his or her life, and on his or her death to convey to another in fee, the legal estate during the life of the tenant for life is vested in him or her, and the remainder in the trustees.[3] If property is devised to a trustee in trust to pay the rents and profits to the cestui que trust, the trustee retains the legal title, but the cestui que trust, acquiring an equitable title, is entitled to possession of the property, unless the testator clearly indicates his or her intention that the cestui que trust is not to have possession.[4] But if the cestui que trust, to whom the rents and profits are directed to be paid, is not the only person beneficially interested in the property, it rests in the discretion of the court to decide whether the actual possession is to remain with the cestui que trust or the trustee.[5]

1. *Spencer v. Registrar of Titles*, [1906] A.C. 503 (P.C. [Aus.]); *Fair v. McCrow* (1871), 31 U.C.Q.B. 599; *Gamble v. Rees* (1850), 6 U.C.Q.B. 396.

2. *Romanes v. Smith* (1880), 8 P.R. 323 (Ont. Ch.); *Doe d. Leicester v. Biggs* (1809), 127 E.R. 1017; *Doe d. Shelley v. Edlin* (1836), 111 E.R. 906.

3. *Doe d. Noble v. Bolton* (1839), 113 E.R. 386; *Adams v. Adams* (1845), 6 Q.B. 860; *Re Hooper* (1914), 7 O.W.N. 104 (H.C.).

4. *Whiteside v. Miller* (1868), 14 Gr. 393.

5. *Orford v. Orford* (1884), 6 O.R. 6 (Ch.).

§**119**   The Statute of Uses executes only the first use; hence, if lands are conveyed by grant "to and to the use" of T in trust for or to the use of C, C acquires an equitable interest and the legal title remains in T, unaffected by the statute.[1]

1. *Gamble v. Rees* (1850), 6 U.C.Q.B. 396 (however, if conveyance being by bargain and sale, not necessary to insert "to and to the use" of bargainee to prevent Statute of Uses executing use, because in that form of conveyance, first use arising by pecuniary consideration acknowledged to be paid; statute executing that use and leaving any subsequent uses untouched); *Doe d. Lloyd v. Passingham* (1827), 108 E.R. 465; *Tyrrel's Case* (1557), 73 E.R. 336.

§**120**   In a conveyance operating under the Statute of Uses, an estate in fee simple may be validly created to take effect after a prior fee simple upon the happening of some named contingency.[1] Where, by an instrument, land is limited to uses, all uses thereunder, whether immediate or future, contingent or executory, or to be declared under any power therein contained, will take effect when and as they arise by force of the estate and seisin originally vested in the person seised to the uses.[2]

1. *Bayliss v. Balfe* (1917), 38 O.L.R. 437 (H.C.) (grantor conveying land to T and T's heirs to hold to use of grantor and grantor's heirs until intended marriage, and to use of intended spouse and spouse's heirs; on marriage, spouse acquiring estate in fee simple; however, if use not inserted, grantor by conveyance cannot create fee simple upon fee simple); **but see** *Re Chauvin* (1920), 18 O.W.N. 178 (H.C.) (in will, fee simple can be limited to take effect after prior fee simple on happening of contingency without intervention of use).

2. Conveyancing and Law of Property Act, R.S.O. 1990, c. C.34, s. 35; *Thuresson v. Thuresson* (1901), 2 O.L.R. 637, per Maclennan J.A.

§**121**   If lands are conveyed to A and A's heirs to such uses as B may appoint, and until appointment to the use of A and A's heirs, A acquires an estate in fee simple until the power of appointment is exercised.[1] If, in such a case, the interest of A is extinguished by the fact that a stranger has been in possession of the lands for the period prescribed by the Limitations Act, an exercise of the power of appointment does not constitute a new starting point for the statute; and thus an appointment of the use, after the extinction of A's interest by the Limitations Act, is of no effect.[2]

1. *Thuresson v. Thuresson* (1901), 2 O.L.R. 637.

2. Limitations Act, R.S.O. 1990, c. L.5; *Thuresson v. Thuresson* (1901), 2 O.L.R. 637, per Maclennan J.A. ("The title of the grantees consisted of two things: the seizin and the use. A power when exercised operates on the use, and the Statute of Uses operates on the seizin and attracts it to the use. But when the title is extinguished there is neither seizin nor use to be operated upon either by the power or by the statute. . . . Indeed it seems to me an absurdity to say that when the title in fee simple is extinguished it nevertheless still continues to exist, for the purpose of being transferred by appointment to a new owner.").

VIII   Dower and Curtesy

§**122**   The Dower Act[1] has been repealed except with respect to a right to dower that vested prior to March 31, 1978.[2] The common law right of a widower to curtesy has been abolished.[3]

1. Dower Act, R.S.O. 1970, c. 135.

2. Family Law Reform Act, S.O. 1978, c. 2, s. 70(2), (4).

3. Succession Law Reform Act, R.S.O. 1990, c. S.26, s. 48.

IX   Powers of Appointment

1. DEFINITION

§123   The essential characteristic of a power of appointment[1] is that it gives the donee of the power the ability to shift beneficial ownership from one or more persons to whom it has been given, to one or more other persons.[2] The power arises where a person is authorized to appoint or create actual interests in land for the benefit of him or herself in some cases and for the benefit of third persons in other cases.[3]

1. See Wills (as to whether, on construction, will giving power of appointment to beneficiary, and if so, whether power general or special); Trusts and Executors and Administrators (as to powers in trust or trusts in form of powers).

2. Morris and Leach, The Rule Against Perpetuities, 1956, p. 126:"The usual type of power of appointment is easily recognizable, e.g., 'to A for life, and then to such persons as A shall by deed or will appoint, and, in default of appointment, to A's children'. There is, however, one type of power which is essentially a power of appointment but is sometimes not recognized as such, namely a discretionary trust, e.g., a trust 'to pay the income to A for life, then to pay the income among the children of A in such proportions as the trustees shall from time to time determine', with appropriate provisions for disposition of the capital. In this case the power in the trustees to determine the shares in which income shall be paid among the children of A is, in essence, a power of appointment."

3. Cheshire's Modern Real Property, 7th ed., p. 219.

2. GENERAL AND SPECIAL POWERS DISTINGUISHED

§124   A general power is such as the donee can exercise in favour of such person or persons as the donee pleases, including him or herself or his or her executors and administrators. A special power can be exercised only in favour of certain specified persons or classes.[1]

1. *Re King* (1925), 57 O.L.R. 144 (C.A.); *Higginson v. Kerr* (1898), 30 O.R. 62 (Ch.).

3. OPERATION, EXERCISE AND VALIDITY OF POWERS

§125   At common law, it was necessary that the terms of the power, and all the formalities required by it, be strictly complied with in the exercise of a power.[1] But a power to be appointed by deed or other non-testamentary written instrument may be validly executed by a deed executed in the presence of and attested by two or more witnesses, notwithstanding that it is especially required that the deed or instrument in writing, made in exercise of such power, is to be executed or attested with some additional or other form of execution or attestation or solemnity.[2]

1. *Marjoribanks v. Hovenden* (1843), 6 I. Eq. R. 238.

2. Conveyancing and Law of Property Act, R.S.O. 1990, c. C.34, s. 25(1), (3) (nothing in s. 25 preventing donee of power from executing it conformably to power).

§126   Where the instrument creating the power does not prescribe the manner in which it is to be executed, the exercise of the power is valid if the Statute of Frauds is complied with; and in such a case it is not necessary that it be executed in the manner prescribed by the Conveyancing and Law of Property Act.[1]

1. *Spellman v. Litovitz* (1918), 44 O.L.R. 30 (H.C.) (legislation intended to give relief from burdensome and needless requirements sometimes contained in instruments creating such powers, not to make manner of execution more burdensome in cases where no burden imposed by creator of power; had enactment not been passed, all that would have been necessary in this case is that Statute of Frauds and Registry Act be complied with, as admittedly they were); **see also** Statute of Frauds, R.S.O. 1990, c. S.19; Registry Act, R.S.O. 1990, c. R.20.

§127   But if the deed or instrument creating the power directs that the consent of some person must be obtained to exercise the power, or that some act having no relation to the mode of executing or attesting the instrument exercising the power must be performed, the power cannot be validly executed unless that consent is obtained or the required acts are performed.[1]

1. Conveyancing and Law of Property Act, R.S.O. 1990, c. C.34, s. 25(2).

§128   An appointment of land in Ontario made by will, in exercise of any power, is not valid unless the will is executed in the manner prescribed by the Succession Law Reform Act.[1]

1. Succession Law Reform Act, R.S.O. 1990, c. S.26, s. 9; **see also** *Tabashniuk v. Barrett* (1979), 3 E.T.R. 251 (Ont. H.C.); *Spellman v. Litovitz* (1918), 44 O.L.R. 30 (H.C.) (notwithstanding strong words of statute, there may be appointments validly made by foreign wills not made in manner required by Wills Act); *Re Price*, [1900] 1 Ch. 442 (appointment of personalty); *Pouey v. Hordern*, [1900] 1 Ch. 492; *Re Simpson*, [1916] 1 Ch. 502; *Re Wilkinson's Settlement*, [1917] 1 Ch. 620 at 627.

§129   An appointment made by will, under any power, may be validly exercised with respect to the execution and attestation thereof if the will is executed in accordance with the Succession Law Reform Act notwithstanding that it is expressly required that a will made in the exercise of such power is to be executed with some additional or other forms of execution or solemnity.[1]

1. Succession Law Reform Act, R.S.O. 1990, c. S.26, s. 9.

§130 A power to appoint by will cannot be executed in any other manner than by will.[1] Where a power is to be appointed by will only, the court has no authority to authorize the donee of the power to exercise it in his or her lifetime.[2]

> 1. *Collard v. Duckworth* (1889), 16 O.R. 735 at 736 (H.C.) (intention of creator of power taken to be that donee not to deprive him or herself of right to select such objects of power as donee deems proper); *Smith v. King* (1917), 13 O.W.N. 54 (H.C.).
>
> 2. *Re Newton* (1912), 3 O.W.N. 948 (Ch.).

§131 Since a will is essentially revocable, an exercise of a power to appoint by will contained in the last will of the donee cannot be affected by an exercise of the power in a revoked will, even though there is a covenant by the donee of the power not to revoke the prior will.[1]

> 1. *Collard v. Duckworth* (1889), 16 O.R. 735 at 736 (H.C.) (such appointment would breach covenant and render covenantor liable in damages, but would not affect title of appointee under later appointment; by terms creating it, power to be executed only by will; any attempt by donee to execute power by irrevocable instrument cannot bind person taking under later will); **but see** *Drew v. McGowan* (1901), 1 O.L.R. 575 (K.B.) (lands to widow for life, then to D for life, with power to D to devise in fee; held that D could agreed for valuable consideration not to execute power, that such agreement would operate as release of power, and that widow and D, and heirs of testator ascertained at time of death, could make good title).

§132 A power which, by the instrument creating it, is to be executed by deed cannot be validly executed by will, even though the will is under seal.[1]

> 1. *Shore v. Shore* (1891), 21 O.R. 54 (C.A.); **but see** *McDermott v. Keenan* (1887), 14 O.R. 687 (H.C.) (must be considered as overruled by *Shore v. Shore*).

§133 Equity will aid a defective execution of a power if the intended appointee is a purchaser from the person intending to exercise the power, or a creditor of such person, or a spouse, or child, or if the appointment is for a charitable purpose.[1] On equitable principles, the court will aid a defective execution of a power for the benefit of children, but not where the effect would be to take away the property from several children who would be entitled on default of appointment, for the benefit of one child who would be entitled under the defective appointment.[2] Nor will the court aid a defective execution of a power for the benefit of an illegitimate child of the appointer so as to deprive the legitimate children of their rights in default of appointment.[3]

> 1. *Lucena v. Lucena* (1843), 49 E.R. 573; *Re Walker*, [1908] 1 Ch. 560.
>
> 2. *Shore v. Shore* (1891), 21 O.R. 54 (C.A.).
>
> 3. *Shore v. Shore* (1891), 21 O.R. 54 (C.A.).

§134   An appointment in excess of the power conferred is void, and under such an excessive execution of a power nothing passes to the appointee.[1]

> 1. *Scane v. Hartwick* (1854), 11 U.C.Q.B. 550 (widow having power to appoint estate in fee tail and purporting to appoint estate in fee simple; devise in fee simple being void execution of power given to widow by husband's will); **see also** *Archer v. Urquhart* (1893), 23 O.R. 214 (power given to married woman to appoint use by deed or will among heirs of her body in fee tail; appointment to use to benefit of husband and children absolutely held excessive exercise of power which was void and entirely inoperative); *Re Matthews* (1924), 56 O.L.R. 406 (H.C.) (widow given power to divide husband's estate among three named sons; appointing in favour of two sons and of infant son of third son, who had predeceased testator; although appointment as to grandson invalid, appointment in favour of two sons severable and valid).

§135   A donee of a power, whether or not that power is coupled with an interest, may by deed disclaim or release or contract not to exercise the power.[1] A donee so disclaiming cannot afterwards exercise or join in the exercise of the power; and on such disclaimer the power may be exercised by the other or others or the survivor or survivors of the others of the persons to whom the power is given, unless the contrary is expressed in the instrument creating the power.[2]

> 1. Conveyancing and Law of Property Act, R.S.O. 1990, c. C.34, s. 26(1); **see also** *Lee v. Shaw* (1932), 42 O.W.N. 92 (H.C.); **but see** *Collard v. Duckworth* (1889), 16 O.R. 735 at 736 (H.C.) (section not conferring on donee of power to be exercised by will right to confer on purchaser good title by covenanting not to exercise power by will); *Drew v. McGowan* (1901), 1 O.L.R. 575 (K.B.) (testator devising lands to his widow for life, then to D for life, with power to D to devise fee; held that if D covenanting in conveyance not to exercise power, then widow, D and testator's heirs able to confer good title on purchaser).

> 2. Conveyancing and Law of Property Act, R.S.O. 1990, c. C.34, s. 26(2).

§136   An appointment made in exercise of any power or authority is valid and effectual, notwithstanding that any one or more will not thereunder or in default of such appointment take more than an insubstantial, illusory or nominal share, or take no share of the property subject to such power.[1]

> 1. Conveyancing and Law of Property Act, R.S.O. 1990, c. C.34, s. 28.

§137   Property over which a testator executes by will a general power of appointment vests in the personal representative of the testator and is subject to the payment of the testator's debts.[1] With respect to the execution of a general power of appointment by will, a married person has a legal personality that is independent, separate and distinct from that of his or her spouse.[2]

> 1. Estates Administration Act, R.S.O. 1990, c. E.22, s. 2(1), (2).

> 2. Family Law Act, R.S.O. 1990, c. F.3, s. 64(1).

§138 A general devise of the real property of the testator, or of the real property of the testator in any place or in the occupation of any person mentioned in the will, or otherwise described in a general manner, is construed to include any real property or any real property to which the description extends, which he or she may have power to appoint in any manner he or she thinks proper, and operates as an execution of such power unless a contrary intention appears in the will.[1]

> 1. Succession Law Reform Act, R.S.O. 1990, c. S.26, s. 25; *Smith v. Chisholme* (1888), 15 O.A.R. 738; *Re Wilson* (1899), 30 O.R. 553; *Re Ross* (1910), 1 O.W.N. 867; *Osborne v. Campbell* (1918), 15 O.W.N. 48 (H.C.); *Re Hammond* (1920), 18 O.W.N. 253 (H.C.); *Re King* (1925), 57 O.L.R. 144 at 147 (C.A.) (applying only to disposition of property over which testator had general power of appointment under general devise or bequest; no application to special or limited power of appointment); *Re Cochrane* (1908), 16 O.L.R. 328 at 335 (C.A.); *Re Gilkinson* (1930), 38 O.W.N. 26 (H.C.); affirmed (1930), 39 O.W.N. 115 (C.A.).

§139 If a general power is given to A to appoint the use by will or by a writing under hand and seal, so that it appears that the exercise of the power is to be personal to A, A cannot delegate by will the execution of that power to B; but A can execute the power by appointing it to B to such uses as B may appoint.[1] If A has an absolute power of appointment, A may appoint to certain persons or classes of persons in such shares as B will nominate, since this implies an actual execution of the power by A.[2]

> 1. *Smith v. Chisholme* (1888), 15 O.A.R. 738 (husband delegating to wife exercise of general power of appointment to which he had been entitled).
>
> 2. *White v. Wilson* (1852), 61 E.R. 466; *Smith v. Chisholme* (1888), 15 O.A.R. 738.

§140 A donee of a special power must exercise the power in good faith for the end designed; otherwise the execution of the power is void.[1] The execution of the power may be fraudulent and void on the ground that it was made in pursuance of an antecedent agreement by the appointee to benefit persons not objects of the power, or on the ground that it was made for purposes foreign to the power, even though such purposes were not communicated to the appointee previous to the appointment and even though the appointer derived no personal benefit.[2] Appointments which are thus fraudulent and void cannot be severed so as to be good to the extent to which they are bona fide executions of the power but bad as to the remainder, except where some consideration has been given which cannot be restored, and it has consequently become impossible to rescind the transaction in toto, or where the court can sever the intentions of the appointer and distinguish the good from the fraudulent.[3]

> 1. *Bell v. Lee* (1883), 8 O.A.R. 185; *Aleyn v. Belchier* (1758), 28 E.R. 634; *Portland (Duke) v. Lady Topham* (1864), 11 H.L. Cas. 32.

2. *Bell v. Lee* (1883), 8 O.A.R. 185; *Portland (Duke) v. Lady Topham* (1864), 11 H.L. Cas. 32.

3. *Bell v. Lee* (1883), 8 O.A.R. 185.

§141   Although the exercise of a power pursuant to an arrangement by which the appointer benefits is generally invalid, the power will be upheld if it is exercised as part of a family arrangement.[1]

1. *Matthews, Re* (1924), 56 O.L.R. 406 (H.C.) (widow appointing in favour of two sons, who were only objects of special power; sons at once conveying their appointed shares back to mother: appointment upheld).

§142   A power the exercise of which does not affect the estate of the donee of the power in the land is termed a power collateral or in gross. If there is no specific limitation as to the time of the exercise of the power, the whole period of the life of the donee is allowed for the execution of the power.[1]

1. *Cowan v. Besserer* (1883), 5 O.R. 624 (H.C.).

§143   If a mere power is vested in two persons' nomination, without any reference to an office in its nature liable to survivorship, such as an executorship, the power cannot be exercised by the survivor of the two persons.[1]

1. *Re Roach* (1930), 38 O.W.N. 189 (H.C.); affirmed (1930), 39 O.W.N. 109 (C.A.); affirmed [1931] S.C.R. 512.

§144   If property is devised to A for life with a general power of appointment, the property passes to the next of kin of the testator if A dies without exercising the power.[1]

1. *Re Gilkinson* (1930), 38 O.W.N. 26 (H.C.); affirmed (1930), 39 O.W.N. 115 (C.A.); *Henderson v. Henderson* (1922), 52 O.L.R. 440 (H.C.); *Re Pellett* (1907), 9 O.W.R. 587 (effect of failure to exercise special or limited power of appointment).

§145   A power which is not to arise until a future or contingent event happens or until a condition is fulfilled cannot be exercised until the event happens or the condition is fulfilled, for until then it has in fact no existence.[1]

1. *Rathbone v. White* (1892), 22 O.R. 550 (Ch.); **see also** *Smith v. King* (1917), 13 O.W.N. 54 (H.C.) (property devised to A for life with power on death to divide among children of testator; held that good title not able to be made unless A and all children being sui juris and unless all joined in conveyance).

§146   If a donee has a power which he or she can exercise by will only, the court has no authority to authorize the exercise of the power in the donee's lifetime.[1]

1. *Re Newton* (1912), 3 O.W.N. 948 (Ch.).

§147 A general power over the whole estate to appoint the use may exist simultaneously with the common law seisin in fee, in one person.[1]

1. *Re Hazell* (1925), 57 O.L.R. 166 (H.C.); varied (1925), 57 O.L.R. 290 (C.A.) (no doubt really existing on point since judgment in *Ray v. Pung*, (1822), 5 B. & A. 561); **see also** *Osborne v. Campbell* (1918), 15 O.W.N. 48 (H.C.); *Strauss v. Fierstein* (1924), 26 O.W.N. 304 (H.C.); *Morris v. Chertkoff* (1925), 56 O.L.R. 665 (C.A.); *Maundrell v. Maundrell* (1804), 32 E.R. 228; *Moody v. King* (1825), 130 E.R. 378; *Lyster v. Kirkpatrick* (1886), 26 U.C.Q.B. 217 at 228 (C.A.).

§148 If an estate is limited to such uses as A appoints, an appointment by A to such uses as B appoints is valid and effectual to pass the legal estate to B's appointee.[1]

1. *Re Hazell* (1925), 57 O.L.R. 166 (H.C.); varied (1925), 57 O.L.R. 290 (C.A.), per Logie J.; *Morley v. Kent*, [1966] 2 O.R. 368 (H.C.) (exercise of power of appointment under statute operating as transfer of fee free of dower).

§149 An appointment of the use by way of mortgage does not necessarily exhaust the power, but the extent to which such an appointment operates depends entirely on the intention to be collected from the deed of appointment taken as a whole.[1] If land is conveyed to A in fee simple to such uses as A may appoint, and A appoints the use by way of mortgage to B, the execution and registration of a discharge of that mortgage will operate to vest in the mortgagor not the original power of appointment, but the legal seisin in fee.[2]

1. *Re Hazell* (1925), 57 O.L.R. 166 (H.C.); varied (1925), 57 O.L.R. 290 (C.A.), per Logie J.

2. *Re Hazell* (1925), 57 O.L.R. 166 (H.C.); varied (1925), 57 O.L.R. 290 (C.A.).

X Joint Tenancy and Tenancy in Common

1. GENERAL

(a) Effect of Grants or Devises to Two or More Persons

§150 Where land has been or is granted, conveyed or devised to two or more persons[1] other than executors or trustees in fee simple or for any less estate by any letters patent, assurance or will made and executed after July 1, 1834, it will be considered that such persons took or take as tenants in common and not as joint tenants, unless sufficient intention appears on the face of such letters patent, assurance or will that such persons are to take as joint tenants.[2] If a will does not manifest a contrary intention, a gift to a named person "and family"creates a tenancy in common.[3] This applies notwithstanding that one of such persons is the spouse or same-sex partner of another of them.[4]

> 1. See 2 Bl. (7th ed., 1775) at 179 (as to estates held in severalty, joint tenancy, coparcenary and common); coparceners expressly mentioned in: Partition Act, R.S.O. 1990, c. P.4, s. 2; Limitations Act, R.S.O. 1990, c. L.15, s. 11; Settled Estates Act, R.S.O. 1990, c. S.7, s. 18(2); **see also** Estates Administration Act, R.S.O. 1990, c. E.22, s. 14; *Central Trust Co. v. McCann Estate* (1987), 59 O.R. (2d) 488 (H.C.) (deed of settlement referring to property held "jointly"; as used, "jointly" broad enough to encompass property held by parties both as tenants in common and as joint tenants); Family Law (as to joint tenancy and tenancy in common by spouses).
>
> 2. Conveyancing and Law of Property Act, R.S.O. 1990, c. C.34, s. 13(1); **see also** *Re Quebec* (1929), 37 O.W.N. 271 (H.C.) (devise to mother and son "jointly" creating joint tenancy); *Re MacDonell* (1929), 36 O.W.N. 338 (H.C.); *Central Trust Co. v. McCann Estate* (1987), 59 O.R. (2d) 488 (H.C.).
>
> 3. *Re Quebec* (1929), 37 O.W.N. 271 (H.C.).
>
> 4. Conveyancing and Law of Property Act, R.S.O. 1990, c. C.34, s. 13(2) [am. 1999, c. 6, s. 13(1)].

§151 The intention that two or more persons to whom a conveyance is made in fee simple are to take as joint tenants and not as tenants in common "sufficiently appears" so as to bring the case within the exception in s. 13(1) of the Conveyancing and Law of Property Act if such intention clearly appears anywhere on the face of the deed; it need not appear in either the habendum or the granting clause.[1]

> 1. Conveyancing and Law of Property Act, R.S.O. 1990, c. C.34, s. 13(1); *Billett v. Davidson* (1920), 18 O.W.N. 425 (H.C.).

(b) Estates Administration Act

§152 Where real property is vested under the Estates Administration Act in two or more persons beneficially entitled under the Act, such persons take as tenants in common in proportion to their respective rights, unless in the case of a devise they take otherwise under the deceased's will.[1]

 1. Estates Administration Act, R.S.O. 1990, c. E.22, s. 14.

(c) Land Held by Trustee

§153   The Land Titles Act requires that where two or more owners are described as trustees, the property must be held to be vested in them as joint tenants unless the contrary is expressly stated.[1]

 1. Land Titles Act, R.S.O. 1990, c. L.5, s. 69(3).

(d) Acquisition of Land by Two or More
Persons by Length of Possession

§154   Where two or more persons acquire land by length of possession, they are to be considered to hold as tenants in common and not as joint tenants.[1]

 1. Conveyancing and Law of Property Act, R.S.O. 1990, c. C.34, s. 14.

(e) Settled Estates

§155   Where two or more persons are entitled as tenants in common, joint tenants or coparceners, any or either of them may apply to the court to exercise the powers conferred by the Settled Estates Act.[1]

 1. Settled Estates Act, R.S.O. 1990, c. S.7, s. 18(2).

(f) Coparceners

§156   Coparceners are not, strictly speaking, within either of the terms "joint tenants" or "tenants in common", differing in some incidents from both.[1]

 1. *Gregory v. Connolly* (1850), 7 U.C.Q.B. 500; see 2 Bl. (7th ed., 1775) at 187ff (estate held in coparcenary where lands of inheritance descending from ancestor to two or more persons; arising either by common law or by particular custom; material differences between coparceners and joint tenants being: claim by descent, not purchase; unity of time unnecessary; and coparceners not having entirety of interest, with no jus accrescendi or survivorship between them).

(g) Liability for Waste

§157   Tenants in common and joint tenants are liable to their co-tenants for waste, or, in the event of a partition, the part wasted may be assigned to the tenant committing the waste, with the value of the waste to be estimated as if no such waste had been committed.[1]

1. Conveyancing and Law of Property Act, R.S.O. 1990, c. C.34, s. 31; Courts of Justice Act, R.S.O. 1990, c. C.43, s. 100; *Lassert v. Salyerds* (1870), 17 Gr. 109 (not general practice of court of equity to enjoin one joint tenant, at instance of co-tenant, from committing waste; rule being otherwise where bill already filed for partition).

(h) Purchase at Tax Sale

§158 Where one of two or more joint tenants of land purchase the land at a tax sale, there being no prior agreement between them that the purchase must be for their joint benefit, and no fraud, the purchaser is entitled to hold the lands for his or her own benefit.[1] The rule is the same where the parties are tenants in common.[2]

1. *Janisse v. Stewart* (1925), 28 O.W.N. 446 (H.C.); *Fleet v. Fleet* (1925), 28 O.W.N. 193 (C.A.).

2. *Kennedy v. De Trafford*, [1896] 1 Ch. 762 (C.A.); affirmed [1897] A.C. 180 (H.L.).

§159 Where land owned by joint tenants is sold for taxes, any one of the joint tenants may redeem, and it is not necessary that all the co-tenants join in redeeming.[1]

1. *Ray v. Kilgour* (1907), 9 O.W.N. 641 (C.A.).

2. JOINT TENANCY

(a) Characteristics of Joint Tenancy

§160 The fourfold unity is the great characteristic of an estate in joint tenancy.[1] The joint tenancy must arise out of the same deed, will or claim; there must be unity of title. The estate must vest in the tenants simultaneously; there must be unity of time. Each tenant must take the same estate; there must be unity of interest. And each tenant takes an undivided moiety of the whole; there must be unity of possession.[2]

1. *Myers v. Ruport* (1904), 8 O.L.R. 668 (C.A.) (right of joint tenant to dispose of parcel); **see also** *Dean v. Coyle*, [1973] 3 O.R. 185 (Co. Ct.) (vendor owning one parcel absolutely and adjacent parcel by joint tenancy not requiring consent pursuant to Planning Act to sell first parcel, since, as joint tenant of other parcel, her right to dispose of such not absolute; "fee" in Act held to refer to interest involving absolute right of disposal).

2. *Myers v. Ruport* (1904), 8 O.L.R. 668 (C.A.); *Armstrong v. Currie* (1932), 7 M.P.R. 135 (N.B.Q.B.); affirmed, 6 M.P.R. 591 (N.B.C.A.); *Miles v. Conkin*, [1995] B.C.W.L.D. 1163 (B.C.S.C.); affirmed (1996), 24 R.F.L. (4th) 211 (B.C. C.A.) (court-ordered partition and sale; each party entitled to original contribution plus equal division of equity; registration in joint tenancy merely a way to secure plaintiff's small financial contribution towards purchase price in event of defendant's death); **see also** *Simpson v. Ziprick* (1995), 8 E.T.R. (2d) 1 (B.C.C.A.); leave to appeal to S.C.C. granted (1996), 199 N.R. 157n (S.C.C.) (transfer of property in joint tenancy void where evidence rebutting presumption of advancement).

§161   A deed conveying property to a husband and wife or same-sex partner as joint tenants is an "assurance" under the Conveyancing and Law of Property Act.[1] The deed creates a joint tenancy and not a tenancy by entireties, which, in addition to the four unities of possession, interest, time and title, also requires the conjugal unity of the parties.[2]

> 1. Conveyancing and Law of Property Act, R.S.O. 1990, c. C.34, s. 13 [am. 1999, c. 6, s. 13].
>
> 2. *Demaiter v. Link*, [1973] O.R. 140 (H.C.).

(b) Creation of Joint Tenancy

§162   A joint tenancy may be created by disseisin as well as by deed or devise, and if two or more persons disseise another of lands or tenements to their own use, they become joint tenants thereof. Also, where two or more persons in lawful possession of property under a title which comes to an end remain in possession without any title, upon such wrongful possession they become joint tenants of the property.[1]

> 1. *Myers v. Ruport* (1904), 8 O.L.R. 668 (C.A.); *McLaughlin v. Mitchell*, [1949] O.R. 105 (C.A.); affirmed [1950] S.C.R. 291 (each purchaser paying half of purchase price; deed made to purchasers as joint tenants); *Re Deeley Estate* (1995), 10 E.T.R. (2d) 30 (Ont. Gen. Div.) (registration and physical delivery of deed to transferee not required to create joint tenancy; **see also** *Steeves v. Haslam House* (1975), 8 O.R. (2d) 165 (H.C.) (deed describing grantees as joint tenants, but making no other references to joint tenancy; sufficient intention shown on face of documents that grantees joint tenants).

(c) Severance and Extinguishment of Joint Tenancy

§163   Destruction of any one of the four unities of joint tenancy, namely possession, interest, title or time, will terminate the tenancy and therewith the right of survivorship. The maintenance of these unities is essential to the continued existence of this right. Not every dealing with the interest of one of the joint tenants will operate to sever or terminate the tenancy. For example, a lease for years of his or her share by one of two joint tenants in fee does not sever the tenancy; but where the joint tenants hold for a term of years only, it will do so. Where one of two joint tenants in fee grants his or her interest to a stranger for life, the joint tenancy is merely suspended; if during such life estate either of the joint tenants dies, there is no proof of survivorship and the joint estate is permanently severed; but if the life tenant dies before either of the joint tenants does, the joint estate is revived.[1]

> 1. *Power v. Grace*, [1932] O.R. 357 (C.A.); *Worobel Estate v. Worobel* (1989), 67 O.R. (2d) 151 (H.C.); *Schobelt v. Barber*, [1967] 1 O.R. 349 (H.C.) (effect of murder of one joint tenant by other on right of survivorship); **see also** *Ontario (Attorney General) v. Yeotes* (1981), 31 O.R. (2d) 589 (C.A.); leave to appeal to S.C.C. refused,

37 N.R. 356 (S.C.C.) (owners of large tracts of land securing partition orders by consent to effect subdivision; partition orders not falling within prohibited methods or instruments under Act); *Kozub v. Timko* (1984), 45 O.R. (2d) 558 (C.A.) (conveyance being disposal of interest under s. 42(1) and properly set aside under s. 44; conveyance ineffective to sever joint tenancy); *Sampaio Estate v. Sampaio* (1992), 22 R.P.R. (2d) 314 (Ont. Gen. Div.) (deceased and defendant former wife intending to sever all ties, as evidenced by separation agreement; deceased's intention to purchase defendant's share of condominium unit clearly demonstrating that deceased intending to sever joint tenancy; this being inconsistent with joint tenancy; plaintiff wife discharging onus and showing course of dealing sufficient to intimate that interests of all being mutually treated as constituting tenancy in common); *Lamanna v. Lamanna* (1983), 32 R.F.L. (2d) 386 (Ont. H.C.) (spouses having joint tenancy of matrimonial home; wife conveying her interest to herself; not "disposition"; joint tenancy severed); *Bendix v. Jonas* (1982), 27 R.P.R. 163 (Ont. H.C.) (conveyance of joint tenancy interest in farm by one spouse without consent of other; matrimonial home located on farm; conveyance set aside with respect to home; conveyance effective as to balance of farm, thus severing joint tenancy; surviving spouse taking matrimonial home portion as surviving joint tenant); *Robichaud v. Watson* (1983), 42 O.R. (2d) 38 (H.C.) (plaintiff administratrix of son's estate applying for declaration that joint tenancy severed prior to murder of son; declaration granted; plaintiff satisfying court that at some stage joint tenants by conduct intending during their lifetime to treat interests as severed; negotiations through counsel indicating joint tenants considered interests severed); *Cochrane v. Cochrane* (1980), 28 O.R. (2d) 57 (Ont. Co. Ct.) (application under Planning Act refused; no appeal taken; subsequent partition application by spouse; no matrimonial proceedings; attempt to circumvent Planning Act; partition refused); *Van Dorp v. Van Dorp* (1980), 30 O.R. (2d) 623 (Co. Ct.) (husband's conveyance of his interest in home to himself severing joint tenancy; wife not consenting; wife having standing to set aside conveyance after husband's death; conveyance set aside, as disposition not made for value, not in good faith, and without notice that property being matrimonial home); *Bank of Montreal v. Bray* (1997), 33 R.F.L. (4th) 335 (Ont. C.A.) (husband and wife owning home as joint tenants; without informing wife, husband signing guarantee for business debt and later acknowledging guarantee; husband transferring home to wife when business failing; conveyance valid as between husband and wife, but void as against creditors; by conveyance, husband destroying unity of title, unity of interest, and right of survivorship; creditor bank entitled to one-half interest in home upon husband's death).

§**164**   There is no survivorship in a joint tenancy except upon the death of one of the joint tenants. The joint tenancy may be severed by operation of law, as upon the bankruptcy of a joint tenant, whether the property held in joint tenancy is real or personal. Where a debtor conveys lands owned by the debtor and his or her spouse as joint tenants, and some years afterward makes an authorized assignment for the benefit of creditors, the assignment severs the joint tenancy and creates a tenancy in common, and, under the Bankruptcy and Insolvency Act,[1] the trustee is entitled to a one-half interest in the property.[2]

1. Bankruptcy and Insolvency Act, R.S.C. 1985, c. B-3, s. 67(1) [renumbered 1992, c. 27, s. 33; am. 1997, c. 12, s. 59].

2. *Re White* (1928), 8 C.B.R. 544 (Ont. H.C.).

§165   The interest of one joint tenant can be sold under an execution, and the purchaser at the sheriff's sale is entitled to partition.[1]

    1. *Re Craig* (1928), 63 O.L.R. 192 (C.A.); *Toronto Hospital for Consumptives v. Toronto* (1930), 38 O.W.N. 196 (C.A.); **see also** *Maroukis v. Maroukis* (1981), 33 O.R. (2d) 661 (C.A.); affirmed [1984] 2 S.C.R. 137 (matrimonial home to be vested in wife subject to rights of bank under executions filed prior to trial judge's order; until judge making order, matrimonial home held in joint tenancy, and executions against husband filed prior to that date attaching to his interest; trial judge having no jurisdiction to vest property in wife free of executions).

§166   If the joint tenant against whom an execution is lodged in the sheriff's office dies before any steps are taken by the sheriff against the lands, the survivor holds free from the execution. Delivery of the writ of fi. fa. to the sheriff is not execution.[1] This rule operates only in the case of death.

    1. *Power v. Grace*, [1932] O.R. 357 (C.A.); **see also** *Morris v. Butler* (1980), 27 O.R. (2d) 765 (Prov. Ct.) (deceased and common law partner owning property as joint tenants; title passing to surviving partner on death of one; writ of execution, filed against deceased's land nine days after death, not affecting jointly owned property; deceased having no interest in property at time writ filed).

§167   By virtue of the Execution Act,[1] the writ binds the lands from the time of the delivery thereof, so that if the interest of the life tenant is exigible, and the joint tenancy thereby severable, then any purchaser from the parties takes subject to the rights of the debtor's execution creditor.[2]

    1. Execution Act, R.S.O. 1990, c. E.24, s. 10(1).

    2. *Re O'Brien*, [1943] O.W.N. 436 (H.C.).

§168   A conveyance in fee to A by B, the survivor of two joint tenants, "of his undivided half of the lot" puts an end to the joint tenancy and makes the joint tenant B, until death, a tenant in common with A, and B may by will devise the moiety he or she has not by his or her deed to A.[1] The joint interest in real property is severable, and one of such interests may be sold under execution. A joint interest in an equity of redemption may be sold under a writ of execution.[2] A joint tenancy held by a husband and wife is severable and the interest of one of them can be sold under execution.[3]

    1. *Doe d. Eberts v. Montreuil* (1850), 6 U.C.Q.B. 515.

    2. *Klagsbrun v. Stankiewicz*, [1953] O.W.N. 910 (H.C.); *Re Craig* (1928), 63 O.L.R. 192 (C.A.); *Kates v. Morrison*, [1951] O.W.N. 701 (H.C.); *Tully v. Tully*, [1953] O.W.N. 661.

    3. *Re O'Brien*, [1943] O.W.N. 436 (H.C.).

§169   Where lands are held by joint tenants and are subject to a mortgage, the filing of a writ of execution in the sheriff's office does not bind the lands.

The Execution Act sets out the rights of execution creditors in respect of lands that are not subject to mortgage,[1] and in respect of lands where the execution debtor owns only an equity of redemption.[2] Because an equity of redemption is a unit, whole and indivisible, and anyone having an interest is entitled to redeem the whole, the share of one joint tenant is not exigible under a writ of execution against that tenant, and the writ does not bind the lands or that tenant's share of the equity of redemption. The mere filing of the execution with the sheriff does not create a severance of the joint tenancy. The equity of redemption of joint tenants not being exigible, the purchaser takes clear title and the rights of the execution creditors are limited to following the purchase moneys into the hands of the execution debtor.[3]

1. Execution Act, R.S.O. 1990, c. E.24, s. 10.

2. Execution Act, R.S.O. 1990, c. E.24, s. 28

3. *Tully v. Tully*, [1953] O.W.N. 661; **but see** *Klagsbrun v. Stankiewicz*, [1953] O.W.N. 910 (H.C.).

§170 The conduct of the parties may be sufficient to sever a joint tenancy. Thus, where one joint tenant dies before the hearing of an application for partition brought by the other joint tenant, the joint tenancy is severed by the conduct of the parties which established a course of dealing "sufficient to intimate that the interests of all were mutually treated as constituting a tenancy in common".[1] It would appear, however, that making an application for partition is not, by itself, sufficient to sever a joint tenancy.[2]

1. *Re Walters* (1978), 16 O.R. (2d) 702 (H.C.); affirmed, 17 O.R. (2d) 592 (C.A.).

2. *Rodrigue v. Dufton* (1976), 13 O.R. (2d) 613 (H.C.).

§171 Joint tenants, although seised in whole and in part, for the purposes of alienation, have separate shares and can release these shares to a co-tenant or transfer them to a stranger, effectively changing the character of the joint tenancy to that of a tenancy in common.[1] The non-alienating joint tenant's claim to title by survivorship is extinguished.[2]

1. *Stonehouse v. British Columbia (Attorney General)*, [1962] S.C.R. 103; **see also** *Re Cameron* (1957), 11 D.L.R. (2d) 201 (H.C.); *Wright v. Gibbons* (1948), 78 C.L.R. 313 (Aus. H.C.).

2. *Stonehouse v. British Columbia (Attorney General)*, [1962] S.C.R. 103; **see also** *Horne v. Evans* (1986), 54 O.R. (2d) 510 (H.C.); affirmed (1987), 60 O.R. (2d) 1 (C.A.)

§172 The fact that a spouse leaves the property does not terminate the joint tenancy. A separation, even followed by annulment of the marriage, does not affect the joint tenancy.[1]

1. *Crawford v. Crawford*, [1953] O.W.N. 781 (Master); *Dunbar v. Dunbar*, [1909] 2 Ch. 639; *Boon v. Thomas* (1997), 29 O.T.C. 97 (Ont. Small Cl. Ct.) (common law couple taking title to home as joint tenants; relationship breaking down; nothing in conduct indicating intention to sever joint tenancy which subsisted to time of sale of home).

§172.1 However, under the Limitations Act,[1] possession of joint tenants is separate possession from the time one joint tenant takes possession of the entirety.[2]

1. Limitations Act, R.S.O. 1990, c. L.15, s. 11.

2. *Hurren v. Hurren* (1995), 11 R.F.L. (4th) 12 (Ont. Gen. Div.) (separate possessions occurring when wife leaving home; husband having continuous exclusive possession for 17 years thereafter; husband having possession for sufficient time to extinguish wife's interest under s. 4 of Limitations Act).

§173 The unilateral act of one joint tenant in conveying to him or herself is sufficient to sever the tenancy; there is no need to resort to the cumbersome device of a deed to a third person to the use of the grantor, since the joint tenant's conduct is sufficient to sever the tenancy even without the agreement of the other joint tenant as to the severance.[1]

1. Conveyancing and Law of Property Act, R.S.O. 1990, c. C.34, s. 41; *Murdoch v. Barry* (1975), 10 O.R. (2d) 626 (H.C.); *Re Cameron* (1957), 11 D.L.R. (2d) 201 (H.C.) (registrability of transfer of joint tenant's interest to third party without concurrence of other joint tenant); **see also** *Re Sammon* (1979), 22 O.R. (2d) 721 (C.A.) (husband, separated from wife, executing deed to uses of half interest to himself and delivering deed to solicitor; solicitor not to register deed until after husband's death, for fear of wife discovering it; deed not effective to sever joint tenancy) *Strong v. Colby* (1978), 20 O.R. (2d) 356 (H.C.) (husband executing deed and conveying to himself and others half interest in matrimonial home; wife's subsequent application for partition and sale opposed on ground of husband's acquisition of possessory title of wife's interest through adverse possession; partition and sale ordered where husband's possession not accompanied by requisite intention to exclude wife); *Horne v. Evans* (1986), 54 O.R. (2d) 510 (H.C.); affirmed (1987), 60 O.R. (2d) 1 (C.A.) (husband and wife owning matrimonial home as joint tenants; shortly before his death, husband conveying his interest to himself for purpose of severing joint tenancy; s. 42 of Family Law Reform Act not proscribing severance of joint tenancy in such manner).

§174 A joint tenancy may be severed by one joint tenant entering into an option to purchase.[1]

1. *National Trust Co. v. McKee* (1974), 49 D.L.R. (3d) 689 (Ont. H.C.); reversed on other grounds, 56 D.L.R. (3d) 190 (C.A.).

(d) Voluntary Bestowment in Joint Tenancy

§175 The requirements to establish a gift inter vivos or a donatio mortis causa are distinct from those which go to create a voluntary bestowment in joint tenancy. In the case of a joint tenancy, the four unities must exist, namely unity of interest, title, time and possession.[1]

1. *Weese v. Weese* (1916), 37 O.L.R. 649 (H.C.); *Re Ryan* (1900), 32 O.R. 224 (H.C.); *Everly v. Dunkley* (1912), 27 O.L.R. 414 (C.A.).

(e) Rights of Joint Tenants Inter Se

§176   There is no fiduciary relationship between joint tenants or tenants in common of real estate,[1] and the mere fact that one co-tenant receives the rents and pays interest and taxes and generally manages the property does not create any such fiduciary relationship.[2]

1. *Mastron v. Cotton* (1925), 58 O.L.R. 251 (C.A.); *Re Sorenson* (1932), 41 O.W.N. 261 (H.C.) (agreement to buy land as joint tenants; death of one tenant); *McLaughlin v. Mitchell*, [1949] O.R. 105; affirmed, (*sub nom.* Randall v. McLaughlin) [1950] S.C.R. 291 (rights of survivor; rents or profits; limitation of actions); *Grant v. Grant*, [1952] O.W.N. 641 (Master) (liability to account; revenues derived by wife from roomers and boarders; wife conducting business alone, at own financial risk and without help from husband; wife not required to account to husband for profits).

2. *Fleet v. Fleet* (1925), 28 O.W.N. 193 (C.A.) (co-tenants being joint tenants and husband and wife); *Gerace v. Thompson* (1977), 15 O.R. (2d) 689 (H.C.) (mode of conveyance by one joint tenant to another); **see also** *Canadian Life Assurance Co. v. Kennedy* (1978), 21 O.R. (2d) 83 (C.A.) (one joint tenant making improvements to land; other joint tenant's interest subject to mortgage; agreement showing intention that improvements create lien; co-tenant having priority over mortgagee with respect to improvements); *Janisse v. Stewart* (1925), 28 O.W.N. 446 (H.C.).

(f) Corporation as Joint Tenant

§177   A corporation is capable of acquiring and holding real property in joint tenancy in the same manner as if it were an individual.[1] When such a corporation is dissolved, the property devolves on the other joint tenant.[2]

1. Conveyancing and Law of Property Act, R.S.O. 1990, c. C.34, s. 43(1).

2. Conveyancing and Law of Property Act, R.S.O. 1990, c. C.34, s. 43(2)

3. TENANCY IN COMMON

(a) Characteristics of Tenancy in Common

§178   The essential unity which characterizes a tenancy in common is that of possession; such tenants occupy the position of one single owner with respect to all persons other than themselves. Their ownership, like that of all tenants who hold pro indiviso, is per my et per tout.[1]

1. *Gunn v. Burgess* (1884), 5 O.R. 685 at 688 (H.C.); *Lasby v. Crewson* (1891), 21 O.R. 255 at 260 (Ch.).

§179   As tenants in common may hold under titles altogether distinct, they cannot join in a demise.[1]

    1. *Doe d. McNab v. Sieker* (1837), 5 U.C.Q.B. (O.S.) 323.

§180   One tenant in common may acquire a title by possession as against the other where there are only two, or against all others where there are more than two; likewise, two tenants in common can acquire title by possession against the third where there are three, or against all others where there are more than three.[1]

    1. *Re Hipkiss*, [1956] O.W.N. 725.

(b) Creation of Tenancy in Common

§181   Where there is an issue whether a joint tenancy or a tenancy in common has been created, the court will lean toward finding a tenancy in common, and will prefer such a finding where there is a doubt.[1]

    1. Family Law Act, R.S.O. 1990, c. F.3, s. 14; *McEwan v. Ewers*, [1946] O.W.N. 573 (H.C.) (devise to two persons "jointly"; intention of testator; creation of tenancy in common; Conveyancing and Law of Property Act, R.S.O. 1990, c. C.34, s. 12); *Re Jay* (1925), 28 O.W.N. 214 (C.A.) (purchase of land by husband and wife; presumption of advancement and tenancy in common); **see also** *L.M. Rosen Realty Ltd. v. D'Amore* (1982), 132 D.L.R. (3d) 648 (Ont. H.C.); reversed in part on other grounds (1984), 45 O.R. (2d) 405 (C.A.) (parties agreeing to purchase property as tenants in common; trust agreement between parties providing that each party to pay own share of money due under agreement for sale, or to repay other parties for advances plus interest; simple, not compound, interest payable; no express agreement to pay compound interest); *Re Crow* (1984), 48 O.R. (2d) 36 (H.C.) (testator devising certain land to grandsons for their natural lives with gift over to their children; will creating tenancy in common unless contrary intention shown by will; codicil and will of testator not showing such contrary intention).

(c) Rights of Tenants in Common Inter Se

(i) GENERAL

§182   The court will refuse to restrict a tenant in common in the legitimate enjoyment of the estate, because an undivided occupation is of the very essence of a tenancy in common, and to interfere with the legitimate exercise of that right would be to deny an essential quality of the title. A tenant in common, therefore, is not entitled to an injunction where the co-tenant is exercising his or her rights in a legitimate manner. The co-tenant must proceed by partition if he or she desires relief. But when a tenant in common enters not by virtue of the right as tenant in common, but under a lease from the co-tenant, or enters as tenant in common and proceeds to destroy the common property, an injunction may be granted.[1] It is clear that a tenant in common does not have an unlimited power to do as he or she will with the estate; for although the court is slow to interfere between tenants in common, where one commits any act amounting to destruction, he or she will be restrained.[2]

1. *Dougall v. Foster* (1853), 4 Gr. 319; *Goodenow v. Farquhar* (1873), 19 Gr. 614 (one of two tenants in common leasing part of land as quarry; co-tenant entitled to injunction against further quarrying, and to accounting against lessee for moiety of amount already quarried).

2. *Dougall v. Foster* (1853), 4 Gr. 319.

§183   The mere fact that one tenant in common holds possession of the whole property does not render him or her liable to a co-tenant, who may also enter and enjoy the possession with the other.[1]

1. *Bates v. Martin* (1866), 12 Gr. 490.

§184   An entry by one co-tenant in common is not an entry also by the co-tenant.[1]

1. *Harley v. Maycock* (1897), 28 O.R. 508 at 516; *Harris v. Mudie* (1882), 7 O.A.R. 414 at 419.

§185   There is no fiduciary relationship between co-tenants such as will prevent one from buying in for his or her own benefit at a bona fide sale under a power of sale in a mortgage, and the mere fact that one co-tenant has been allowed to receive the rents, pay interest and taxes therewith, and generally manage the property does not create any such fiduciary relationship.[1]

1. *Fleet v. Fleet* (1925), 28 O.W.N. 193 (C.A.).

§186   The same rule applies also to a purchase by one co-tenant at a tax sale, whether the tenants be joint tenants or tenants in common.[1]

1. *Janisse v. Stewart* (1925), 28 O.W.N. 446 (H.C.).

(ii) RENT

§187   Each tenant in common has a right to receive his or her share of the rent,[1] and payment of the whole rent to one tenant in common, after notice of the joint interest, is not a good payment to the other or others, who, notwithstanding such payment, may distrain for their portions of the rent.[2]

1. *McPherson v. McPherson* (1883), 10 P.R. 140 (Ont. H.C.) (tenant in common receiving more than his or her proportion of rent; co-tenants claiming against his or her share of land for excess of rent received; executions being in sheriff's hands, and execution creditors coming in under decree in cause; execution creditors having

priority over claimants; claimants merely claiming debt, for which action might be brought, and having no actual charge until obtaining judgment at law or decree in equity).

2. *Bradburne v. Shanly* (1859), 7 Gr. 569; *Harrison v. Barnby* (1793), 101 E.R. 138; *Vasiloff v. Johnson* (1932), 41 O.W.N. 139 (H.C.) (discussion of incidents of tenancy in common).

§188   Unless a co-tenant in possession is charged with an occupation rent, such tenant is not entitled to be repaid for substantial repairs and lasting improvements on any part of the property.[1] There is nothing of a fiduciary character in the relationship of tenants in common; such a tenant is not accountable for an occupation rent.

1. *Rice v. George* (1873), 20 Gr. 221 at 222; *Curry v. Curry* (1898), 25 O.A.R. 267; *Field v. Field* (1910), 8 E.L.R. 374 (P.E.I.S.C.).

§189   Although liable to account as bailiff for rents and profits received, a tenant in common can in no sense be considered a trustee for a co-tenant.[1]

1. *McIntosh v. Ontario Bank* (1873), 20 Gr. 24.

(iii) CROPS

§190   One tenant in common cannot maintain an action of trespass or trover against a co-tenant for the mere act of harvesting a crop on the land,[1] but may do so if the co-tenant has consumed the crop or dealt with it so that the first co-tenant cannot retake it or pursue a remedy against the persons who have possession of it.[2]

1. *Wemp v. Mormon* (1846), 2 U.C.Q.B. 146 (parties agreeing to divide crops from each other's farms; defendant ejected; plaintiff unable to refuse to divide crops with defendant, and unable to maintain trespass against defendant for entering and taking half of crops).

2. *Brady v. Arnold* (1868), 19 U.C.C.P. 42.

(iv) FELLING TIMBER

§191   Where land of which plaintiff and defendant are tenants in common is valuable only for the timber on it and not as farm land,[1] the taking of timber by the defendant is substantially a destruction of the subject matter of the tenancy and is not a legitimate mode of enjoyment of the right of occupation arising out of the defendant's title. The plaintiff will be granted an injunction restraining further cutting of timber by the co-tenant.[2]

1. *Rice v. George* (1873), 20 Gr. 221 at 222.

2. *Proudfoot v. Bush* (1859), 7 Gr. 518; *Christie v. Saunders* (1851), 2 Gr. 670; *Dougall v. Foster* (1853), 4 Gr. 319.

§192   Where a tenant in common of one moiety who is trustee of the other moiety under a will fells timber for his or her own individual advantage, that tenant's powers of disposition and rights of ownership over his or her own moiety are to be exercised in subordination to the duty as trustee of the other moiety, and an injunction will be granted restraining the cutting of timber on the moiety of the cestui que trust, the effect of which is to prevent the cutting of timber on any part of the lot.[1]

   1.   *Christie v. Saunders* (1851), 2 Gr. 670.

(v)   COMPENSATION FOR IMPROVEMENTS

§193   An action cannot be maintained by one tenant in common against another for the value of improvements alone. But in a partition action in equity such an allowance is always made.[1]

   1.   *Handley v. Archibald* (1899), 30 S.C.R. 130 at 141; *Griffies v. Griffies* (1863), 8 L.T. 758.

§194   One tenant in common making improvements and repairs to the common property is not entitled to be paid therefor unless that tenant consents to be charged with occupation rent, and if so charged, that tenant is entitled to contribution from the co-tenant for taxes and water rates paid.[1]

   1.   *Wuychik v. Majewski* (1920), 19 O.W.N. 207 (H.C.); *Rice v. George* (1873), 20 Gr. 221 at 222.

§195   No tenant in common is entitled to execute repairs or improvements upon property held in common and charge the co-tenant with the costs thereof while the property is enjoyed in common. But in a suit for partition it is usual to have an inquiry as to those expenses of which nothing could be recovered so long as the parties enjoyed their property in common. When it is decided to put an end to that state of things, it is then necessary to consider what was expended in improvements or repairs, as the property held in common has been increased in value by the improvements and repairs. And regardless whether the property is divided or sold by court decree, one party cannot take the increase in value without making allowance for what has been expended in order to obtain that increased value; in fact, the execution of the repairs and improvements is adopted and sanctioned by accepting the increased value.[1] But where improvements are made by one co-tenant before the tenancy in common begins in fact, e.g., during a prior life tenancy, then the equitable doctrines attaching to improvements made during tenancies in common do not arise.[2]

   1.   *Lasby v. Crewson* (1891), 21 O.R. 255 at 259 (Ch.).

2. *Lasby v. Crewson* (1891), 21 O.R. 255 at 259 (Ch.); *Wuychik v. Majewski* (1920), 19 O.W.N. 207 (H.C.) (to entitle one co-tenant to occupation rent, must be shown that there has been exclusion of a co-tenant or that co-tenant in possession in actual receipt of rent from third parties).

§**196**   Apart from contract, the right of a tenant in common who has made repairs the benefit of which a co-tenant has taken is limited to an equitable right to an accounting, which can be asserted only in a suit for partition; a lien or charge on the property itself is not acquired. A purchaser from the registered owner of an undivided fractional share in a parcel of land is not put upon inquiry as to the state of the accounts between his or her vendor and the latter's co-tenants.[1]

1. *Ruptash v. Zawick*, [1956] S.C.R. 347; *Toronto Dominion Bank v. Morison* (1984), 47 O.R. (2d) 524 (H.C.) (bank lending money to company and taking collateral mortgage on company's interest in property; co-tenant agreeing to make improvements upon bank's consent that co-tenant to have priority for amount of improvements, to be secured by rents; bank sending attornment notices to tenants; bank acting in bad faith; if tenant denied priority, bank unjustly enriched).

§**197**   If a tenant in common is in beneficial occupation of property and has made improvements, he or she must, if seeking compensation in any shape for the improvements, account for the profits derived from the occupation.[1]

1. *Rice v. George* (1873), 20 Gr. 221 at 226; *Lasby v. Crewson* (1891), 21 O.R. 255 (Ch.).

(vi) APPOINTMENT OF AGENT

§**198**   Where joint owners of land who are tenants in common and not joint tenants appoint an agent to collect their rents, the concurrence of all the joint owners in the appointment is not necessary.[1]

1. *Bradburne v. Shanly* (1859), 7 Gr. 569.

(vii) WASTE

§**199**   Where a suit by one co-tenant on behalf of the entire tenancy to restrain waste is necessary and proper, and the suit results in benefit to the co-tenants, the co-tenants must share in the costs of the suit according to the advantage they might be shown to have respectively derived.[1]

1. *Gage v. Mulholland* (1869), 16 Gr. 145; **see** Costs.

§**200**   A tenant in common does not have unlimited power over the estate, for though the court is slow to interfere between tenants in common, a tenant who commits any act amounting to destruction will be restrained. When the acts complained of amount only to equitable waste, the court will not restrain a tenant in common, but when the acts amount to destruction, it will grant an injunction.[1]

1. *Dougall v. Foster* (1853), 4 Gr. 319; *Goodenow v. Farquhar* (1873), 19 Gr. 614 (one tenant in common leasing part of land as quarry; co-tenant granted injunction restraining further quarrying; accounting decreed against lessee for moiety of what already quarried); **see also** *Proudfoot v. Bush* (1859), 7 Gr. 518.

(d) Dissolution of Tenancy in Common

§201   Estates in common are dissolved in two ways: by uniting all the titles or interests in one tenant, by purchase or otherwise, which brings the whole to one severalty; and by partition.[1]

1. *Rutherford v. Rispin* (1926), 59 O.L.R. 506 at 512 (H.C.).

(e) Party Walls

§202   Where two adjoining buildings, both owned by the same person, have a party wall dividing them which is necessary for the support of each, and one building is sold and conveyed to a purchaser, the description in the conveyance being by street address, the vendor and purchaser are tenants in common of the party wall.[1]

1. *Lewis v. Allison* (1899), 30 S.C.R. 173; **see also** *Salter v. Everson* (1913), 4 O.W.N. 1457 (H.C.) (unsuccessful claim to right of way by plaintiff claiming title under one of two tenants in common); see Boundaries, Easements (as to party walls generally).

(f) Trespass

§203   One tenant in common may commit trespass[1] by expelling another co-tenant and wrongfully taking the whole enjoyment of the estate.[2] As long as one tenant in common is lawfully exercising rights as a tenant in common, no action lies for trespass; but if the acts are equivalent to an exclusion of the co-tenants, then there is an ouster, and trespass will lie.[3]

1. **See** Damages, Trespass (as to measure of damages for trespass or damage to land).

2. *Petrie v. Taylor* (1847), 3 U.C.Q.B. 457; *Culver v. Macklem* (1854), 11 U.C.Q.B. 513 (case of chattel).

3. *Monro v. Toronto Railway* (1902), 4 O.L.R. 36 at 42 (Div. Ct.); reversed on another point (1903), 5 O.L.R. 483 (C.A.).

§204   One joint tenant or tenant in common cannot maintain an action of trespass against another in respect of the exercise of any acts of ownership by the latter that are consistent with the right of the former, except for an actual expulsion or a destruction of some part of the common property.[1]

1. *Lehman v. Hunter* (1939), 13 M.P.R. 533 (N.B.S.C.); **see also** *Carson v. McMahon* (1940), 15 M.P.R. 109 (N.B.C.A.).

§205   A demand of possession by one tenant in common and a refusal by the other, stating that the tenant claimed the whole, is evidence of an actual ouster of the co-tenant.[1] For example, where a defendant railway company insists that a lease of land made to it by the co-tenants of the plaintiff during the plaintiff's infancy is valid and binding on the plaintiff despite repudiation, thereby claiming the whole land and denying possession to its co-tenants, this amounts to a virtual exclusion, from which an ouster might properly be inferred, and the plaintiff is entitled to damages either for trespass or by way of allowance for mesne profits.[2]

1. *Doe d. Hellings v. Bird* (1809), 103 E.R. 922; *Adamson v. Adamson* (1889), 17 O.R. 407; *Monro v. Toronto Railway* (1902), 4 O.L.R. 36 at 42 (Div. Ct.); reversed on another point (1903), 5 O.L.R. 483 (C.A.) (railway putting itself in position of one tenant in common in possession claiming whole and denying possession to other; these acts alone, without reference to manner of company's user of premises, which in itself amounting to virtual exclusion, being acts and conduct from which ouster may properly be inferred); **see also** *Herr v. Weston* (1872), 32 U.C.Q.B. 402 (action for trespass by one tenant in common bringing action as owner of whole; defence that defendant being lessee of other co-tenant good defence).

2. *Monro v. Toronto Railway* (1902), 4 O.L.R. 36 at 42 (Div. Ct.); reversed on another point (1903), 5 O.L.R. 483 (C.A.).

§206   A tenant in common suing in ejectment can recover, even from a trespasser, only in respect of the share to which title is proved.[1]

1. *Barnier v. Barnier* (1892), 23 O.R. 280 (Q.B.); *Lyster v. Kirkpatrick* (1866), 26 U.C.Q.B. 217; *Lyster v. Ramage* (1866), 26 U.C.Q.B. 233.

(g) Parent and Child

§207   Where parent and child are entitled to undivided shares in land as tenants in common, ordinarily the possession of the parent is that of the child; but the presumption that the parent's possession was as bailiff or agent as to the child's share in the land depends upon the facts and is rebuttable.[1]

1. *Fry v. Speare* (1915), 34 O.L.R. 632 (H.C.); affirmed, 36 O.L.R. 301 (C.A.); **see** Infants and Children; Limitation of Actions.

§208   The relationship of principal and agent may be dissolved by circumstances; the child's attainment of age 21 is not enough in itself to dissolve the relationship, provided there is no break in possession.[1]

1. *Fry v. Speare* (1915), 34 O.L.R. 632 (H.C.); affirmed, 36 O.L.R. 301 (C.A.) (also held, on facts, that infants could not be heard in court of equity to say that stepmother's possession being their possession).

4. PARTITION

§209   A partition is void at law unless made by deed.[1]

> 1. Conveyancing and Law of Property Act, R.S.O. 1990, c. C.34, s. 9; *Barchuk v. Valentini* (1980), 27 O.R. (2d) 53 (Div. Ct.) (partition order effectively severing land without necessity of compliance with Planning Act).

§210   All joint tenants, tenants in common and co-parceners, all mortgagees or other creditors having liens on, and all parties interested in, to or out of any land in Ontario may be compelled to make or suffer partition or sale of the land or any part thereof whether the estate is legal and equitable or equitable only.[1]

> 1. Partition Act, R.S.O. 1990, c. P.4, s. 2; *Re Craig* (1928), 63 O.L.R. 192 (C.A.) (partition ordered at instance of purchaser of one joint tenant's interest sold under writ of execution); **see also** *Garnet v. McGoran* (1980), 30 O.R. (2d) 742 (H.C.); affirmed (1981), 32 O.R. (2d) 514 (Div. Ct.) (mortgagee required to show right of possession superior to that of present occupants in order to enforce judgment for possession; proceedings brought by wife possibly confirming that wife's right superior; mortgagee's application for partition and sale not to be considered until completion of wife's proceedings); *Hay v. Gooderham* (1979), 24 O.R. (2d) 701 (Div. Ct.) (termination of co-tenancy; right to partition); *Kuz v. Kuz* (1980), 15 R.P.R. 165 (Ont. H.C.) (right to partition; effect of planning considerations in partition application); *Van Harten v. Van Harten* (1980), 15 R.P.R. 161 (Ont. Co. Ct.) (land use committee refusing application to sever land; applicant seeking partition to effect severance; partition application intended merely to defeat severance provision of Act; application dismissed); *Vandongen v. Royal* (1990), 72 O.R. (2d) 533 (Dist. Ct.) (male applicant and female respondent cohabiting for three years on applicant's farm; parties subsequently purchasing property as tenants in common; property sold; each party to be reimbursed to extent of original contribution and remainder divided equally; since parties not spouses, rules respecting spouses as co-owners not applying; general rules on partition between tenants in common applying instead).

§210.1   Any person interested in land in Ontario, or the guardian of a minor entitled to the immediate possession of an estate therein, may bring an action or make an application for the partition of such land or for the sale thereof under the directions of the court if such sale is considered by the court to be more advantageous to the interested parties.[1]

> 1. Partition Act, R.S.O. 1990, c. P.4, s. 3(1); *Ferrier v. Civiero*, 1999 CarswellOnt 4197 (Ont. S.C.J.); affirmed, 2000 CarswellOnt 5277 (Ont. Div. Ct.); affirmed (2001), 42 R.P.R. (3d) 12 (Ont. C.A.) (execution creditor not person entitled to "immediate possession of an estate"; sheriff and creditor, having neither legal interest nor right to possession, unable to bring application for partition and sale).

§211   The Partition Act can be invoked not only where compulsion is required but also where the parties mutually desire the partition and thus the respondent consents to the application. A tenant in common has a prima facie right to partition and hence a corresponding obligation to permit partition.[1]

1. Partition Act, R.S.O. 1990, c. P.4, s. 2; *Hay v. Gooderham* (1979), 24 O.R. (2d) 701 (Div. Ct.); **see also** *Bisson v. Luciani* (1982), 37 O.R. (2d) 257 (H.C.) (claims of mortgagees and execution creditors not permitted to interfere where partition otherwise proper; rights of innocent co-owners not to be fettered by acts of other partners).

§212　　The court has discretion to refuse an order for partition or sale of property in which two or more persons have undivided interests. The discretion must be exercised judicially, on the basis of the circumstances of each case.[1]

1. *Hutcheson v. Hutcheson*, [1950] O.R. 265 (C.A.); *Byall v. Byall*, [1942] O.W.N. 339 (H.C.); *Dickson v. Dickson*, [1948] O.W.N. 325 (H.C.); *M v. H*, 1996 CarswellOnt 4882 (Ont. Gen. Div.) (plaintiff severing joint tenancy and then requesting partition and sale alleging a desperate need for funds; request denied; parties would suffer significant mortgage penalty if property sold); *MacDonald v. Bezzo (Litigation Guardian of)* (1998), 38 B.L.R. (2d) 1 (Ont. C.A.) (deed of property on which hunt club located naming members of club as owners as tenants in common; club rules requiring outgoing members to execute deed conveying interest in club's property; contrary to rules, member conveying property to his son and seeking order compelling partition and sale of property; court finding members understood and agreed their respective interests in lands of club were subject to club rules; no basis upon which any one member could effectively dissolve club; conveyance to son void); *Rouse v. Rouse* (1999), 27 R.P.R. (3d) 288 (Ont. Gen. Div.) (fairness dictating that weight of first wife's larger interest in property be recognized; partition inconsistent with intended use of property contemplated by original owners; order for sale serving interests of both parties and preserving integrity of property); **see also** *Brown v. Brown*, [1952] O.W.N. 725 (H.C.); *Steele v. Weir* (1914), 6 O.W.N. 400 (H.C.); varied (1914), 7 O.W.N. 99 (C.A.); *McCully v. McCully* (1911), 23 O.L.R. 156 (C.A.); *Davis v. Davis*, [1954] O.R. 23 (C.A.) (right to partition, and exercise of discretion of court); *Hearty v. Hearty*, [1970] 2 O.R. 344 (H.C.); *Cook v. Johnston*, [1970] 2 O.R. 1 (H.C.); *Morris v. Howe* (1982), 38 O.R. (2d) 480 (H.C.) (farm property willed to applicant for life, remainder to respondent; applicant wishing to have property sold; respondent reasonably refusing; sale refused); *Dibattista v. Menecola* (1990), 14 R.P.R. (2d) 157 (C.A.) (s. 3(1) of Partition Act, R.S.O. 1980, c. 369, providing for sale only where court considering sale to be more advantageous to interests of parties; land developer taking calculated risk by purchasing land and then interest of one of two tenants in common in adjacent lands, knowing purchase of other half might not be possible; sale advantageous only to developer; judgment overemphasizing issue of good land development rather than rights of parties under Act; land partitioned).

§213　　A person who has an undivided interest in lands in Ontario has a prima facie right to an order for partition; and where there is a prima facie legal claim which is sought to be enforced without vexation or oppression, the court is bound, in the exercise of a judicial discretion, to grant the order even though there may be circumstances in the case which incline the court to look with disfavour upon the application.[1]

1. *Szuba v. Szuba*, [1950] O.W.N. 669 (H.C.); *Brown v. Brown*, [1952] O.W.N. 725 (H.C.); **see also** *Roblin v. Roblin*, [1960] O.R. 157 (H.C.) (mere inconvenience not sufficient ground to refuse application); *MacDonald and MacDonald* (1976), 14 O.R. (2d) 249 (Div. Ct.); *581352 Ontario Ltd. v. Greenbanktree Power Corp.* (1994), 71

O.A.C. 338 (Div. Ct.) (tenant in common of commercial property having prima facie right to partition and sale in absence of malicious, vexatious or oppressive conduct; where mortgagee notified and not objecting, tantamount to consent).

§214   Only those entitled to possession of their shares in land are entitled to ask for partition. Having a charge on the land for a sum of money does not give a right to partition.[1]

1. *Morrison v. Morrison* (1917), 39 O.L.R. 163 (C.A.); *Bunting v. Servos*, [1931] O.R. 409 (C.A.) (possession by lessee of life tenant not being possession of such interest in land as giving right to partition under Partition Act); *Fidler v. Seaman*, [1948] O.W.N. 454 (H.C.); **see also** *Toronto Dominion Bank v. Morison* (1984), 47 O.R. (2d) 524 (H.C.) (mortgagee bank applying for partition and sale; application dismissed; bank having no status to bring application, as having no estate in or immediate right to possession).

§215   Partition or sale should not be ordered where there is no common title, no interest in common. If the defendants claim only an easement to which the plaintiff is also entitled, but assert that if the plaintiff has title to the land itself, he or she is free to sell it subject to their easement, it is not open to the plaintiff, by admitting an ownership in the defendants which they do not assert, to obtain a sale by partition proceedings and thus force the defendants to either protect their easement, if any, by purchasing, or permit it to be destroyed by selling all their rights to the plaintiff or a stranger.[1]

1. *Stroud v. Sun Oil Co.* (1904), 7 O.L.R. 704 (K.B.); affirmed, 8 O.L.R. 748 (Div. Ct.); **see also** *Tolosnak v. Tolosnak*, [1957] O.W.N. 273 (H.C.) (right to partition; essential that applicant have interest in lands); *Davis v. Davis*, [1959] O.W.N. 41 (H.C.) (no jurisdiction in partition application; proceedings on reference stayed to enable applicant to amend order of reference).

§216   An honest dispute as to ownership of the land must be settled before partition can be ordered.[1]

1. *Kulczycki v. Kulczycki*, [1949] O.W.N. 177 (C.A.); *Ames v. Bond* (1992), 39 R.F.L. (3d) 375 (Ont. C.A.) (order for sale of jointly owned property under Partition Act not to be made where party having made claim for sole ownership of disputed property sufficiently serious to raise genuine issue for trial); see *Farlinger v. Farlinger*, [1950] O.W.N. 413 (H.C.) (counterclaim for partition in action for alimony); **see also** *Blackhall v. Jardine*, [1958] O.W.N. 457 (C.A.) (question of ownership should be tried by court and not by master); *Rush v. Rush* (1960), 24 D.L.R. (2d) 248 (Ont. C.A.); *Tait v. Tait* (1970), 4 R.F.L. 125 (Ont. H.C.) (spouses holding property; both parties signing agreement not to commence partition proceedings; neither party feeling bound by agreement; agreement not impediment to wife applying for partition).

§217   Where land is held in joint tenancy or tenancy in common or coparcenary by reason of a devise or an intestacy, no proceedings can be taken until one year after the decease of the testator or intestate in whom the land was vested.[1]

1. Partition Act, R.S.O. 1990, c. P.4, s. 3(2); *Morrison v. Morrison* (1917), 39 O.L.R. 163 (C.A.) (provisions in s. 3(2) prohibiting proceedings thereunder until one year after death not in conflict with view that as long as land vested in personal representative to enable him or her to perform duties, there can be no right to compel partition; prohibition enacted at time when land of intestate and testator devolving not upon personal representative but upon persons beneficially entitled, and so giving right to partition at once; prohibition being of exercise of that right, so as to provide reasonable time to learn whether land needed for payment of debts, in which event administration would follow ordinarily and render partition, if obtained, useless; now, not only is time extended, but right to land which formerly gave right to partition is taken away and given to personal representative; no need for prohibition of exercise of right to compel partition when such right not existing).

§218   Where only one of several tenants desires partition, a part may be allotted to him or her while the remainder continues to be held jointly or in common by the others as before.[1]

1. *Devereux v. Kearns* (1886), 11 P.R. 452 (Ch.).

§219   Where one tenant in common takes proceedings for partition and an accounting of the profits of the estate from the co-tenant, such tenant is entitled to such accounting where it is shown that the co-tenant received a greater share from the estate than he or she was entitled to.[1]

1. *Curtis v. Coleman* (1875), 22 Gr. 561 (one of several tenants in common, in sole possession of plaster bed, selling portions of plaster; ordered to account to co-tenants for receipts therefrom); *Shields v. London & Western Trust Co.*, [1924] S.C.R. 25 (at time of 1916 proceedings for partition and sale of land having belonged to deceased father of parties, one of parties and tenant in common with the others, S, having had exclusive possession for less than ten years; five of parties, including S, declared to be owners, and partition and sale not proceeding; in 1922, partition proceedings again taken, in which S claiming statutory title by possession of whole land; 1916 judgment having interrupted continuance of possession by S, and his title not having accrued).

§220   On a reference in partition proceedings, payments on account of a joint liability of the parties were held not to be matters for accounting, since the liability was not a charge on the lands that were the subject of the partition proceedings.[1]

1. *MacDonald v. MacDonald*, [1953] O.W.N. 232 (H.C.).

§221   Remaindermen are not entitled to sale or partition if the life tenant objects.[1]

1. *Murcar v. Bolton* (1884), 5 O.R. 164; *Rajotte v. Wilson* (1904), 3 O.W.R. 737; *Bunting v. Servos*, [1931] O.R. 409 (C.A.); **see also** *Graham v. Graham* (1858), 6 Gr. 372; *Angus v. Heinze* (1909), 42 S.C.R. 416.

§222   Since a partition of an equity of redemption cannot be done by an actual partition of the land, the equity of redemption should be sold and the proceeds divided between the joint tenants.[1]

  1. *Fleet v. Fleet* (1925), 28 O.W.N. 193 (C.A.).

§223   While the general rule is that one joint tenant may not sue another for use and occupation unless ousted by the co-tenant, the court may, in proceedings where a joint tenancy is terminated by an order for partition or sale, make all just allowances, and should give such directions as will do to complete equity between the parties.[1]

  1. *Mastron v. Cotton* (1925), 58 O.L.R. 251 (C.A.) (right to recover for use and occupation in event of ouster of one joint tenant by another mentioned); *Gage v. Mulholland* (1869), 16 Gr. 145; **see also** Family Law Act, R.S.O. 1990, c. F.3, s. 40 [am. 1999, c. 6, s. 25(18)] (as to right to remain in matrimonial home); *Murray v. Hall* (1849), 137 E.R. 175; *Vasiloff v. Johnson* (1932), 41 O.W.N. 139 (H.C.) (in action for ejectment and trespass, right to recover for use and occupation being by way of damages); *Crawford v. Crawford*, [1953] O.W.N. 781 (Master) (in case of joint tenants, right to recover for use and occupation also being by way of damages); *Szuba v. Szuba*, [1951] O.W.N. 61 (H.C.); *Talbutt v. Talbutt*, [1953] O.W.N. 63 (H.C.); *Re Pearce*, [1934] O.W.N. 223 (C.A.); *Spatafora v. Spatafora*, [1956] O.W.N. 628 (Master); *Jollow v. Jollow*, [1954] O.R. 895 (C.A.); *Robichaud v. Watson* (1983), 42 O.R. (2d) 38 (H.C.) (order declaring severance usually requiring further order directing reference and accounting; co-owner dying and leaving modest estate; sufficient evidence available to calculate interests).

§224   What is just and equitable depends upon the circumstances of each case. For instance, if the tenant in occupation claims for upkeep, taxes, mortgage interest and repairs, the court usually requires, as a term of such allowance, that the claimant submit to an allowance for use and occupation.[1] However, a joint owner with only constructive possession of an unoccupied property is not liable to be charged occupation rent if he or she claims, on an accounting in partition proceedings, an allowance for taxes, interest and repairs.[2] And if one tenant has made improvements which have increased the selling value of the property, the other tenant cannot take the advantage of such increase without submitting to an allowance for the improvements. Also, where one tenant has paid more than his or her share of encumbrances, that tenant is entitled to an allowance for such surplus.[3]

  1. *Mastron v. Cotton* (1925), 58 O.L.R. 251 (C.A.); *Rice v. George* (1873), 20 Gr. 221; *Szuba v. Szuba*, [1951] O.W.N. 61 (H.C.); **see also** *Talbutt v. Talbutt*, [1953] O.W.N. 63 (H.C.); *Robichaud v. Watson* (1983), 42 O.R. (2d) 38 (H.C.) (declaration incorporating accounting; plaintiff's son to be charged occupation rent from time of sole possession until death; rent to be set off against claim for mortgage payments and estimated improvements; defendant entitled to credit for mortgage payments and moneys expended in connection with property).

2. *MacDonald v. MacDonald,* [1953] O.W.N. 232 (H.C.).

3. *Mastron v. Cotton* (1925), 58 O.L.R. 251 (C.A.); *Curry v. Curry* (1898), 25 O.A.R. 267; **see also** *Merritt v. Shaw* (1868), 15 Gr. 321; *McDougall v. McDougall* (1868), 14 Gr. 267; *Shields v. London & Western Trust Co.,* [1924] S.C.R. 25; *Smith v. Smith* (1901), 1 O.L.R. 404 (Div. Ct.); *Stroud v. Sun Oil Co.* (1904), 7 O.L.R. 704 (K.B.); affirmed (1904), 8 O.L.R. 748 (Div. Ct.); *Cartwright v. Diehl* (1867), 13 Gr. 360.

§225   The court will not decree the partition of lands the title to which is vested in the Crown, and neither will it decree the sale of such lands at the instance of the representatives of a deceased locatee.[1] In making partition of lands when the fee is in the Crown, the Crown must recognize the locatee's right to improvements.[2]

1. *Abell v. Weir* (1877), 24 Gr. 464.

2. *Pride v. Rodger* (1896), 27 O.R. 320 (C.A.).

§226   Where a plaintiff, upon attaining the age of majority, repudiates a lease to the defendant company of land of which he and his or her brother and sister were tenants in common, made when the plaintiff was an infant, and has made a partition by deed with the brother and sister to which the company is not a party, the brother and sister are necessary parties to the plaintiff's action for partition as against the company in respect of its possession under the lease.[1] Where the defendant on a motion for partition or sale claims to be the beneficial owner of the land, the registered title being in the name of the defendant's deceased spouse, the defendant is permitted to bring an action to establish his or her claim; and should the defendant not do so, partition may be ordered.[2]

1. *Monro v. Toronto Railway* (1903), 5 O.L.R. 483 (C.A.).

2. *Noel v. Noel* (1903), 2 O.W.R. 628.

§227   The Partition Act provides for the appointment of a guardian of the interest of anyone interested in the land who has not been heard of for three years, and of those who, if such person is dead, take his or her share.[1]

1. Partition Act, R.S.O. 1990, c. P.4, s. 4; *Stroud v. Mandell* (1929), 65 O.L.R. 4 (H.C.).

§228   While the institution of an action for partition does not destroy the joint tenancy, its continuation to the point where judgment for sale results has that effect.[1]

1. *Grant v. Grant,* [1952] O.W.N. 641 (Master).

§229   In partition suits, commission in lieu of costs should be divided into fractional parts, and allowance made to the parties in proportion to the amount of work done by and the responsibility imposed upon each.[1]

1. *Wuychik v. Majewski* (1920), 19 O.W.N. 207 (H.C.); *Adrienne Slan Ltd. v. Mountbirch Ltd.* (1984), 47 C.P.C. 49 (Ont. Master) (pursuant to R. 660, each party in partition action entitled to commission on value of property partitioned unless otherwise ordered by judge; respondent M allowed costs pursuant to rule, limited to application for order for reference and closing of sale, but not otherwise).

§230　The Superior Court of Justice has jurisdiction to order partition.[1]

1. Partition Act, R.S.O. 1990, c. P.4, s. 1("court").

§231　An appeal lies to the Divisional Court from any order made under the Partition Act.[1]

1. Partition Act, R.S.O. 1990, c. P.4, s. 7; *Fitzpatrick v. Fitzpatrick* (1976), 3 C.P.C. 59 (Ont. Div. Ct.) (report on reference being order and subject to appeal to Divisional Court by virtue of s. 9 [now s. 7]).

5.　PARTNERSHIP

§232　None of joint tenancy, tenancy in common, joint property, common property, or part ownership of itself creates a partnership as to anything so held or owned, whether or not the tenants or owners share any profits made by the use thereof.[1]

1. Partnerships Act, R.S.O. 1990, c. P.5, s. 3(1); **see also** *Mason v. Parker* (1869), 16 Gr. 81 (H and R carrying on business in partnership on lands in their joint possession and owned by H; H mortgaging property to defendants; mortgage containing power of distress in case of default; mortgagees distraining on partnership property; both partners becoming insolvent; assignee of R seeking injunction to restrain mortgagees from selling goods seized; not apparent whether partnership agreement being in writing or containing any provision as to land in question, or whether R knowing of execution of mortgage, or when having notice of it; injunction granted to afford opportunity to ascertain facts before deciding rights of parties); **see** Partnership.

§233　Where co-owners of an estate or interest in any land that is not itself partnership property are partners as to profits arising from the use of that land or estate, and where such co-owners purchase other land or estate out of such profits, to be used in like manner, the land or estate so purchased belongs to them, in the absence of an agreement to the contrary, not as partners but as co-owners for the same respective estates and interests as they held in the original land or estate as at the date of purchase of the new land.[1]

1. Partnerships Act, R.S.O. 1990, c. P.5, s. 21(3); *Rathwell v. Rathwell* (1866), 26 U.C.Q.B. 179 (doctrine of non-survivorship extending to partners generally).

6.　ACTION FOR ACCOUNTING

§234　At common law there could be no action for an accounting by one tenant in common or joint tenant against another unless there had been an appointment of one by the other as bailiff.[1] The Imperial Statute[2] enabled one tenant in common to bring an action of account against a co-tenant for receiving more than a just share or proportion from the common property.[3]

1. *Gregory v. Connolly* (1850), 7 U.C.Q.B. 500 at 501.

2. Imperial Statute, 4 & 5 Anne, c. 16, s. 27.

3. *Re Kirkpatrick* (1883), 10 P.R. 4; **see also** *Munsie v. Lindsay* (1883), 10 P.R. 173 (Ont. Master); varied (1886), 11 O.R. 520 (Ch.).

§235   Notwithstanding the extinction of the title of a joint tenant, a co-tenant who receives an excess share of the rents and profits arising from the land is legally obliged to account for the excess received within the limitation period prior to the date of the extinction of such title.[1] Such a co-tenant is not answerable for taking the whole enjoyment of the property where there was no exclusion or ouster,[2] or for any profit made thereout by the employment of his or her industry and capital by tilling and manuring or by feeding and grazing cattle,[3] or for cutting down trees of a suitable age and growth,[4] or for other acts of waste,[5] or for cutting and taking away a crop of hay, the whole produce of the common property.[6]

1. *Isaryk v. Isaryk*, [1955] O.W.N. 487 (H.C.).

2. *Re Kirkpatrick* (1883), 10 P.R. 4, citing *Nash v. McKay* (1868), 15 Gr. 247.

3. *Re Kirkpatrick* (1883), 10 P.R. 4, citing *Henderson v. Eason* (1852), 117 E.R. 1451.

4. *Re Kirkpatrick* (1883), 10 P.R. 4, citing *Martyn v. Knowllys* (1799), 101 E.R. 1313; *Rice v. George* (1873), 20 Gr. 221; **see also** *Munsie v. Lindsay* (1883), 10 P.R. 173 (Ont. Master); varied (1886), 11 O.R. 520 (Ch.).

5. *Re Kirkpatrick* (1883), 10 P.R. 4, citing *Griffies v. Griffies* (1863), 8 L.T. 758.

6. *Re Kirkpatrick* (1883), 10 P.R. 4, citing *Jacobs v. Seward* (1869), L.R. 4 C.P. 328.

§236   The accounting extends only to whatever has been paid or given by tenants or occupants of the common property that is more than the co-tenant's just share or proportion.[1]

1. Courts of Justice Act, R.S.O. 1990, c. C.43, s. 122; *Re Kirkpatrick* (1883), 10 P.R. 4; *Janisse v. Stewart* (1925), 28 O.W.N. 446 (H.C.); *Zegil v. Opie* (1994), 8 R.F.L. (4th) 91 (Ont. Gen. Div.); additional reasons (1995), 18 R.F.L. (4th) 347 (Ont. Gen. Div.); reversed (1997), 28 R.F.L. (4th) 405 (Ont. C.A.); leave to appeal refused (1997), 225 N.R. 398 (note) (S.C.C.) (co-tenant entitled to one half of rent that property would attract, less one-half of expenses chargeable against it, as compensation for exclusive use of property by other co-tenant).

§237   If joint tenants secure a joint and several debt by mortgaging the lands, each is, in the absence of some agreement to the contrary, under an implied obligation to indemnify the other in respect of any payment in excess of his or her share of the debt.[1]

1. *McMillan v. National Trust Co.* (1931), 66 O.L.R. 601 at 610 (C.A.).

7. SALE

§238   A spouse who is a joint tenant is not liable to a purchaser for damages for breach of contract by not having signed an agreement of purchase and sale.[1]

>   1. *Dresler v. Alexson* (1977), 1 R.P.R. 158 (Ont. H.C.).

8. MORTGAGES

§239   A payment to the surviving mortgagee of two or more mortgagees operates as a discharge of the mortgage,[1] even if the mortgagees were not joint tenants.[2]

>   1. *McIntosh v. Ontario Bank* (1872), 19 Gr. 155; varied (1873), 20 Gr. 24 (C.A.) (what being sufficient notice to mortgagee making advance to one of several co-tenants that borrower not sole owner of security offered).
>
>   2. Mortgages Act, R.S.O. 1990, c. M.40, s. 12 [am. 2000, c. 26, Schedule B, s. 14]; *Re Alderson* (1924), 26 O.W.N. 277 (H.C.).

9. LIMITATION OF ACTIONS

§240   Where one of two tenants in common has been in possession as against a co-tenant, the bringing of an action of ejectment in their joint names and the entry of judgment thereon against a third party in actual possession interrupt the prescription[1] then accruing in favour of one tenant against the other.[2]

>   1. Limitations Act, R.S.O. 1990, c. L.15, s. 11; **see also** Limitation of Actions.
>
>   2. *Handley v. Archibald* (1899), 30 S.C.R. 130.

§241   Where a tenant out of possession acquires another undivided share from one of several tenants in possession, the ten years not yet having run, the limitation period runs as to both shares from the time the last one was acquired.[1]

>   1. *Hill v. Ashbridge* (1892), 20 O.A.R. 44; *Meyers v. Doyle* (1860), 9 U.C.C.P. 371 (as defendant in ejectment action claiming through one of several tenants in common, possession of part to be considered possession of whole); **see also** *Doe d. Hill v. Gander* (1844), 1 U.C.Q.B. 3 (defendant having possession of part of plaintiff's land as trespasser without title; title by 20 years possession limited to land actually occupied).

§242   Where only one of several tenants in common had gone into possession, believing she was the sole grantee, some 18 years before the action in defence to which she sought to establish her title by possession, it was held that, as possession by one tenant in common is not to be considered possession by any other,[1] and as the tenant had continued in quiet, peaceable, continuous and undisturbed possession of the land down to the issuing of the writ, she was entitled to the declaration she sought.[2]

1. *Harris v. Mudie* (1882), 7 O.A.R. 414.

2. *Foisy v. Lord* (1911), 2 O.W.N. 1217 (H.C.); affirmed (1911), 3 O.W.N. 373 (C.A.).

§242.1   Under the Limitations Act,[1] possession of joint tenants is separate possession from the time one joint tenant takes possession of the entirety.[2]

1. Limitations Act, R.S.O. 1990, c. L.15, s. 11.

2. *Hurren v. Hurren* (1995), 11 R.F.L. (4th) 12 (Ont. Gen. Div.) (separate possessions occurring when wife leaving home; husband having continuous exclusive possession for 17 years thereafter; husband having possession for sufficient time to extinguish wife's interest under s. 4 of Limitations Act).

10. PRACTICE

§243   All persons found in possession of land may be made defendants, without reference to whether their possession is joint or several.[1]

1. *Bannerman v. Dewson* (1886), 17 U.C.C.P. 257; **see also** *Bradley v. Terry* (1861), 20 U.C.Q.B. 563 (several plaintiffs, each holding undivided interest, may maintain joint action upon separate titles without having to prove some joint titles or connection with one another in some way, e.g., as joint tenants or tenants in common).

§244   An action for possession by one joint tenant is improperly constituted and must fail.[1]

1. *Tepper v. Abramsky*, [1937] O.W.N. 142 (C.A.).

XI   Conveyance

1.   TRANSFER OF FREEHOLD ESTATES

§245   At common law, an estate of freehold in possession could be transferred[1] only by feoffment with livery of seisin. Livery of seisin, without which a deed of feoffment created a mere estate at will, was a pure feudal investiture of delivery of corporeal possession of the land or tenement, which was absolutely necessary to complete the donation.[2] However, a grant from the Crown by letters patent did not have to be accompanied with livery of seisin, since the notoriety which the common law insisted upon in conveyances of land was obtained by a different mode in the case of letters patent from the Crown.[3]

1.   *See Also* Deeds and Documents; Sale of Land.

2.   *Weaver v. Burgess* (1871), 22 U.C.C.P. 104 at 109 (transfer of estate of freehold in possession "then only perfect when fit juris et seisinae conjunctio", the object of livery of seisin being to give notoriety to transfer; citing Blackstone); **see also** *McDonald v. McGillis* (1867), 26 U.C.Q.B. 458 (C.A.) (indenture executed in 1826, although purporting to convey estate in fee simple, not operating to convey such estate where absence of livery of seisin); *Spears v. Miller* (1882), 32 U.C.C.P. 661; *Wilmot v. Larabee* (1858), 7 U.C.C.P. 407 (at common law, life estate created only by livery of seisin); *Acre v. Livingstone* (1867), 26 U.C.Q.B. 282.

3.   *Weaver v. Burgess* (1871), 22 U.C.C.P. 104 at 109; **see also** *Greenlaw v. Fraser* (1874), 24 U.C.C.P. 230 (letters patent from Crown, which themselves constituting title by record, operating by way of feoffment with livery of seisin to patentee); *Clench v. Hendricks* (1826), Taylor 403.

§246   By statute, it is provided that all corporeal tenements and hereditaments, as regards the conveyance of the immediate freehold thereof, lie in grant as well as in livery.[1]

1.   Conveyancing and Law of Property Act, R.S.O. 1990, c. C.34, s. 2; **see also** *Smith v. Dale* (1919), 46 O.L.R. 403 (H.C.) (effect of section being to abrogate old rule of common law that feoffment not able be made to operate in futuro); *Nicholson v. Dillabough* (1862), 21 U.C.Q.B. 591; *Acre v. Livingstone* (1867), 26 U.C.Q.B. 282; **but see** *Savill Brothers v. Bethell*, [1902] 2 Ch. 523 (formerly, deed of grant being mode of assurance applicable only to incorporeal hereditaments, including reversions and remainders in land; 8-9 Vict., c. 106, s. 2 enacting that corporeal hereditaments, regarding conveyance of immediate freehold thereof, to be deemed to be in grant as well as in livery; this in no way altering rules of law with respect to creation of estates).

§247   Any feoffment of lands is void unless it is made by deed.[1] A deed is any document which is under seal, although the word "deed" is most frequently used in the popular sense of a conveyance of real estate.[2]

1. Conveyancing and Law of Property Act, R.S.O. 1990, c. C.34, s. 3; **see also** Statute of Frauds, R.S.O. 1990, c. S.19, ss. 1, 2.

2. *Eastview v. Roman Catholic Episcopal Corp. of Ottawa* (1918), 44 O.L.R. 284 at 295, per Riddell J.

§248   A "conveyance" is defined as including assignment, appointment, lease, settlement and other assurance, made by deed, on a sale, mortgage, demise or settlement of any property, or on any other dealing with or for any property.[1]

1. Conveyancing and Law of Property Act, R.S.O. 1990, c. C.34, s. 1(1)("conveyance"); *Bard v. Duggan*, [1955] O.W.N. 246 (H.C.).

§249   In a conveyance, it is not necessary, in the limitation of an estate in fee simple, to use the word"heirs".[1] A limitation in a conveyance or will which before May 27, 1956 would have created an estate tail must now be construed as an estate in fee simple or the greatest estate that the grantor or testator had in the land.[2]

1. Conveyancing and Law of Property Act, R.S.O. 1990, c. C.34, s. 5(1); *Armstrong v. Brown*, [1951] O.W.N. 877 (H.C.); reversed [1952] O.W.N. 55 (C.A.).

2. Conveyancing and Law of Property Act, R.S.O. 1990, c. C.34, s. 4.

§250   On a sale, the purchaser is not entitled to require that the conveyance be executed in his or her presence or that of his or her solicitor, but the purchaser may require that it be attested by a person appointed by the purchaser, which appointee may be the purchaser's solicitor.[1]

1. Conveyancing and Law of Property Act, R.S.O. 1990, c. C.34, s. 8.

§251   A partition, an exchange of land, an assignment of a chattel interest in land, and a surrender in writing of land not being an interest which might by law have been created without writing, are void at law unless made by deed.[1]

1. Conveyancing and Law of Property Act, R.S.O. 1990, c. C.34, s. 9.

§252   Contingent, executory and future interests and possibilities connected with an interest in land and rights of entry, whether immediate or future and whether vested or contingent, may be disposed of by deed.[1]

1. Conveyancing and Law of Property Act, R.S.O. 1990, c. C.34, s. 10; **see also** *Baldwin v. Wanzer* (1892), 22 O.R. 612; *Re Melville* (1886), 11 O.R. 626 (Ch.); *Soper v. Windsor (City)* (1914), 32 O.L.R. 352 (C.A.); *Re Craig* (1928), 63 O.L.R. 192 (C.A.); *Kimniak v. Anderson* (1928), 63 O.L.R. 428 (C.A.).

2. PARTIES TO CONVEYANCE

§253 Although parol evidence as to the identity of a party to a conveyance is always admissible, the indicia of identity afforded by the conveyance itself are of paramount importance.[1]

    1. *Shan v. Shun*, [1918] A.C. 403.

§254 A conveyance to a grantee who is dead at the date of the conveyance does not operate retroactively so as to vest an estate in the deceased grantee during his or her lifetime, and the only value of such a conveyance is as a piece of evidence operating in the nature of an estoppel against the grantor.[1]

    1. *O'Donnell v. Nicholson* (1920), 48 O.L.R. 187 (H.C.).

§255 As a general rule, a person not named as a party to a conveyance, in the clause containing the names of the persons who are formally made parties, cannot take any benefit under the conveyance or sue upon any covenant contained therein.[1]

    1. *O'Donnell v. Nicholson* (1920), 48 O.L.R. 187 (H.C.).

§256 It is not essential that the parties to a deed be described with complete accuracy; it is enough if the court is able to identify the respective parties by the intent collected from the deed itself.[1]

    1. *Galbraith v. Kerrigen* (1917), 39 O.L.R. 519 (H.C.); *Mill v. Hill* (1852), 10 E.R. 330; *Lord Say & Seal's Case* (1712), 88 E.R. 617 (names of parties left blank, and in operative clause grantor not named but grantee named; deed good); *McDonald v. Clarke* (1870), 30 U.C.Q.B. 307; *Coghlan v. Tilbury East School Section No. 4* (1874), 35 U.C.Q.B. 575; **see also** *Elevated Construction Ltd. v. Nixon*, [1970] 1 O.R. 650 (H.C.) (conveyance made by all general partners of limited partnership; limited partners also specifically named; not necessary for limited partners to execute deed).

§257 A person who signs, seals and delivers a conveyance containing a covenant cannot avoid liability by signing a name which he or she uses but which is not in fact his or her own, nor can such liability be saddled on the person whose name is so used unless the user is the duly constituted attorney of such person.[1]

    1. *Shan v. Shun*, [1918] A.C. 403.

3. RECITALS AND RECEIPTS IN CONVEYANCE

§258 Recitals are put in a deed for the purpose of placing some fact upon record. They may operate as an estoppel, but they do not have the effect of conveying anything to the grantees. In some cases, a recital may contain statements so specific and particular as to preclude the parties to the deed from averring the contrary, but such recitals must be clear and unambiguous. These recitals bind only those who are parties to the deed or those claiming under them.[1]

> 1. *Sherlock v. Green*, [1949] O.W.N. 506 (H.C.).

§259   A recital in a conveyance may operate by way of an estoppel, and such an estoppel is binding upon all persons claiming under or through the person estopped by the recital.[1]

> 1. *Bain v. Leslie* (1894), 25 O.R. 136 (H.C.); **see also** *Eyre v. Burmester* (1862), 46 E.R. 987 (estoppel binding those claiming through or under party estopped, and not those claiming by title paramount to party estopped); Estoppel.

§260   If a recital in a conveyance that is a deed inter partes is intended to be the statement of one party only, the estoppel is confined to that party.[1] Whether a recital is to be considered a statement of one party only or of all parties is a question of intention to be gathered from the construction of the conveyance.[2]

> 1. *Roe v. McNeil* (1864), 14 U.C.C.P. 424; *Minaker v. Ash* (1861), 10 U.C.C.P. 363.
>
> 2. *Roe v. McNeil* (1864), 14 U.C.C.P. 424; *Gamble v. Rees* (1850), 6 U.C.Q.B. 396; *Boulton v. Boulton* (1898), 28 S.C.R. 592.

§261   A recital in a conveyance cannot operate to estop a party thereto unless the recital is direct, precise and particular.[1]

> 1. *Gamble v. Rees* (1850), 6 U.C.Q.B. 396.

§262   A receipt for money or other consideration in the body of a conveyance is a sufficient discharge to the person paying or delivering the same without any receipt being endorsed on the conveyance.[1] In actions for specific performance of a contract for the sale and purchase of land, as in other cases, evidence is admissible to prove that there was in fact valuable consideration although only a nominal consideration is recited in the option or in the conveyance.[2]

> 1. Conveyancing and Law of Property Act, R.S.O. 1990, c. C.34, s. 6; *Patterson v. Wurm* (1915), 9 O.W.N. 195 (H.C.).
>
> 2. *Riches v. Burns* (1924), 27 O.W.N. 203 (H.C.).

§263   A vendor is never estopped by a statement in the conveyance that the purchase money has been paid, or by an endorsed receipt for the money signed by the vendor, so as to exclude the enforcement of a vendor's lien against the purchaser.[1] A receipt for money or other consideration, included in the body of a conveyance or endorsed thereon, is, in favour of a subsequent purchaser not having notice that such consideration was not in fact paid, sufficient evidence of the payment or giving of the whole amount thereof.[2] This provision of the Conveyancing and Law of Property Act is not confined merely to claims that might be made upon alleged vendor's liens for unpaid purchase money; rather, it is a positive enactment that for all purposes, in favour of purchasers without notice, a receipt for the consideration is sufficient evidence of payment in fact.[3]

1. *Equitable Fire & Accident Office Ltd. v. Hong*, [1907] A.C. 96 (where vendor having given receipt in conveyance, he could not prove that part of purchase money not in fact paid); *Harrison v. Preston* (1873), 22 U.C.C.P. 576; *Casey v. McCall* (1868), 19 U.C.C.P. 90; *Ketchum v. Smith* (1861), 20 U.C.Q.B. 313; *Sparling v. Savage* (1866), 25 U.C.Q.B. 259.

2. Conveyancing and Law of Property Act, R.S.O. 1990, c. C.34, s. 7; *Jones v. McGrath* (1888), 16 O.R. 617 (C.A.) (party to conveyance may be estopped from denying fact recited, as against third parties who act upon recital); *Rice v. Rice* (1853), 61 E.R. 646; **see also** Land Titles Act, R.S.O. 1990, c. L.5, s. 101 (transfers of charges subject to state of account between chargor and chargee).

3. *Jones v. McGrath* (1888), 16 O.R. 617 (C.A.).

4. GRANTING OR OPERATIVE CLAUSE OF CONVEYANCE

(a) General

§264   It is not necessary to use the word"grant" in the operative clause of a conveyance of freehold; "transfer" is sufficient.[1] "Demise" is also an effective word to convey an estate of freehold, and is equivalent to "grant".[2]

1. *Nicholson v. Dillabough* (1862), 21 U.C.Q.B. 591; *Re Airey* (1921), 21 O.W.N. 190 (H.C.); **see also** *McDonald v. McGillis* (1867), 26 U.C.Q.B. 458 (grant worded "doth grant, demise, and to farm let to the 'grantee', his heirs and assigns" being grant of fee simple).

2. *Spears v. Miller* (1882), 32 U.C.C.P. 661; **see also** *Roan v. Kronsbein* (1886), 12 O.R. 197 (words "be permitted to occupy her house during his life" being sufficient to pass life estate so as to give effect to parties' intention); *Johnston v. Kraemer* (1885), 8 O.R. 193 (C.A.).

§265   Either of the words "assign" or"convey" is sufficient to pass an estate of freehold when used in the operative clause of a deed of grant.[1] The words"release and quit claim" in the operative clause of a conveyance are adequate to pass an estate in fee simple, where the intention to convey is plain.[2] The words "remise, release and quit claim" are sufficient to pass an estate of freehold by deed of grant.[3]

1. *Fraser v. Fraser* (1864), 14 U.C.C.P. 70 ("assign" sufficient); *Saylor v. Cooper* (1883), 8 O.A.R. 707 ("convey" sufficient); *Watt v. Feader* (1862), 12 U.C.C.P. 254 ("assign, transfer and set over" sufficient); *Bright v. McMurray* (1882), 1 O.R. 172 ("convey, assign, release and quit claim" sufficient).

2. *Nicholson v. Dillabough* (1862), 21 U.C.Q.B. 591; **see also** *Doe d. Wilkinson v. Tranmarr* (1757), 125 E.R. 1383; *Shove v. Pincke* (1793), 101 E.R. 72 (words "limit and appoint" operating as grant; intention of parties being that deed operate as appointment to uses); *Bright v. McMurray* (1882), 1 O.R. 172 (Ch.).

3. *Pearson v. Mulholland* (1889), 17 O.R. 502 (C.A.); *Acre v. Livingstone* (1867), 26 U.C.Q.B. 282; *Cameron v. Gunn* (1865), 25 U.C.Q.B. 77; **see also** *Bright v.* McMurray (1882), 1 O.R. 172 (Ch.); **but see** *Collver v. Shaw* (1873), 19 Gr. 599; *Spears v. Miller* (1882), 32 U.C.C.P. 661.

§266   An exchange or a partition of any tenements or hereditaments does not imply any condition in law, and the word"give" or the word "grant" in a conveyance does not imply any covenant in law, except so far as"give" or "grant" may, by force of any Act in force in Ontario, imply a covenant.[1] If, by a conveyance or will executed after July 1, 1834, lands are granted, conveyed or devised to two or more persons other than executors or trustees in fee simple, or for any less estate, it is to be considered that such persons take as tenants in common and not as joint tenants, unless an intention sufficiently appears on the face of such letter, assurance or will that they are to take as joint tenants.[2] This is so notwithstanding that one of such persons is the spouse or same-sex partner of another of them.[3]

1. Conveyancing and Law of Property Act, R.S.O. 1990, c. C.34, ss. 11, 12 (s. 11 not extending to anything executed or done before January 1, 1850).

2. Conveyancing and Law of Property Act, R.S.O. 1990, c. C.34, s. 13(1); **see also** *Billett v. Davidson* (1920), 18 O.W.N. 425 (H.C.); *Re Giffen* (1925), 57 O.L.R. 634 (H.C.).

3. Conveyancing and Law of Property Act, R.S.O. 1990, c. C.34, s. 13(2) [am. 1999, c. 6, s. 13(1)].

(b) Reservations and Exceptions

§267   A grantor in the conveyance of a fee simple can reserve a life estate unto him or herself.[1] But if a grantor wishes to reserve any rights over the land granted, it must be done expressly.[2]

1. *Simpson v. Hartman* (1868), 27 U.C.Q.B. 460 (deed conveying land in fee simple, reserving nevertheless to grantor's "own use, benefit and behalf the occupation, rents, issues and profits of the said above-granted premises, for and during the term of my natural life"; instrument being conveyance of fee simple, and not mere testamentary paper which grantor could revoke by subsequent deed); **see also** *Hartman v. Fleming* (1870), 30 U.C.Q.B. 209 (grantor conveying to daughter in fee, adding after habendum: "Reserving nevertheless to my own use, benefit and behalf, the occupation, rents, issues and profits of the said above granted premises, for and during the term of my natural life"; reservation not void; deed might be construed as covenant to stand seized of reversion to use of daughter, with life estate remaining in grantor); *Doe d. Bennet v. Murdock* (1880), 20 N.B.R. 317 (C.A.).

2. *Majestic Mines Ltd. v. Alberta (Attorney General)*, [1941] 2 W.W.R. 353 (Alta. T.D.); affirmed [1942] 1 W.W.R. 321 (C.A.); affirmed [1942] S.C.R. 402.

§268   There may be a severance of the mines and minerals from the owner-ship of the surface. The mines and minerals so severed are a separate tene-ment capable of being held for the same estates as other hereditaments. A separate estate in fee simple may be held in mines and minerals in, on or under land, apart from the ownership of the surface.[1]

1. *Algoma Ore Properties Ltd. v. Smith*, [1953] O.R. 634 (C.A.); **see also** *Knight Sugar Co. v. Alberta Railway & Irrigation Co.*, [1936] 1 W.W.R. 416 (Alta. C.A.); affirmed [1938] 1 W.W.R. 234 (P.C.).

§269   Where by the terms of a conveyance a right of way or easement is reserved or excepted from the land transferred or charged, such reservation or exception is effectual and is to be deemed always to have been effectual to vest the right of way or other easement in the transferor or chargor of the land, notwithstanding that the transferee or chargee does not execute the instrument.[1]

1. Conveyancing and Law of Property Act, R.S.O. 1990, c. C.34, s. 44.

5. HABENDUM

§270   A habendum[1] is not an essential part of a conveyance; the granting or operative clause is sufficient of itself to pass the estate created.[2]

1. *See Also* §§15-21

2. *Dunlap v. Dunlap* (1883), 6 O.R. 141 at 144; reversed on other grounds, 10 O.A.R. 670 (form of conveyance set out in Sched. A to Short Forms of Conveyances Act not containing habendum).

§271   The proper purpose of the habendum is to determine what estate or interest is granted by the deed, though this may be done in the operative clause. The habendum may explain or qualify but not totally contradict or be repugnant to the estate created by the operative clause.[1] If the habendum has the effect of cutting down the estate given in the premises, it is repugnant and void, and if the grant is of a fee simple, the grantees would take the fee.[2] The habendum is the proper part of the conveyance in which to create trusts or uses.[3]

1. *Gold v. Rowe* (1913), 4 O.W.N. 642 at 643 (H.C.); *Langlois v. Lesperance* (1892), 22 O.R. 682 (H.C.); *Purcell v. Tully* (1906), 12 O.L.R. 5 (C.A.); *Doe d. Meyers v. Marsh* (1852), 9 U.C.Q.B. 242; *Owston v. Williams* (1858), 16 U.C.Q.B. 405; *Doe d. Wood v. Fox* (1846), 3 U.C.Q.B. 134.

2. *Sherlock v. Green*, [1949] O.W.N. 506 (H.C.); *Diesebourg v. James*, [1950] O.W.N. 565 (H.C.).

3. *Bayliss v. Balfe* (1917), 38 O.L.R. 437 (H.C.); **see also** *Hunter v. Munn*, [1962] O.W.N. 250 (C.A.) (habendum making fee simple subject to life interest of grantors).

§272   Although the habendum cannot retract the gift in the premises, it may construe and explain the sense in which the words in the premises should be taken.[1]

> 1. *Spencer v. Registrar of Titles*, [1906] A.C. 503 (P.C. [Aus.]), per Lord Davey.

6. DESCRIPTION OF PROPERTY CONVEYED

§273   Unless the contrary appears to be the intent of the instrument,[1] where the "mining rights" in respect of any land are granted or reserved, such grant or reservation will be construed to convey or reserve the ores, mines and minerals on or under the land, together with such right of access for the purpose of winning the ores, mines and minerals as is incidental to a grant thereof.[2] Similarly, unless the contrary appears to be the intent, where the "surface rights" in respect of land are granted or reserved, such grant or reservation will be construed to convey or reserve the land therein described, with the exception of the ores, mines and minerals on or under the land and such right of access for the purpose of winning the ores, mines and minerals as is incidental to a grant thereof.[3]

> 1. *Doe d. Murray v. Smith* (1848), 5 U.C.Q.B. 225 (land described generally in deed as being part of lot 4; particular and specific description given afterwards clearly showing parcel to embrace part of lot 3 as well as lot 4; specific description, not general one, governing); **see also** *Gillen v. Haynes* (1873), 33 U.C.Q.B. 516; *Wilson v. Gilmer* (1882), 46 U.C.Q.B. 545; *Iler v. Nolan* (1861), 21 U.C.Q.B. 309; *Thomson v. Neil* (1974), 7 O.R. (2d) 438 (Co. Ct.) (whether "mill privilege" constituting term of description or term of usage); Deeds and Documents (as to rules of construction applicable to conveyances generally); Mines and Minerals (as to grants of "surface rights" or "mining rights"); **see also** Boundaries.
>
> 2. Conveyancing and Law of Property Act, R.S.O. 1990, c. C.34, s. 16.
>
> 3. Conveyancing and Law of Property Act, R.S.O. 1990, c. C.34, s. 17.

§274   The conventional line principle applies only where there is no other means of establishing a boundary.[1]

> 1. *Bea v. Robinson* (1977), 18 O.R. (2d) 12 (H.C.) (boundaries determinable from description in deeds).

7. PROPERTY PASSING UNDER CONVEYANCES AS APPURTENANT TO PREMISED DESCRIBED

§275   Every conveyance of land made after July 1, 1886 which purports to convey an estate in fee simple includes the reversion or reversions, the remainder and remainders, the yearly and other rents, issues and profits of the same land and every part and parcel thereof, and all the estate, right, title, interest, inheritance, use, trust, property, profit, possession, claim and demand whatsoever of the grantor into, out of or upon the same land, and every part and parcel thereof, with their and every of their appurtenances.[1]

> 1. Conveyancing and Law of Property Act, R.S.O. 1990, c. C.34, s. 15.

§276   Every conveyance of land made after July 1, 1886, unless an exception is specially made therein, includes all houses, out-houses, edifices, barns, stables, yards, gardens, orchards, commons, trees, woods, underwoods, mounds, fences, hedges, ditches, ways, waters, watercourses, light, liberties, privileges, easements, profits, commodities, emoluments, hereditaments, and appurtenances whatsoever to such land belonging or in anywise appertaining, or with the same demised, held, used, occupied and enjoyed or taken or known as part or parcel thereof.[1] However, a conveyance can only include something that, in some form, had an existence at the time of the conveyance.[2]

    1. Conveyancing and Law of Property Act, R.S.O. 1990, c. C.34, s. 15; **see also** *Hill v. Broadbent* (1898), 25 O.A.R. 159.

    2. *Carpenter v. Smith*, [1951] O.R. 241 (H.C.).

§277   Under the Conveyancing and Law of Property Act,[1] a conveyance does not operate to pass, as appurtenant to the parcel described in the conveyance, land which has not been built upon, even though it is shown that such land was held, used, occupied or enjoyed as part of the described parcel.[2] Nor does a such conveyance operate to pass land covered by a building if no part of that building lies upon the parcel described in the conveyance, even though the building is used and enjoyed as part of the parcel described.[3] But if there is a building on the parcel described in the conveyance, the conveyance will operate, under this section, to pass any land covered by such a building which is not included in the description in the conveyance.[4]

    1. Conveyancing and Law of Property Act, R.S.O. 1990, c. C.34, s. 15.

    2. *McNish v. Munro* (1875), 25 U.C.C.P. 290; *Hill v. Broadbent* (1898), 25 O.A.R. 159.

    3. *Hill v. Broadbent* (1898), 25 O.A.R. 159.

    4. *Fraser v. Mutchmor* (1904), 8 O.L.R. 613 (H.C.); *Weeks v. Rogalski*, [1956] O.R. 109 (C.A.); Easements (as to creation and conveyance of easements under s. 15); **see also** *Woodrow v. Connor* (1922), 52 O.L.R. 631 (C.A.); *Winfield v. Fowlie* (1887), 14 O.R. 102 (H.C.); *St. Mary's Milling Co. v. St. Mary's (Town)* (1916), 37 O.L.R. 546 (C.A.); *Brenzel v. Rabinovitch* (1918), 42 O.L.R. 394 (H.C.); *Hickman v. Warman* (1918), 44 O.L.R. 257 (C.A.); *Re Rogers* (1920), 47 O.L.R. 82 (H.C.); *Reid v. Mimico (Town)* (1926), 59 O.L.R. 579 (C.A.); *Fowler v. Caulfield* (1925), 29 O.W.N. 245 (H.C.).

8. COVENANTS

§278   At common law, in the absence of any privity of estate, the burden of a covenant[1] touching and concerning land does not run with the land.[2]

1. **See** Pt. XII (restrictive covenants); **see also** Deeds and Documents; Contracts; Sale of Land.

2. *Austerberry v. Oldham Corp.* (1885), 29 Ch. D. 750, cited in *Freeman v. Camden (Township)* (1917), 41 O.L.R. 179 (H.C.); **see** §§369-73 (as to enforcement of restrictive covenants upon equitable principles).

§279   Covenants running with the land must have the following characteristics: they must be made with a covenantee who has an interest in the land to which they refer; and they must concern or touch the land. The covenant must either affect the land as regards mode of occupation, or be such as, per se and not merely from collateral circumstances, affects the value of the land.[1]

1. *Rowan v. Eaton* (1927), 60 O.L.R. 245 (C.A.); **see also** *Rogers v. Hosegood*, [1900] 2 Ch. 388; *Thompson v. Trepil Realty Ltd.*, [1962] O.R. 956 (H.C.) (covenant in agreement to sell but not embodied in subsequent deed of conveyance); *Sinclair v. Milligan*, [1971] 3 O.R. 735 (H.C.) (agreement registered as deposit on title permitting use of cabin and surrounding land for 50 years; creation of interest in land binding subsequent purchaser with notice).

§280   A "covenant" within the meaning of the rules as to the burdens and benefits thereof, running with the land, is confined to a contract contained in an instrument under seal.[1] However, the benefit of a covenant runs with the land without privity of estate, and a purchaser of the fee simple can sue upon a covenant as to title contained in a prior conveyance.[2]

1. *Ontario (Attorney General) v. Great Lakes Paper Co.* (1921), 50 O.L.R. 78 at 97 (H.C.).

2. *Gamble v. Rees* (1850), 6 U.C.Q.B. 396 (assignee acquiring right to sue upon breach of covenant and to recover damages when showing grantor having either no title or not good title when first deed made, at least when not shown that either deed must have been wholly inoperative to pass any estate, not merely by reason of first grantor having no interest when he assumed to convey, but by reason of having been evicted before assignment); *Clark v. Bogart* (1880), 27 Gr. 450.

§281   A covenant relating to land of inheritance or to land held for the life of another is deemed to be made with the covenantee and his or her heirs and assigns, and it has effect as if the heirs and assigns were expressed, whereas a covenant relating to land not of inheritance or not held for the life of another is deemed to be made with the covenantee and his or her executors, administrators and assigns, and takes effect as if the executors, administrators and assigns were expressed.[1]

1. Conveyancing and Law of Property Act, R.S.O. 1990, c. C.34, s. 24.

§282   It is no objection to an action brought upon a covenant for title by the assignee of the covenantee against the original covenantor that the covenant was broken the instant it was made and therefore could not be assigned.[1]

1. *Scott v. Fralick* (1850), 6 U.C.Q.B. 511; *Gamble v. Rees* (1850), 6 U.C.Q.B. 396.

§283 Upon an action of covenant as to title brought by an assignee of the covenantee, it is not essential for the plaintiff to show that a legal estate passed to him or her under the conveyance, because the cause of action lies in the fact that the plaintiff has not obtained the interest which he or she supposed he or she was acquiring and which he or she would have obtained if the title of the covenantor who executed the first deed had been good.[1]

   1. *Gamble v. Rees* (1850), 6 U.C.Q.B. 396.

§284 An assignee of part of the land may sue upon a covenant as to title and recover damages in proportion to his or her interest.[1]

   1. *Keyes v. O'Brien* (1860), 20 U.C.Q.B. 12, citing Sugden on Vendors 508.

§285 An action for breach of covenant as to title does not lie where the grantor has a good title but the grantee meets with obstruction and delay in gaining possession.[1]

   1. *Kerr v. Gordon* (1852), 9 U.C.Q.B. 249.

§286 Delay in the performance of a covenant for further assurances, which is an independent covenant, does not entitle a purchaser to rescission of an executed conveyance and recovery of the purchase money.[1]

   1. *Bowlen v. Canada Permanent Trust Co.*, [1925] S.C.R. 672 [Alta.].

§287 Whether covenants are dependent or independent turns upon the intention of the parties, to be deduced from the language used in the instrument.[1]

   1. *Wilson v. Wittrock* (1860), 19 U.C.Q.B. 391; *Tisdale v. Dallas* (1861), 11 U.C.C.P. 238; *McCrae v. Backer* (1885), 9 O.R. 1 (C.A.); *Armstrong v. Auger* (1891), 21 O.R. 98; *Re Canada Niagara Power Co.* (1899), 30 O.R. 185 (Div. Ct.).

§288 No action lies upon a covenant to maintain and keep in repair a right of way, where performance of that covenant becomes impossible because the land over which the right of way existed has washed away.[1]

   1. *Kerrigan v. Harrison* (1921), 62 S.C.R. 374; **see also** Contracts.

§289 In an action brought upon a covenant for quiet enjoyment, contained in a conveyance of real property, the measure of damages is to be ascertained by applying the rule in *Hadley v. Baxendale*,[1] and the covenantee or his or her assignee is entitled to such damages as may fairly and reasonably be considered either arising naturally, i.e., according to the usual course of things, from such breach of the covenant, or such as may reasonably be supposed to have been in contemplation of both parties, at the time they entered into the covenant, as the probable result of the breach of it.[2]

1. *Hadley v. Baxendale* (1854), 9 Exch. 341.

2. *Goodison v. Crow* (1920), 48 O.L.R. 552 (C.A.).

§290   No particular form of words is necessary to create a covenant; it is sufficient if, from the construction of the whole deed, it appears that the party intended to bind him or herself; and a covenant may take the form of a condition, a proviso or a stipulation.[1]

1. *Pearson v. Adams* (1912), 27 O.L.R. 87 (Div. Ct.); reversed (1913), 28 O.L.R. 154 (C.A.); which was reversed (1914), 50 S.C.R. 204 (stipulation in conveyance that property "to be used only as a site for a detached brick or stone dwelling house" constituting covenant, not condition); **see also** *Great Northern Railway v. Harrison* (1852), 138 E.R. 1032 (no particular form of words necessary to form covenant; but wherever court can collect from instrument an engagement on one side to do or not do something, that amounts to covenant, whether found in recital or in any other part of instrument); *Bank of Montreal v. Lingham* (1940), 7 O.L.R. 164 (C.A.); *Whitby (Town) v. Grand Trunk Railway* (1901), 1 O.L.R. 480 (C.A.) (recital of agreement, contained in bond executed under corporate seal, constituting covenant on company's part).

§291   Where a stipulation would be ineffectual as a condition because no right of entry is reserved for breach of the stipulation, the stipulation should be treated as a covenant, on the principle ut res magis valeat.[1]

1. *Pearson v. Adams* (1912), 27 O.L.R. 87 (Div. Ct.); reversed (1913), 28 O.L.R. 154 (C.A.); reversed (1914), 50 S.C.R. 204, per Anglin J.

§292   Conditions are not favoured in law; and if it is doubtful whether a clause in a conveyance is a condition or a covenant, the courts do not favour construing the clause as a condition.[1]

1. *Rawson v. Inhabitants of School District No. 5 in Uxbridge* (1863), 89 Mass. (7 Allen) 125; *Pearson v. Adams* (1912), 27 O.L.R. 87 (Div. Ct.); reversed (1913), 28 O.L.R. 154 (C.A.); reversed (1914), 50 S.C.R. 204.

§293   In construing covenants to ascertain their scope and effect, regard must be had to the objects and purposes they were designed to accomplish.[1]

1. *Pearson v. Adams* (1912), 27 O.L.R. 87 at 91 (Div. Ct.); reversed (1913), 28 O.L.R. 154 (C.A.); which was reversed (1914), 50 S.C.R. 204

§294   No covenant will arise by implication of law on any matter as to which the parties have inserted an express covenant in a conveyance.[1]

1. *Eccles v. Mills*, [1898] A.C. 360.

§295   A covenant for quiet possession free from encumbrances is not broken until the grantee is proved to have actually been disturbed in possession or enjoyment, as by ejectment or by entry or by user contrary to the grantee's rights.[1]

1. *Julien v. Labelle* (1923), 25 O.W.N. 388 (H.C.); *Nottidge v. Dering*, [1910] 1 Ch. 297; **see also** *Shuter v. Patten* (1921), 51 O.L.R. 428 (H.C.); *Leeming v. Smith* (1877), 25 Gr. 256; *Canavan v. Meek* (1883), 2 O.R. 636 (Q.B.).

§296 A purchaser who accepts the conveyance and goes into possession of the property thereby waives any objection to title or any right he or she might have had while the contract was executory to rescind the transaction or have it set aside; and thereafter the purchaser's only remedy as to defects of title lies in the right of action which he or she may have on the covenants as to title contained in the conveyance.[1]

1. *Wallace v. Hesslein* (1898), 29 S.C.R. 171; *Julien v. Labelle* (1923), 25 O.W.N. 388 (H.C.).

§297 Under a covenant for further assurance, a purchaser can compel the vendor to pay off an encumbrance created by the vendor.[1] Municipal taxes due are an encumbrance, but if the covenant as to quiet possession free from encumbrances is confined to the acts of the vendor, there is no breach of the covenant if the tax arrears accrued prior to the vendor's ownership.[2]

1. *Tripp v. Griffin* (1859), 5 U.C.L.J. 117; **see also** *Clark v. Bogart* (1880), 27 Gr. 450 (lands subject to encumbrances created by vendor; vendor covenanting with purchaser to pay off encumbrances; mortgagee from purchaser entitled to benefit of vendor's covenant; vendor ordered to pay off encumbrances).

2. Local Improvement Act, R.S.O. 1990, c. L.26, s. 71 (special rates charged on land for local improvements, except so much of them as are in arrears, not to be deemed encumbrance as respecting covenant against encumbrances); *Harry v. Anderson* (1863), 13 U.C.C.P. 476; *Silverthorne v. Lowe* (1876), 40 U.C.Q.B. 73; *Re Kennedy* (1878), 26 Gr. 33.

§298 In every conveyance for valuable consideration made after July 1, 1886, the following covenants by the person who conveys and is expressed to convey as beneficial owner are deemed to be included and implied in the conveyance: a covenant for right to convey; a covenant for quiet enjoyment; a covenant for freedom from encumbrances; and a covenant for the further assurance, according to the forms of covenants for such purposes set out in the Short Forms of Conveyances Act.[1] The benefit of such an implied covenant is annexed and incident to and goes with the estate or interest of the implied covenantee, and is capable of being enforced by every person in whom that estate or interest is for the whole or any part thereof from time to time vested.[2]

1. Short Forms of Conveyances Act, R.S.O. 1980, c. 472 [NC/NR by R.S.O. 1990], Sched. B.; Conveyancing and Law of Property Act, R.S.O. 1990, c. C.34, s. 23(1) [am. 1992, c. 32, s. 5], (2).

2. Conveyancing and Law of Property Act, R.S.O. 1990, c. C.34, s. 23(3).

§299   No right of action lies against a grantee on a covenant contained in a conveyance unless the grantee has executed the conveyance.[1] However, a restrictive covenant contained in a conveyance will be enforced against a grantee, even though he or she does not execute the conveyance, if the covenant is part of the transaction under which the grantee acquires the land.[2]

> 1. *Crédit Foncier Franco-Canadien v. Lawrie* (1896), 27 O.R. 498 (Ch.) (plaintiffs claiming as assignee of a covenant to pay encumbrance contained in deed which had not been executed by defendant; no action lying); **see also** *Polak v. Swartz* (1917), 12 O.W.N. 252 (Div. Ct.).
>
> 2. *Re Wheeler* (1926), 59 O.L.R. 223 at 234 (C.A.), per Middleton J.A.

§300   Every covenant made after March 24, 1950 which, but for the Conveyancing and Law of Property Act, would be annexed to and run with land and which restricts the sale, ownership, occupation or use of land because of race, creed, colour, nationality, ancestry or place of origin of any person, is void and of no effect.[1]

> 1. Conveyancing and Law of Property Act, R.S.O. 1990, c. C.34, s. 22.

9. EXECUTION OF CONVEYANCE

(a) General

§301   A conveyance is "executed" when all the acts necessary to render it complete – the signing, sealing and delivering – have been performed.[1]

> 1. *Re Metropolitan Theatres* (1917), 40 O.L.R. 345 (H.C.); **see also** *Cherry v. Heming* (1849), 154 E.R. 1367.

(b) Signing

§302   A person who signs, seals and delivers a conveyance containing a duplicate covenant cannot avoid liability by signing a name which he or she uses but which is not in fact his or her own, nor can liability be saddled on the person whose name is so used unless the user is the duly constituted attorney of such person.[1]

> 1. *Shan v. Shun*, [1918] A.C. 403; *McMeekin v. Furry* (1907), 39 S.C.R. 378.

§303   A defendant's plea of non est factum to an action brought upon a covenant in a conveyance will be upheld if it is proved that the defendant is illiterate and that the contents of the conveyance were falsely explained to him or her.[1] The authorities are clear that where a party executing a document cannot read or write except to provide a signature, even when the document is drafted in his or her own language, it is held not to be executed where a request that the document be read by the party putting it forward is refused; or where the document is misread; or where the contents of the document are misrepresented.[2]

1. *J.R. Watkins Co. v. Minke*, [1928] S.C.R. 414; *Letourneau v. Carboneau* (1904), 35 S.C.R. 110, per Nesbitt J.; **see also** *Murray v. Jenkins* (1898), 28 S.C.R. 565 [N.S.]; *Owens v. Thomas* (1857), 6 U.C.C.P. 383; *Hatton v. Fish* (1851), 8 U.C.Q.B. 177; see Fraud and Misrepresentation (as to right of party to have conveyance set aside on ground of fraud, misrepresentation, duress or undue influence); Mistake, Contracts (as to plea of non est factum by person executing conveyance who is mistaken as to nature of instrument signed).

2. See *Letourneau v. Carboneau* (1904), 35 S.C.R. 110, per Nesbitt J.

(c) Sealing

§304 A conveyance of a freehold interest can be made by deed only, and a seal is essential to render an instrument a deed.[1] Although at one time it was held that a seal had to be of wax impressed upon the document, the modern view is more lenient: anything attached to the document, or any physical interference with the document, such as an impression or a perforation, may constitute a valid seal if the party executing the document intended to adopt it as his or her seal.[2] There is no technical rule as to the sealing of a conveyance that the party executing must place his or her hand on the seal.[3]

1. Conveyancing and Law of Property Act, R.S.O. 1990, c. C.34, s. 3; *Zwicker v. Zwicker* (1899), 29 S.C.R. 527; *Eastview v. Roman Catholic Episcopal Corp. of Ottawa* (1918), 44 O.L.R. 284 (H.C.).

2. *Bell v. Black* (1882), 1 O.R. 125 (H.C.) (visible impression in form of circular scroll, made with pen, in which was inscribed word"seal" being good seal); *Hamilton v. Dennis* (1866), 12 Gr. 325 (where ribbon woven through slits cut in document, document sealed); **see also** *Clement v. Donaldson* (1852), 9 U.C.Q.B. 299 (mere marking of paper with poker opposite signature, without signer acknowledging mark as being own seal, not rendering paper sealed instrument).

3. *Hatton v. Fish* (1851), 8 U.C.Q.B. 177.

§305 Even if no mark or impression appears on the paper, if the testimonium clause states that the document has been sealed, a presumption arises that the document has in fact been sealed.[1] If a corporation has a common seal, the affixing of that seal to a conveyance and the delivery thereof will render the conveyance operative without any signature.[2]

1. *Bell v. Black* (1882), 1 O.R. 125 (H.C.); *Re Buff Pressed Brick Co.* (1924), 56 O.L.R. 33 (H.C.); **see also** *Stewart v. Clark* (1863), 13 U.C.C.P. 203 (seal slipping off document after signing).

2. *Eastview v. Roman Catholic Episcopal Corp. of Ottawa* (1918), 44 O.L.R. 284 (H.C.).

(d) Delivery

§306 A conveyance has no operation until delivery.[1] Delivery may be effective by words alone or, without words, by acts or conduct from which can be inferred the intent to deliver the deed as an instrument binding upon the conveyor.[2]

> 1. *Xenos v. Wickham* (1866), L.R. 2 H.L. 296; *Goddard's Case* (1584), 76 E.R. 396; *Re Metropolitan Theatres Ltd.* (1917), 40 O.L.R. 345 (H.C.); *Zwicker v. Zwicker* (1899), 29 S.C.R. 527; *Re Giffen* (1925), 57 O.L.R. 634 (H.C.).

> 2. Co. Litt. 36a, 49b; *Thoroughgood's Case* (1612), 77 E.R. 925; *Xenos v. Wickham* (1866), L.R. 2 H.L. 296; *Zwicker v. Zwicker* (1899), 29 S.C.R. 527; *Macedo v. Stroud*, [1922] 2 A.C. 330 (P.C.).

§307 A conveyance is not be be presumed inoperative for want of delivery merely because the grantor retains it in his or her possession; a deed is delivered as soon as there are acts or words by the party executing which show that he or she considers it as his or her deed, presently binding upon him or her.[1] Whether a deed has been delivered is a question of fact, and delivery may be inferred from the execution of the deed in the presence of an attesting witness.[2]

> 1. *Zwicker v. Zwicker* (1899), 29 S.C.R. 527 (deed held to have been delivered, notwithstanding that grantor retaining it in possession and continuing to use property conveyed, and notwithstanding that conveyance covering all property of grantor); **see also** *Xenos v. Wickham* (1866), L.R. 2 H.L. 296; *Tupper v. Foulkes* (1861), 142 E.R. 314; *Re Giffen* (1925), 57 O.L.R. 634 (H.C.); *Anning v. Anning* (1916), 38 O.L.R. 277; *McDonald v. McDonald* (1879), 44 U.C.Q.B. 291.

> 2. *Moore v. Hazelton* (1864), 9 Allen (Mass.) 102, quoted with approval in *Zwicker v. Zwicker* (1899), 29 S.C.R. 527.

§308 Since a conveyance cannot be registered unless it is a complete and operative instrument, it follows that it ought to be an impossible task to establish that a deed which has been registered, with the full knowledge and approval of the grantor, has not been delivered.[1]

> 1. *Anning v. Anning* (1916), 38 O.L.R. 277.

§309 Knowledge by the grantee of the conveyance is not essential to delivery and operation of the conveyance.[1]

> 1. *Zwicker v. Zwicker* (1899), 29 S.C.R. 527; *Doe d. Garnons v. Knight* (1826), 108 E.R. 250; *Hall v. Palmer* (1844), 67 E.R. 491.

§310 Although a conveyance is presumed to have been delivered on the day of its date, evidence may be produced to prove that it was actually delivered on some other date, in which event the conveyance will take effect from that date.[1]

1. *Heron v. Lalonde* (1916), 53 S.C.R. 503.

(e) Delivery in Escrow

§311 A grantor may deliver the conveyance in such manner as to suspend or qualify its binding effect. The maker of a deed may declare that it is to have no effect until a certain time has arrived or some condition has been performed; but when the time has arrived or the condition has been performed, the delivery becomes absolute and the maker of the deed is absolutely bound by it whether or not he or she has parted with the possession of it. Until the specified time has arrived or the condition has been performed, the instrument is not a deed; it is a mere escrow.[1]

1. *Xenos v. Wickham* (1866), L.R. 2 H.L. 296, per Lord Cranworth.

§312 The evidence produced to establish an escrow of an instrument, the terms of which show it was intended to operate at once, must be express and clear.[1] The old common law rule that a deed could not be handed over to a grantee as an escrow but had to be handed to a stranger, is no longer law.[2]

1. *Molson's Bank v. Cranston* (1918), 44 O.L.R. 58 (C.A.); *Carter v. Canadian Northern Railway* (1911), 23 O.L.R. 140 (Div. Ct.); reversed (1911), 24 O.L.R. 370 (C.A.).

2. *Molson's Bank v. Cranston* (1918), 44 O.L.R. 58 (C.A.); **but see** *Confederation Life Assn. v. O'Donnell* (1866), 13 S.C.R. 218.

§313 An escrow cannot be handed over to take effect only on the grantor's death, since a conveyance delivered as an escrow to take effect on the grantor's death is necessarily testamentary and must be executed in conformity with the requirements of the Succession Law Reform Act.[1] Upon the performance of the condition on which the conveyance was handed over, it takes effect and becomes operative without any further delivery, even though the grantor or grantee or both are dead or have ceased to be sui juris.[2]

1. Succession Law Reform Act, R.S.O. 1990, c. S.26; *Foundling Hospital Governors v. Crane*, [1911] 2 K.B. 367 at 379, per Farwell L.J.; *Habergham v. Vincent* (1793), 101 E.R. 53; *In the Goods of Morgan* (1866), 14 W.R. 1022 (where grantor delivering writing as deed, to be delivered to grantee at grantor's death or upon some future event, deed possessing present interest to be enjoyed in future); *Riddell v. Johnston* (1931), 66 O.L.R. 554 (H.C.).

2. *Re Giffen* (1925), 57 O.L.R. 634 (H.C.); *Perryman's Case* (1599), 77 E.R. 181; *Graham v. Graham* (1791), 30 E.R. 339; *Coare v. Giblett* (1803), 102 E.R. 763.

§314 Where the executors of an estate convey lands by a conveyance which is absolute in form but is not intended to so operate, and the grantee is given at the same time an option to purchase, with the understanding that the grantee will reconvey if the option is not exercised, the executors will be entitled to a reconveyance and an accounting upon the grantee's failing to exercise the option.[1]

1. *Cartwright v. Cartwright*, [1940] S.C.R. 659.

(f) Effect of Execution by Some of Parties

§315 If a conveyance is expressed to be made by several persons, and if the object of the conveyance appears from the recitals and can be attained only by execution of the conveyance by all the named parties, then the execution by one person will not bind that person in the absence of execution by the others.[1] A clause in a deed which provides that parties who execute the instrument are bound notwithstanding non-execution by other parties, is of no force unless and until the instrument itself becomes operative.[2]

1. *Moore v. Irwin* (1926), 59 O.L.R. 245 (H.C.); affirmed (1926), 59 O.L.R. 546 (C.A.).

2. *Molson's Bank v. Cranston* (1918), 44 O.L.R. 58 (C.A.).

10. EFFECT OF CONVEYANCE TO GRANTEE WITH NO KNOWLEDGE OF CONVEYANCE

§316 If a conveyance has been signed, sealed and delivered by the grantor, it operates to vest the title in the grantee even though the grantee has no knowledge of the conveyance, subject to the grantee's right to repudiate the conveyance; but until such repudiation the title is in the grantee.[1]

1. *Purdom v. Northern Life Assurance Co. of Canada* (1928), 63 O.L.R. 12 (C.A.); affirmed [1930] S.C.R. 119; *London & City Banking Co. v. London & River Plate Bank* (1888), 21 Q.B.D. 535 (C.A.) (donee's acceptance of gift to be presumed until dissent signified, even though donee not aware of gift); *Butler & Baker's Case* (1591), 76 E.R. 684; *Standing v. Bowring* (1886), 31 Ch. D. 282.

11. EFFECT OF CONVEYANCE UPON AFTER-ACQUIRED PROPERTY

§317 If a grantor purports to convey by deed an interest in land to which he or she is not entitled as at the date of the deed but subsequently acquires, the benefit of the subsequent acquisition vests automatically in the grantee by reason of the doctrine of "feeding the estoppel", without the necessity of a new conveyance.[1] But if the grantor intends the conveyance to pass only whatever interest he or she has in the property as at that date, any subsequently acquired interest will not pass to the grantee under the conveyance.[2]

1. *Rajapakse v. Fernando*, [1920] A.C. 892 (P.C.); *Trust & Loan Co. of Upper Canada v. Ruttan* (1877), 1 S.C.R. 564 (and cases cited therein); *Edinburgh Life Assurance Co. v. Allen* (1876), 23 Gr. 230; *Kapoor Sawmills Ltd. v. Deliko*, [1941] 2 W.W.R. 554 (B.C.S.C.); **see also** Estoppel.

2. *Stuart v. Prentiss* (1861), 20 U.C.Q.B. 513; *Standard Life Assurance Co. v. Kraft* (1919), 45 O.L.R. 323 at 325 (C.A.).

§318   This doctrine of "feeding the estoppel" does not apply where the grantor acquires the subsequent interest in a different capacity, e.g., as trustee.[1]

1. See *Nevitt v. McMurray* (1886), 14 O.A.R. 126.

§319   The estoppel operates only against the grantor and those claiming under him or her, and not against anyone claiming by a title paramount to the grantor's.[1]

1. See *Eyre v. Burmester* (1862), 46 E.R. 987.

12.   SHORT FORMS OF CONVEYANCES ACT

(a) General

§320   If a contract for the sale and purchase of land does not refer to the form of deed[1] to be given by the vendor, the purchaser has the right to demand only a deed in the form set out in the Short Forms of Conveyances Act.[2]

1. *See Also* §21.

2. Short Forms of Conveyances Act, R.S.O. 1980, c. 472 [NC/NR], Sched. A; *McKay v. McKay* (1880), 31 U.C.C.P. 1 at 20; *Julien v. Labelle* (1923), 25 O.W.N. 388 (H.C.).

§321   Unless a conveyance is made according to the form set forth in the Act, or is expressed to be made in pursuance of the Act, or refers to the Act, any covenants inserted in it will not have the extended meaning and effect set out in the Act.[1]

1. Short Forms of Conveyances Act, R.S.O. 1980, c. 472, s. 2 [am. 1984, c. 32, s. 23], Sched. A; *Julien v. Labelle* (1923), 25 O.W.N. 388 (H.C.) (covenant for quiet possession free from encumbrance); **see also** *Seaton v. Lunney* (1879), 27 Gr. 169 (form in Sched. A using only word"grant" and not containing habendum).

§322   If the statement that the conveyance is made pursuant to the Short Forms of Conveyances Act has been omitted by mutual mistake, the conveyance may be rectified to bring it into accordance with the intention of the parties.[1]

1. *Julien v. Labelle* (1923), 25 O.W.N. 388 (H.C.); *Hickman v. Warman* (1918), 44 O.L.R. 257 (C.A.).

§323   Although the Interpretation Act[1] provides that where a form is prescribed, deviations therefrom not affecting substance or calculated to mislead do not vitiate it, it is nevertheless essential, in order for the Short Forms of Conveyances Act to operate, that the words prescribed by that Act be used before the extended meaning set out in that Act can be attributed to them.[2]

1. Interpretation Act, R.S.O. 1990, c. I.11, s. 28(d).

2. *Wood v. Rosenthal* (1922), 52 O.L.R. 502 (H.C.) (discharge of mortgage, although not mentioning assignments of mortgage as required by statutory form, being nevertheless effective for purpose of reconveying property to mortgagor; case not analogous to use of short form of conveyance where certain words when used have attributed to them some extended meaning quite different from original meaning of words actually used; there, in order for statute to operate, essential that prescribed words be used before such effect can be attributed to them); *Bills v. Sims* (1922), 53 O.L.R. 57 (H.C.) (discharge of mortgage not containing statement required by form in Registry Act that "such mortgagee is thereby discharged" not operating to reconvey property to mortgagor, as omission being one affecting substance); *Emmett v. Quinn* (1882), 7 O.A.R. 306; *Barry v. Anderson* (1891), 18 O.A.R. 247 at 251; *Gilchrist v. Island* (1886), 11 O.R. 537 (H.C.); *Bradshaw v. Ontario (Registrar of Simcoe)* (1867), 26 U.C.Q.B. 464; **see also** *Clarke v. Chamberlain* (1889), 18 O.R. 270 (Ch.) (if words to have any force in registered instrument beyond their ordinary meaning in any instrument, that must be effected by statute; in such case, statutorily prescribed terminology must be strictly followed unless defect curable by Interpretation Act); *Roche v. Allan* (1911), 23 O.L.R. 300 (C.A.) (no assistance available from Short Forms of Conveyances Act in order to extend covenants to include "Assigns" of parties unless statutory words used); *Crozier v. Tabb* (1876), 38 U.C.Q.B. 54; *Clark v. Harvey* (1888), 16 O.R. 159.

(b) Covenant as to Right to Convey

§324   Where a grantor covenants in the conveyance that he or she has a right to convey the lands notwithstanding any act of such grantor, the grantee is entitled to recover damages on this covenant as to a strip of land four feet wide which the grantor had sold to a third party prior to the conveyance, and which is included in the parcel described in the conveyance.[1] A covenant by the grantor that he or she has the right to convey, which covenant does not contain the words "notwithstanding any act of the said grantor", cannot take effect under the Short Forms of Conveyances Act, because it is not in the form prescribed by the Act; but such a covenant binds the covenantor according to its very words, its legal effect being that he or she is seised and has a right to convey in fee simple.[2]

1. *Hickman v. Warman* (1918), 44 O.L.R. 257 (C.A.).

2. *Brown v. O'Dwyer* (1874), 35 U.C.Q.B. 354; *McKay v. McKay* (1880), 31 U.C.C.P. 1 (C.A.).

(c) Covenant for Quiet Possession Free From Encumbrances

§325   An agreement for the sale and purchase of a fee simple carries with it the right of the purchaser to demand proper covenants in the conveyance, and one of these usual or proper covenants is a covenant for quiet enjoyment.[1]

>   1. *Guest v. Cochlin* (1929), 64 O.L.R. 165 (C.A.).

§326   A grantor who covenants that the grantee shall have quiet possession is liable if that covenant is broken, even though the grantor gave the covenant in good faith and without knowledge of the right of any one else to possession of the premises.[1] A covenant for quiet possession is not broken until the grantee has been actually disturbed in the possession or enjoyment, as by ejectment or entry or user contrary to his or her right.[2]

>   1. *Guest v. Cochlin* (1929), 64 O.L.R. 165 (C.A.).
>
>   2. *Julien v. Labelle* (1923), 25 O.W.N. 388 (H.C.); *Nottidge v. Dering*, [1910] 1 Ch. 297.

§327   The covenant as to quiet possession contained in the Short Forms of Conveyances Act[1] entitles the grantee and his or her heirs, executors, administrators, successors and assigns to the quiet possession of the land "with their and every of their appurtenances"; but "appurtenances" does not cover quasi-easements which have never existed or have ceased to exist, as easements properly so called, by reason of unity of ownership.[2]

>   1. Short Forms of Conveyances Act, R.S.O. 1980, c. 472, Sched. B3.
>
>   2. *Ruetsch v. Spry* (1907), 14 O.L.R. 233 at 237 (H.C.); *Harris v. Smith* (1876), 40 U.C.Q.B. 33 at 39; **see also** Easements.

§328   The extended meaning given by the Short Forms of Conveyances Act,[1] to the covenant for quiet possession free from encumbrances does not embrace a judgment or execution obtained or issued against the grantor, but rather one which affects the lands in contravention of the grantor's absolute ownership, i.e., one issued or enforceable against the lands in the grantor's hands, and one which, as against the grantee, the grantor ought to pay.[2]

>   1. Short Forms of Conveyances Act, R.S.O. 1980, c. 472, Sched. B3.
>
>   2. *Chittick v. Lowery* (1903), 6 O.L.R. 547 at 549 (H.C.).

(d) Release Clause

§329   If by a conveyance operating pursuant to the Short Forms of Conveyances Act the grantor releases to the grantee all of his or her claims upon the land, the extended meaning given to such a release by the Act is ample to pass to the grantee whatever interest the grantor has or might in the future acquire in the lands conveyed.[1] The protection afforded by the release clause in the Act is against all claims which a purchaser would not otherwise have to meet were it not for his or her ownership of the land, and the clause applies only to claims on the land, which it is the duty of the vendor to remove in order to assure the purchaser a complete title at the date of the conveyance.[2]

1. *Birdsill v. Birdsill* (1919), 45 O.L.R. 307 at 311 (H.C.); affirmed (1919), 46 O.L.R. 345 (C.A.).

2. *Chittick v. Lowery* (1903), 6 O.L.R. 547 at 549 (H.C.).

XII   Restrictive Covenants

1. CREATION OF RESTRICTIVE COVENANTS

(a) General

§330   The benefit of a restrictive covenant may be attached to an equitable interest in land, and when so attached the benefit will pass with the ownership of that equitable interest.[1]

> 1. *Besinnett v. White* (1925), 58 O.L.R. 125 (C.A.) (equitable interest of creditor in land, arising from oral promise by debtor to convey land to creditor in satisfaction of debt, being sufficient interest in land to which benefit of restrictive covenant could be attached); **see also** *Tulk v. Moxhay* (1848), 41 E.R. 1143 (question in each case being one of substance and reality, not of technicality); *Kuhirtt v. Lamb* (1991), 18 R.P.R. (2d) 122 (Ont. Gen. Div.) (covenants not running with land being merely personal covenants).

§331   A restrictive covenant must be negative in substance and constitute a burden on the covenantor's land analogous to an easement. The covenant must be imposed for the benefit or to enhance the value of the benefited land. The land must be capable of being benefited by the covenant at the time the covenant is imposed.[1] The instrument creating the restrictive covenant must precisely define both the benefited and the burdened land.[2] The land being benefited is not required to be physically adjoining or touching the servient land.[3]

> 1. *Zetland (Marquess) v. Driver*, [1939] Ch. 1; *Hi-Way Housing (Saskatchewan) Ltd. v. Mini-Mansion Construction Co.*, [1980] 5 W.W.R. 367 (Sask. C.A.); reversing [1980] 3 W.W.R. 340 (Q.B.); *Lamvid Inc. v. 427654 Ontario Ltd.* (1985), 50 O.R. (2d) 782 (H.C.); *Amberwood Investments Ltd. v. Durham Condominium Corp. No. 123* (2000), 37 R.P.R. (3d) 144 (Ont. S.C.J.); affirmed, 2002 CarswellOnt 850 (Ont. C.A.) (no exception to general rule that positive covenants cannot run with land has been established in case law).
>
> 2. *Canadian Construction Co. v. Beaver (Alberta) Lumber Ltd.*, [1955] S.C.R. 682 [Alta.]; *Rogers v. Hosegood*, [1900] 2 Ch. 388 (C.A.); *Bank of Montreal v. University of Saskatchewan* (1953), 9 W.W.R. (N.S.) 193 (Sask. Q.B.).
>
> 3. *International Coal & Coke Co. v. Evans* (1909), 11 W.L.R. 463 (C.A.); affirming (1908), 9 W.L.R. 711 (S.C.); *Bowes Co. v. Rankin*, [1924] 4 D.L.R. 406 (Ont. C.A.).

§332   The land registrar may register as annexed to the land a covenant that the land or a specified part thereof is not to be built upon or is not to be used in a particular manner, or any other covenant running with or capable of being legally annexed to the land, unless: the covenantor is the owner of the land to be burdened by the covenant; the covenantee is a person other than the covenantor; the covenantee owns land to be benefited by the covenant, and that land is mentioned in the covenant; and the covenantor signs the application to assume the burden of the covenant.[1]

> 1. Land Titles Act, R.S.O. 1990, c. L.5, s. 119(3), (4).

§333   Where a covenant is not binding upon successors in title or is not stated to run with the land, the covenant cannot be enforced upon subsequent successors in title, as it is merely a personal covenant and not a restrictive one.[1]

> 1. *Harder Homes Ltd. v. Stellar Development Ltd.* (1982), 25 R.P.R. 52 (Sask. Q.B.); **see also** *Hi-Way Housing (Saskatchewan) Ltd. v. Mini-Mansion Construction Co.*, [1980] 5 W.W.R. 367 (Sask. C.A.); reversing [1980] 3 W.W.R. 340 (Q.B.).

(b) Building Schemes

§334   In an action brought by a purchaser of one lot against the purchaser of another lot to enforce a restrictive covenant on the basis of the existence of a building scheme, the following must be proved: that both plaintiff and defendant derive title under a common vendor; that prior to selling the lands the vendor had laid out his estate or a defined portion thereof, including the lands purchased by the plaintiff and defendant respectively, for sale in lots subject to restrictions intended to be imposed on all the lots, and which, though varying in details as to particular lots, are consistent and consistent only with some general scheme of development; that these restrictions were intended by the common vendor to be and were for the benefit of all the lots intended to be sold, whether or not they were also intended to be and were for the benefit of other lots retained by the vendor; and that both the plaintiff and the defendant, or their predecessors in title, purchased their lots from the common vendor upon the footing that the restrictions subject to which the purchases were made were to enure for the benefit of the other lots included in the general scheme whether or not they were also to enure for the benefit of other lands retained by the vendor.[1]

> 1. *Re Wheeler* (1926), 59 O.L.R. 223 (C.A.) (building scheme not existing because of varying nature of covenants exacted from purchasers of different lots and because of absence of any development scheme); *Elliston v. Reacher*, [1908] 2 Ch. 665; *Kelly v. Barrett*, [1924] 2 Ch. 379; *Re Lorne Park* (1914), 33 O.L.R. 51 (C.A.); *Peters v. Waddington* (1920), 18 O.W.N. 115 (H.C.); *Playter v. Lucas* (1921), 51 O.L.R. 492 (Div. Ct.); *Kirk v. Distacom Ventures Inc.* (1996), 4 R.P.R. (3d) 240 (B.C. C.A.); reversing (1995), 45 R.P.R. (2d) 313 (B.C.S.C.) (restrictive covenant unenforceable where identity of dominant lands in doubt); *London Life Insurance v. W.L.M. Construction Ltd.* (1995), 147 N.S.R. (2d) 312 (C.A.) (developer effectively waiving compliance with restrictive covenant); *Berry v. Indian Park Assn.* (1997), 12 R.P.R. (3d) 315 (Ont. Gen. Div.); additional reaons, 1997 CarswellOnt 5054 (Ont. Gen. Div.); affirmed on other grounds (1999), 23 R.P.R. (3d) 169 (Ont. C.A.) (by-laws of association restricting use of private lots not binding land; existence of building scheme not established); **see also** *Reid v. Bickerstaff*, [1909] 2 Ch. 305 (some essentials of building scheme: defined area within which scheme operative; reciprocity of scheme; purchaser of one parcel cannot be subject to implied obligation to purchasers of undefined and unknown area; purchaser must know both extent of burden and extent of benefit; obligations to be imposed within defined area must also be defined; obligations need not be identical; scheme not created by mere fact that owner sells estate in lots and takes varying covenants from various purchasers; must

be notice to various purchasers as to vendors' impositions on definite area); *Re Glengrove Lands Ltd.* (1929), 35 O.W.N. 308 (H.C.); *Miller v. R.*, [1927] Ex. C.R. 52; affirmed [1928] S.C.R. 318; *Smith v. Eggertson* (1922), 66 D.L.R. 774 (C.A.) (covenant stating "any building or dwelling house" erected must be of value of at least stated sum and should be placed at least 20 feet back from street; covenant not prohibiting construction of any building other than dwelling-house); *Torbay Hotel Ltd. v. Jenkins*, [1927] 2 Ch. 225 (building scheme not existing where absence of defined geographical area); *McGregor v. Boyd Builders Ltd.*, [1966] 1 O.R. 424 (H.C.) (full nature of elements of alleged building scheme not proved); *Shen Investments Ltd. v. Mosca*, [1968] 2 O.R. 162 (H.C.) (building scheme not inferred); *White v. Lauder Developments Ltd.*, [1973] 1 O.R. 473 (H.C.); affirmed on other grounds [1973] 3 O.R. 967 (C.A.) (common vendor originally intending to impose on all lots in shopping plaza covenants running with land precluding owners or lessees from operating businesses competing with one another in plaza; failure of common vendor to impose restrictive covenants on some lots conveyed); *Audze v. Innisfil (Township)*, [1973] 2 O.R. 228 (H.C.) (existence of building scheme where block A on registered cottage development plan designated as "area of user common to each property owner in the subdivision"; deeds to cottage owners containing no covenants pertaining to block A); *Dorrell v. Mueller* (1975), 16 O.R. (2d) 795 (Dist. Ct.) (common vendor not necessary to finding that building scheme existing when land registered under Land Titles Act; thus, two vendors selling under "checkerboard" scheme being covenantors; covenants being mutually enforceable); *Re Clarke* (1991), 18 R.P.R. (2d) 109 (Ont. Gen. Div.) (valid building scheme not created if any of four criteria not fulfilled); *Lakhani v. Weinstein* (1980), 31 O.R. (2d) 65 (H.C.) (absence of common vendor being fatal to existence of building scheme; creation of mutual rights and obligations in agreement by predecessors in title not establishing further class of building scheme; held that extension of common law requirements should occur only as result of decision of higher court); *Matthews v. Tucci* (1985), 38 R.P.R. 302 (Ont. Dist. Ct.) (deeds from subdividers to predecessors in title of plaintiff and defendant containing restrictive covenants; restrictions on respective lots meeting requirements of development scheme; benefit and burden of restrictions therefore running with respective lots).

§335　To establish the existence of a building scheme, it is not necessary to find any express contract by the vendor and the several purchasers; a building scheme may be inferred from the circumstances.[1]

1. *West v. Hughes* (1927), 58 O.L.R. 183 (H.C.).

§336　When land is sold upon a building scheme, i.e., where part of a tract is set apart by the vendors for the benefit of the purchasers, either by way of a plan or otherwise, the vendors cannot depart from the plan or scheme which was the foundation of the sales. It may be regarded as an implied covenant or an implied grant of an easement, or it may rest on the principles of estoppel. In any case, the property so dedicated is rendered subject to the rights held out to the purchaser as an inducement to purchase. These rights may exist in perpetuity.[1]

1. *Re Lorne Park* (1914), 33 O.L.R. 51 (C.A.).

§337   The absence of a covenant by the common grantor that he or she is bound by similar restrictions or will exact similar covenants from later purchasers of remaining lots may be a serious obstacle to establishing a building scheme.[1] However, where a covenantor has retained some of the land for the benefit of which the restrictive covenant was exacted, the covenantor may enforce that covenant against subsequent purchasers regardless of whether a building scheme has been created.[2]

1. *Second Church of Christ Scientist v. Dods* (1920), 18 O.W.N. 409 (H.C.).

2. *Shortt v. Griffin*, [1947] O.W.N. 782 (H.C.).

§338   Any restrictions registered against one certain lot fall into the class of restrictions which are personal to the person imposing them, and they negate the existence of a building scheme.[1] If the vendors reserve a discretionary power to modify the restrictions in any manner, there can be no building scheme in effect, and the covenants cannot run with the land and do not bind.[2]

1. *Wallace v. Bremner*, [1954] O.W.N. 826 (H.C.); **see also** *Re Zierler* (1957), 8 D.L.R. (2d) 189 (Ont. H.C.) (application for order declaring that restrictive covenants not binding on certain lots; when plan of subdivision registered, owners contemplating selling most lots for residential purposes with same restrictions throughout; intention to transfer two lots to village for park purposes; application allowed; no building scheme existing, as intention not carried out and owners having failed to exact restrictions respecting all lots sold; vendors not in position to impose restrictions in certain cases and not in others); *Jain v. Nepean (City)* (1989), 7 R.P.R. (2d) 132 (Ont. H.C.); varied on other grounds (1992), 25 R.P.R. (2d) 1 (C.A.); leave to appeal to S.C.C. refused, 150 N.R. 391n (land not benefiting financially from restriction; no restrictive covenant found; right of first option creating personal covenant crystallizing into equitable interest in land upon default of respondent).

2. *Ex parte Little*, [1954] O.W.N. 610 (H.C.); **see also** *Lafortune v. Puccini* (1991), 16 R.P.R. (2d) 16 (Ont. Gen. Div.) (original intent of subdivision agreement and restrictive covenants therein having been varied by conduct of original purchasers and subsequent transferees; significant and substantial change in character of neighbourhood resulting; restrictive covenants no longer enforceable).

§339   In order to constitute a proper building scheme, the original vendor must intend to impose the restrictions in connection with a general scheme of development.[1]

1. *Scharf v. Mac's Milk Ltd.*, [1965] 2 O.R. 640 (C.A.) (enforcement of restrictive covenant against lessee of purchaser).

§340   A building scheme may exist where there are only two parcels of land in the scheme.[1]

1. *Rowan v. Eaton* (1926), 59 O.L.R. 379 (H.C.); affirmed (1927), 60 O.L.R. 245 (C.A.).

§**341** A grantee who does not execute a conveyance containing a restrictive covenant on his or her part is in equity bound by a covenant that is part of the transaction under which he or she acquires the land.[1]

> 1. *Re Wheeler* (1926), 59 O.L.R. 223 (C.A.); *Rowan v. Eaton* (1926), 59 O.L.R. 379 (H.C.); affirmed (1927), 60 O.L.R. 245 (C.A.); *Gilpinville v. Dumaresq*, [1927] 1 D.L.R. 730 (N.S.T.D.).

2. REGISTRATION

§**342** Notice of a restrictive covenant is given to all persons who subsequently acquire an interest in land subject to the restrictive covenant, upon registration of the instrument in which the covenant is contained.[1]

> 1. Registry Act, R.S.O. 1990, c. R.20, s. 74(1); **see also** *Besinnett v. White* (1925), 58 O.L.R. 125 (C.A.) (purchaser bound by restrictive covenants if instrument in which covenants contained registered; purchaser not able to claim freedom from liability on ground that registered instruments not disclosing all facts establishing validity of restrictive covenants).

§**343** Every instrument affecting land in whole or in part will be adjudged fraudulent and void against any subsequent purchaser or mortgagee for valuable consideration without actual notice unless the instrument is registered before the registration of the instrument under which the subsequent purchaser or mortgagee claims.[1]

> 1. Registry Act, R.S.O. 1990, c. R.20, s. 70(1); **see also** *Toronto (City) v. Beck*, [1953] O.W.N. 301 (C.A.); *Babcock v. Archibald* (1981), 34 O.R. (2d) 65 (H.C.) (purchaser aware of prior claim but being advised that claim invalid; no actual notice; specific performance not granted to claimant); **but see** *Maker v. Davanne Holdings Ltd.*, [1954] O.R. 935 (H.C.).

§**344** If restrictive conditions or covenants are filed against land under the Land Titles Act,[1] and if the persons who impose the conditions intend that the benefit of them attach to and run with other lands, those other lands must be clearly defined and set forth in the register and certificate of ownership, because, having regard to the purpose of the Land Titles Act, a person dealing with a parcel of land should be able, by inspecting the certificate of ownership, to determine without further investigation the precise nature and extent of the encumbrances to which the land is subject.[2]

> 1. Land Titles Act, R.S.O. 1990, c. L.5, s. 129 [am. 1998, c. 18, Schedule E, s. 150].
>
> 2. *Campbell v. Cowdy* (1928), 61 O.L.R. 545 (C.A.).

3. DETERMINATION OF VALIDITY

(a) General

§345 A restrictive covenant binding land is a defect in title, and an owner may, by way of originating notice under the Rules of Civil Procedure, raise the question of whether his or her lands are bound by a restrictive covenant.[1]

> 1. Rules of Civil Procedure, R.R.O. 1990, Reg. 194, R. 14.05 [am. O. Reg. 396/91, s. 3; 484/94, s. 5; 292/99, s. 1(2)]; **see also** Rules of Civil Procedure, R.R.O. 1990, Reg. 194, R. 38.06 [am. O. Reg. 171/98, s. 15]; *Rowan v. Eaton* (1926), 59 O.L.R. 379 (H.C.); affirmed (1927), 60 O.L.R. 245 (C.A.); *Keyser v. Daniel J. McA'Nulty Realty Co.* (1923), 55 O.L.R. 136 (C.A.) (application under rule to determine whether anyone may enforce building restriction on certain property; notice of application under R. 610 to be given to everyone interested in question raised); *McGillivray v. Stockdale* (1927), 31 O.W.N. 385 (H.C.); *Re Dinnick*, [1933] O.W.N. 55 (H.C.); *Cosgrave v. Delta Park Ltd.*, [1936] O.W.N. 617 (H.C.); **see also** Practice.

§346 A breach of a restrictive covenant may be restrained by injunction.[1]

> 1. *McEacharn v. Colton*, [1902] A.C. 104 (P.C.); *Doherty v. Allman* (1878), 3 App. Cas. 709; **see also** *Cosgrave v. Delta Park Ltd.*, [1936] O.W.N. 617 (H.C.); *Achilli v. Tovell*, [1927] 2 Ch. 243 (if breach of restrictive covenant causing substantial damage, court not having discretion to award damages in lieu of mandatory injunction); *Sharp v. Harrison*, [1922] 1 Ch. 502; *Playter v. Lucas* (1921), 51 O.L.R. 492 (Div. Ct.) (granting of interlocutory injunction to restrain breach of restrictive covenant); see Injunctions (as to damages in lieu of injunction).

(b) Discriminatory Covenants

§347 Covenants restricting the sale, ownership, occupation or use of land on the basis of race, creed, colour, nationality, ancestry or place of origin of any person is void and of no effect when made after March 24, 1950.[1]

> 1. Conveyancing and Law of Property Act, R.S.O. 1990, c. C.34, s. 22; **see also** Human Rights Code, R.S.O. 1990, c. H.19, ss. 2(1), 10 [am. 1997, c. 16, s. 8; 1999, c. 6, s. 28(8); 2001, c. 13, s. 19; 2001, c. 32, s. 27(2)-(4)]; *Metropolitan Toronto Condominium Corp. No. 624 v. Ramdial* (1988), 49 R.P.R. 182 (Ont. Dist. Ct.); appeal quashed (1988), 49 R.P.R. xxxvi (C.A.) (injunction granted prohibiting sale to person with 16-year-old son intended to reside in unit).

4. DISCHARGE OR MODIFICATION

§348 The Conveyancing and Law of Property Act provides that where there is annexed to land a condition or covenant that the land or a specified part of it is not to be built on, or is to be or not to be used in a particular manner, or any other condition or covenant running with or capable of being legally annexed to land, any such condition or covenant may be modified or discharged by order of a judge of the Superior Court of Justice.[1] An appeal lies to the Divisional Court from such a decision.[2] This provision does not apply to building restrictions imposed by a by-law passed under the Municipal Act or the Planning Act.[3] This provision also does not apply to covenants and easements established under the Agricultural Research Institute of Ontario Act.[4] A clear case must be made before removal of the restriction will be obtained by recourse to this provision.[5]

1. Conveyancing and Law of Property Act, R.S.O. 1990, c. C.34, s. 61(1); *Van Bork v. William Carson Holdings Ltd.*, 1998 CarswellOnt 4300 (Ont. Gen. Div.) (purpose of legislation being to allow court to discharge restriction that is spent).

2. Conveyancing and Law of Property Act, R.S.O. 1990, c. C.34, s. 61(2).

3. Conveyancing and Law of Property Act, R.S.O. 1990, c. C.34, s. 61(3); Municipal Act, R.S.O. 1990, c. M.45; Planning Act, R.S.O. 1990, c. P.13.

4. Conveyancing and Law of Property Act, R.S.O. 1990, c. C.34, s. 61(4) [en. 1994, c. 27, s. 6]; Agricultural Research Institute of Ontario Act, R.S.O. 1990, c. A.13.

5. *Pacific International Equities Corp. v. Royal Trust Co.* (1994), 42 R.P.R. (2d) 66 (Ont. Gen. Div.) (language used in agreements resulting in creation of restrictive covenants under s. 119 of Land Titles Act, and not creation of easements; application for deletion or discharge of covenants from land register dismissed); **see also** Land Titles Act, R.S.O. 1990, c. L.5, s. 119(5) (any such condition or covenant able to be modified or discharged by order of court on proof to satisfaction of court that modification being beneficial to persons principally interested in enforcement of condition or covenant); *Kuhirtt v. Lamb* (1991), 18 R.P.R. (2d) 122 (Ont. Gen. Div.) (covenants merely personal, not running with land; deed containing nothing on face, such as easement, stipulating that building restrictions being for benefit of adjacent land or future owners; since covenants being neither encumbrances nor clouds on title, vendor having no obligation to remove to provide clear title; defendants not entitled to avoid transaction); *Bryers v. Morris* (1931), 40 O.W.N. 572 (H.C.).

§349 If an owner of land, by application under the Conveyancing and Law of Property Act,[1] seeks to be freed from legally binding restrictive covenants, those who in good faith insist upon their rights ought not to be subjected to any expense whatever.[2] Before a judge will vary any restrictions he or she must first satisfy himself that in granting such an application he or she is favouring the balance of convenience having regard to the rights and interests of both parties, or that the benefit to the applicant greatly exceeds any possible detriment to those legally entitled to enforce the restrictions.[3]

1. Conveyancing and Law of Property Act, R.S.O. 1990, c. C.34, s. 61 [am. 1994, c. 27, s. 6].

2. *Rowan v. Eaton* (1926), 59 O.L.R. 379 (H.C.); affirmed (1927), 60 O.L.R. 245 (C.A.).

3. *Re George* (1926), 59 O.L.R. 574 (C.A.); *Re Button* (1925), 57 O.L.R. 161 (C.A.) (no building scheme existing; application to modify opposed by original covenantee, who still retaining land to be benefited; restriction removed; whatever value restriction may have been to covenantee when first imposed absolutely lost by covenantee's failure to impose similar restrictions on neighbouring lands, which afterwards sold); *Re Jackson* (1919), 16 O.W.N. 69 (H.C.); *Re Hawgill*, [1957] O.W.N. 310; *Re*

Eglinton & Bedford Park Presbyterian Church (1927), 61 O.L.R. 430 (C.A.) (church erected where restrictions allowing dwelling-houses only; restrictions having only two years to run, and proposed church being of architectural beauty); *Re Langley* (1929), 37 O.W.N. 87 (H.C.) (application for order for modification refused, even though restrictions having only one year to run; could not be said person opposing application would not be injured if restriction modified); *Re Speer* (1926), 59 O.L.R. 385 (H.C.) (application to modify restriction made under Land Titles Act; modification beneficial to only person having right to enforce covenant, i.e., original grantor; application allowed); *Re St. Timothy's Church* (1930), 39 O.W.N. 93 (H.C.) (restriction modified so as to permit building church; proposed church being of artistic design and ornament to neighbourhood; undertaking inserted that no bell be installed); see *Re Beardmore*, [1935] O.R. 526 (C.A.) (on application to discharge or modify restrictive covenant, applicant must, by evidence, completely satisfy court that if proposed modification allowed, injury to neighbouring owners who object being negligible; court may take into account not only financial effect of change, but effect on amenities of occupation of neighbouring lands); *Re Dinnick*, [1933] O.W.N. 55 (H.C.) (application to modify refused on ground construction of apartment house would materially injure residential properties in neighbourhood); *Re Crocker* (1931), 40 O.W.N. 294; *Re Hastings* (1931), 40 O.W.N. 271 (H.C.).

§350   If the court is of the opinion that those opposing an application to remove a building restriction, although they have a legal right to enforce the restriction, can derive no real or substantial benefit from the enforcement thereof, the restriction will be ordered discharged.[1]

     1. *Re Button* (1925), 57 O.L.R. 161 (C.A.); *Re Speer* (1926), 59 O.L.R. 385 (H.C.).

§351   A judge's power under the Conveyancing and Law of Property Act[1] to modify or discharge building restrictions is not, in its application, confined to building schemes.[2]

     1. Conveyancing and Law of Property Act, R.S.O. 1990, c. C.34, s. 61 [am. 1994, c. 27, s. 6].

     2. *Re Button* (1925), 57 O.L.R. 161 (C.A.).

§352   The statute does not confer upon the court any power to award compensation to a landowner who is prejudicially affected; accordingly, the jurisdiction conferred upon the court is exercised with caution, and an order discharging a restriction will not be made to the prejudice of an adjacent landowner who has real rights.[1]

     1. *Re Ontario Lime Co.* (1926), 59 O.L.R. 646 (C.A.); *Re Howie* (1922), 53 O.L.R. 65 (Div. Ct.) (application to modify refused where proposed modification would prejudice substantial rights of persons entitled to enforce restriction); *Re Findley* (1927), 32 O.W.N. 79 (C.A.); *Re Pugh* (1926), 31 O.W.N. 11 (H.C.); *Re Sellers-Gough Fur Co.* (1925), 28 O.W.N. 255 (H.C.); *Re McSherry* (1924), 26 O.W.N. 125 (H.C.); *Re Western Canada Flour Mills Ltd.* (1923), 25 O.W.N. 219 (H.C.); *Re McMurtry* (1922), 23 O.W.N. 168 (H.C.); affirmed (1922), 23 O.W.N. 346 (C.A.); *Cornell v. Brown* (1928), 34 O.W.N. 179 (C.A.); *Re Davidson Construction Co.* (1929), 36 O.W.N. 91 (H.C.); **see also** *Re Moody*, [1941] O.W.N. 167 (C.A.) (appli-

cation to modify restrictions in district where business premises with residential quarters above allowed, to permit erection of funeral home; application dismissed; power under Act to be used only when character of neighbourhood so changed that order can be made without doing violence to rights of other landowners); *Toronto (City) v. Lot 23 Plan M260*, [1945] O.W.N. 723 (application to be allowed only where any balance of convenience in favour).

§353 The true function of the statute is to enable the court to lift a condition or restriction that is spent or that is so unsuitable as to be of no value, under circumstances when assertion of the condition or restriction would clearly be vexatious.[1]

> 1. *Re Ontario Lime Co.* (1926), 59 O.L.R. 646 (C.A.) (application to modify restriction forbidding use of lot for any purpose but residence, to permit erection of stable; proposed building unquestionably detrimental to beneficial use of adjoining lot; application dismissed, without prejudice to another application proposing scheme not obnoxious to any reasonable user of adjoining lot); *Re Western Canada Flour Mills Ltd.* (1923), 25 O.W.N. 219 (H.C.); *Re Graham* (1922), 23 O.W.N. 413 (H.C.); *Re Long* (1920), 36 O.W.N. 15 (H.C.).

§354 Notice of an application must be given to all persons who have a right to enforce the building restriction, and to all persons having any interest, either legal or equitable, in lands to which the benefit of the restriction has become annexed.[1] If no one has a right to enforce a restrictive covenant, there is no necessity for an application under the statute to have the covenant modified or discharged. If it is doubtful whether anyone has a right to enforce the covenant, the owner of the land may have the question determined by an application under the Rules of Civil Procedure.[2]

> 1. *Re Baillie* (1911), 2 O.W.N. 816 (Ch.); *Re Speer* (1926), 59 O.L.R. 385 (H.C.); *Re McMurtry* (1922), 23 O.W.N. 168 (H.C.); affirmed (1922), 23 O.W.N. 346 (C.A.).
>
> 2. Rules of Civil Procedure, R.R.O. 1990, Reg. 194, R. 38.06(1).

§355 A person who is not the owner but has only entered into an agreement to purchase the land is not entitled to apply for modification or discharge of building restrictions under the Conveyancing and Law of Property Act.[1]

> 1. Conveyancing and Law of Property Act, R.S.O. 1990, c. C.34, s. 61 [am. 1994, c. 27, s. 6]; *Re Bartley*, [1950] O.W.N. 648 (C.A.).

5. ENFORCEMENT OR CONSTRUCTION

(a) General

§356 Although the burden of a restrictive covenant entered into by a grantee in fee simple does not run with the land at common law,[1] nevertheless, on equitable principles such a restrictive covenant will be enforced against anyone on the land, except against a purchaser of the legal estate for value without notice of the restrictive covenant.[2]

1. *See Also Cities Service Oil Co. v. Pauley*, [1931] O.R. 685 at 691 (H.C.) (burden
of covenant not involving grant never running with land except as between landlord
and tenant); *Denison v. Carrousel Farms Ltd.* (1981), 129 D.L.R. (3d) 334 (Ont.
H.C.); affirmed (1982), 138 D.L.R. (3d) 381 (C.A.) (lands having already been subject
to restrictive covenant; lease not constituting contract in restraint of trade; circumstances appropriate for permanent injunction); Landlord and Tenant (as to running of
covenants with land as between landlords and tenants and their assigns).

2. *Besinnett v. White* (1925), 58 O.L.R. 125 (C.A.); *Long Eaton Recreation Grounds
v. Midland Railway* (1901), 17 T.L.R. 775; affirmed [1902] 2 K.B. 574 (C.A.); see
also Federal Real Property Act, S.C. 1991, c. 50, s. 12 (restrictive covenants); *Huron
Woods Inc. v. 499691 Ontario Ltd.* (1992), 3 W.D.C.P. (2d) 467 (Ont. Gen. Div.)
(restrictive covenant requiring preservation of as much of natural landscape and tree
growth as possible; developer seeking interlocutory injunction to require purchaser to
restore backyard to natural grade and vegetation; application dismissed; little or no
inconvenience to developer if relief sought conferred by way of permanent mandatory
injunction after trial); *British United Automobiles Ltd. v. Volvo Canada Ltd.* (1980), 29
O.R. (2d) 725 (H.C.) (dominant tenement necessary for creation of covenant running
with land; covenant not binding on subsequent purchaser); *Lakhani v. Weinstein*
(1980), 31 O.R. (2d) 65 (H.C.) (owners of land agreeing to impose restrictions on land
and intending that benefit of restrictive covenants should run with land; registration of
agreement annexing covenants to land; covenants binding on subsequent purchasers
for value with notice); *Lamvid Inc. v. 427654 Ontario Ltd.* (1985), 50 O.R. (2d) 782
(H.C.) (presumption against covenants running with land not necessarily applicable to
leases; lessee having requisite interest in land; lease manifesting parties' intention that
covenant run with land; senseless to construe non-competition covenant in shopping
centre lease as personal covenant only); *Strus v. New Peel Developments Corp.*
(1986), 54 O.R. (2d) 208 (H.C.) (developer registering restrictive covenants in favour
of railway company after purchasers of condominium units signing agreements of
purchase and sale and taking interim possession; registration after execution of
agreements improper).

§357   The covenantee may sue the covenantor for breach of a restrictive
covenant even though the covenantee has parted with the land for the benefit
of which the covenant was created.[1] However, the covenantee cannot enforce
the covenant against subsequent purchasers unless the covenantee has
retained some of the land for the benefit of which the restrictive covenant was
created.[2] Nor can an assignee of the benefit of a covenant enforce that
covenant against a subsequent purchaser if the assignee has no land to be
benefited by the covenant.[3] And the covenantee is required not only to have
retained such land at the date of the covenant, but to retain it and own it at the
date when enforcement of the covenant is sought.[4]

1. *Hunt v. Bell* (1915), 34 O.L.R. 256 (C.A.); *Russell v. Stokes* (1791), 126 E.R. 323
(Exch. Ch.).

2. *Hunt v. Bell* (1915), 34 O.L.R. 256 (C.A.); *Re Wheeler* (1926), 59 O.L.R. 223
(C.A.); *London County Council v. Allen*, [1914] 3 K.B. 642 (C.A.); *Formby v. Barker*,
[1903] 2 Ch. 539; *Re Nisbet & Potts' Contract*, [1905] 1 Ch. 391; affirmed [1906] 1
Ch. 386; *Millbourn v. Lyons*, [1914] 2 Ch. 231 (C.A.); *London & South Western
Railway v. Gomm* (1882), 20 Ch. D. 562 (equitable doctrine establishing exception to
common law rules, which did not treat such covenant as running with land; not

mattering whether proceeding on analogy to easement or to covenant running with land); *Bowes Co. v. Rankin* (1924), 55 O.L.R. 601 (C.A.) (covenant by grantees not to use conveyed lands for manufacturing canned fruit without consent of grantors); **see also** *Page v. Campbell* (1921), 61 S.C.R. 633; *Keyser v. Daniel J. McA'Nulty Realty Co.* (1923), 55 O.L.R. 136 (C.A.); *Playter v. Lucas* (1921), 51 O.L.R. 492 (Div. Ct.); *Ontario (Attorney General) v. Great Lakes Paper Co.* (1921), 50 O.L.R. 78 (H.C.); *Ex parte Little*, [1954] O.W.N. 610 (H.C.); *Canadian Construction Co. v. Beaver (Alberta) Lumber Ltd.*, [1955] 3 D.L.R. 502 (S.C.C.).

3. *West v. Hughes* (1926), 58 O.L.R. 183 (H.C.).

4. *Playter v. Lucas* (1921), 51 O.L.R. 492 (Div. Ct.); *Ex parte Little*, [1954] O.W.N. 610 (H.C.).

§358   If a covenantee who brings an action against subsequent purchasers to enforce a restrictive covenant does not, at the date of trial, have any of the land for the benefit of which the covenant was exacted, the action will be dismissed even though at the date of issue of the writ the covenantee did have such land.[1] If a lot is subject to the burden of a restrictive covenant and the lot is subdivided, the owner of one part cannot enforce the covenant as against the owner of the other part.[2]

1. *Page v. Campbell* (1921), 61 S.C.R. 633; *London County Council v. Allen*, [1914] 3 K.B. 642 (C.A.).

2. *Harrod v. Hadden* (1924), 25 O.W.N. 581 (H.C.); *King v. Dickeson* (1889), 40 Ch. D. 596; **see also** *Re Pidgeon*, [1938] O.W.N. 292 (C.A.).

§359   A restrictive covenant creates an equitable interest in favour of the covenantee, and is enforceable against one who acquires title to the land by possession, even though that person has no notice of the restrictive covenant.[1]

1. *Re Nisbet & Potts' Contract*, [1905] 1 Ch. 391; affirmed [1906] 1 Ch. 386; *Colchester South (Township) v. Hackett*, [1928] S.C.R. 255.

§360   The equitable principles as to the enforcement of covenants against subsequent purchasers apply only to covenants which restrict the user of the land; a covenant which involves the expenditure of money will never be enforced against purchasers, even if they have notice of the covenant.[1] Moreover, a covenant intended to run with the land and be enforceable against subsequent purchasers with notice must be a covenant affecting the user of the land, and not a mere personal covenant entered into by the owner of the land.[2] If the restrictive covenant is intended for the personal benefit of the grantor and not for the benefit of other lands retained by the grantor, the covenant is not enforceable against subsequent purchasers.[3] It is not necessary, however, that the other lands retained by the grantor be adjoining lands.[4]

1. *Bowes Co. v. Rankin* (1924), 55 O.L.R. 601 (C.A.) (courts will enforce as against subsequent purchasers only those covenants negative in substance); *Clegg v. Hands* (1890), 44 Ch. D. 503 at 519; *Marlay Construction Ltd. v. Mount Pearl (Town)*

(1989), 47 M.P.L.R. 80 (Nfld. T.D.); reversed in part on other grounds (1996), 36 M.P.L.R. (2d) 130 (Nfld. C.A.) (undertaking to pave roads not a restrictive covenant); **see also** *Haywood v. Brunswick Building Society* (1881), 8 Q.B.D. 403 (covenant to build and maintain houses not enforced against purchaser of lands with notice of covenant); *Ontario (Attorney General) v. Great Lakes Paper Co.* (1921), 50 O.L.R. 78 (H.C.) (covenant positive in form may be negative in substance; if negative in substance, equitable principles as to enforcement of restrictive covenants against subsequent purchasers will be applied).

2.   *Ferris v. Ellis* (1920), 48 O.L.R. 374 (H.C.); *Albay Realty Ltd. v. Dufferin-Lawrence Developments Ltd.*, [1956] O.W.N. 302; *Galbraith v. Madawaska Club Ltd.*, [1961] S.C.R. 639 (restraint on alienation in regard to members of club); see also *Ferris v. Ellis* (1921), 49 O.L.R. 264 (H.C.) (owner of land selling fishing rights to syndicate and entering into $10,000 penal bond with syndicate conditioned on owner keeping dam on property in good repair; bond creating purely personal obligation not annexed to or capable of running with land; obligation created by bond not enforceable against purchasers of land, even with notice of bond); *Canadian Petrofina Ltd. v. Rogers*, [1963] 1 O.R. 24 (H.C.) (covenant in mortgage to buy mortgagee's products affirmative in form but restrictive in substance; therefore breach might be enjoined; covenant not running with land, however, and not binding mortgagor's transferee, despite transferee having occupied while premises subject to mortgage); *Fairhill Developments Ltd. v. Aberdeen Properties Ltd.*, [1969] 2 O.R. 267 (H.C.) (agreement for vendor to install appliances required by purchaser for business situate on land not being covenant capable of attaching to and running with land); *Bahnsen v. Hazelwood*, [1960] O.W.N. 155 (C.A.) (condition requiring purchaser to be approved by mortgagee); *Re Clarke* (1991), 18 R.P.R. (2d) 109 (Ont. Gen. Div.) (restrictive covenant not enforceable against subsequent purchasers where land to be benefited not properly and clearly defined in deed; restrictive covenant required to be clearly ascertainable and not merely impliedly identifiable; otherwise covenant being personal and not running with land).

3.   *Bowes Co. v. Rankin* (1924), 55 O.L.R. 601 (C.A.); *Renals v. Cowlishaw* (1878), 9 Ch. D. 125; affirmed (1879), 11 Ch. D. 866 (C.A.); *Spicer v. Martin* (1888), 14 App. Cas. 12; *Re Pidgeon*, [1938] O.W.N. 292 (C.A.) (restrictive covenant not stipulated to be for benefit of adjacent land or its future owners; grantee not executing deed containing such covenant; covenant not operative against subsequent purchaser).

4.   *Cities Service Oil Co. v. Pauley*, [1931] O.R. 685 at 691 (H.C.).

§361   There are three ways in which a plaintiff who is not the original covenantee can become entitled to the benefit of a restrictive covenant: as assignee of the land to which the benefit of the covenant is annexed; or as express assignee of the benefit of the covenant; or where both plaintiff and defendant own land that is subject to a building scheme.[1]

1.   *McGregor v. Boyd Builders Ltd.*, [1966] 1 O.R. 424 (H.C.).

§362   If the restrictive covenant is exacted for the personal benefit of the covenantee, the covenantee may validly release the covenant[1] If the restrictive covenant is exacted by the covenantee for the benefit of his or her adjoining lands, the benefit of the covenant becomes attached to those lands, and on a conveyance thereof the benefit of the covenant passes to the grantee without an express assignment of the covenant itself.[2] If the benefit of the covenant becomes attached to adjoining lands, a grantee of those lands may enforce the covenant even though he or she did not know of the existence of the covenant at the time of purchasing the lands.[3]

1. *Campbell v. Cowdy* (1928), 61 O.L.R. 545 (C.A.); *Page v. Campbell*, [1921] 2 W.W.R. 552 (S.C.C.); *Peters v. Waddington* (1920), 18 O.W.N. 115 (H.C.).

2. *Bowes Co. v. Rankin* (1924), 55 O.L.R. 601 (C.A.); **see also** *Rogers v. Hosegood*, [1900] 2 Ch. 388 (benefit may be annexed to one plot and burden to another; where such clearly done, benefit and burden passing to respective assignees, subject, in case of burden, to proof that legal estate, if acquired, acquired with notice of covenant); *Rowan v. Eaton* (1926), 59 O.L.R. 379 (H.C.); affirmed (1927), 60 O.L.R. 245 (C.A.); *Millbourn v. Lyons*, [1914] 2 Ch. 231.

3. *Rogers v. Hosegood*, [1900] 2 Ch. 388 (benefit clearly annexed to one piece of land, passing by assignment of and running with that land, in contemplation of equity as well as of law, without proof of special bargain or representation upon assignment).

§363 The benefit of a restrictive covenant may be attached to the equitable interest of a mortgagor of land.[1]

1. *Rogers v. Hosegood*, [1900] 2 Ch. 388.

§364 Unless the restrictive covenant is exacted for the benefit of an adjoining lot, the grantee of that adjoining lot has no right to enforce a restrictive covenant contained in a conveyance of another lot.[1] Whether the benefits of restrictive covenants entered into by a grantee with the grantor are to be personal to the grantor or are to be annexed to land retained by the grantor is a question of intention to be determined on the construction of the particular document, having due regard to the nature of the covenant and to the surrounding circumstances.[2]

1. *Reid v. Bickerstaff*, [1909] 2 Ch. 305; *Re Speer* (1926), 59 O.L.R. 385 (H.C.) (covenant exacted for benefit of grantor and not attached to other lots subsequently sold by grantor).

2. *Rowan v. Eaton* (1926), 59 O.L.R. 379 (H.C.); affirmed (1927), 60 O.L.R. 245 (C.A.) (conveyance containing covenants providing that "the said agreements to relate to the lands of the said grantor . . . as well as to the lands hereby conveyed"; intention held to be to attach benefit to lands retained by grantor); *Rogers v. Hosegood*, [1900] 2 Ch. 388; *Gilpinville v. Dumaresq*, [1927] 1 D.L.R. 730 (N.S.T.D.); *West v. Hughes* (1927), 58 O.L.R. 183 (H.C.); *Captain Developments Ltd. v. McDonald's Restaurants of Canada Ltd.* (1988), 49 R.P.R. 1 (Ont. H.C.) (covenant prohibiting use of land for "competitive" fastfood restaurant; plaintiff seeking declaration that covenant not breached by lease of adjoining premises to similar restaurant; action dismissed; restrictive covenant upheld); *Gray v. J.N.S. Developments Ltd.* (1990), 9 R.P.R. (2d) 101 (Ont. H.C.) (plaintiff dentist executing lease providing landlord agreeing not to lease other premises in shopping centre as constituted to another dentist; shopping centre subsequently having additions erected; plaintiff's application for interim injunction preventing lease to dentist dismissed; restrictive covenant ambiguous and intention of parties being in dispute; plaintiff's damages ascertainable and balance of convenience favouring defendants).

§365 For restrictive covenants to be enforceable, the land to be benefited must be owned by the covenantee and must be defined in the instrument creating the covenants. If either of these essentials is missing, the covenants are invalid.[1]

> 1. *Sekretov v. Toronto (City)*, [1972] 3 O.R. 534 (H.C.); affirmed [1973] 2 O.R. 161 (C.A.); *Victoria University v. Heritage Properties Ltd.* (1991), 4 O.R. (3d) 655 (Gen. Div.) (deed containing restrictive covenant not identifying lands of grantor intended to be benefited by covenant; covenant not running to burden purportedly servient lands so as to be binding upon present owners of transferred lands).

§366 Where a grantor exacts a covenant for the benefit of adjoining lots, he or she cannot enforce the covenant against subsequent purchasers after having disposed of all the lots for the benefit of which the covenant was exacted.[1]

> 1. *Page v. Campbell*, [1921] 2 W.W.R. 552 (S.C.C.); *Playter v. Lucas* (1921), 51 O.L.R. 492 (Div. Ct.); *Chambers v. Randall*, [1923] 1 Ch. 149; *London County Council v. Allen*, [1914] 3 K.B. 642 (C.A.).

§367 A purchaser of a lot will be entitled to the benefit of a restrictive covenant contained in the conveyance of another lot, even though the covenant was not exacted for the benefit of the first lot, if the purchaser is an assignee of the covenant, as distinct from being an assignee of the land.[1]

> 1. *Reid v. Bickerstaff*, [1909] 2 Ch. 305; *Renals v. Cowlishaw* (1878), 9 Ch. D. 125; affirmed, 11 Ch. D. 866.

§368 It would appear that restrictive covenants entered into by owners of incorporeal hereditaments are within the equitable rules applicable to restrictive covenants entered into by the owners of land.[1]

> 1. *Ontario (Attorney General) v. Great Lakes Paper Co.* (1921), 50 O.L.R. 78 (H.C.); *Norval v. Pascoe* (1864), 34 L.J. Ch. 82; *Hooper v. Clark* (1867), L.R. 2 Q.B. 200.

(b) Equitable Defences

§369 A purchaser of land is bound by a covenant on that land unless able to establish as a defence the purchase of the legal estate for value without notice.[1]

> 1. Conveyancing and Law of Property Act, R.S.O. 1990, c. C.34, s. 40; *Wilkes v. Spooner*, [1911] 2 K.B. 473; *Besinnett v. White* (1925), 58 O.L.R. 125 (C.A.).

§370 Since the right of a covenantee to enforce a restrictive covenant against a subsequent purchaser exists only in equity, the equitable right may be answered by equitable defences.[1]

> 1. *Miller v. R.*, [1927] Ex. C.R. 52; affirmed [1928] S.C.R. 318.

§371 The right to enforce a restrictive covenant in equity may be lost by laches or acquiescence.[1] But the mere circumstance that a person entitled to enforce a restrictive covenant has endured an evil embraced by the covenant does not prevent the court from subsequently arresting the evil.[2]

1. *Besinnett v. White* (1925), 57 O.L.R. 171 (H.C.); affirmed (1925), 58 O.L.R. 125 (C.A.) (covenantee who permits person bound by covenant to spend money or otherwise alter position in belief that covenantee will not object to use of land in contravention of covenant not entitled to enforce covenant against person so misled).

2. *Besinnett v. White* (1925), 57 O.L.R. 171 (H.C.); affirmed (1925), 58 O.L.R. 125 (C.A.); *Attorney General v. Leeds Corp.* (1870), 5 Ch. App. 583; *Willmott v. Barber* (1880), 15 Ch. D. 96; additional reasons (1881), 17 Ch. D. 772.

§372 Allowing a purchaser to erect a building which does not comply with one restrictive covenant may constitute a waiver of that covenant, but does not constitute a waiver of another, independent covenant.[1]

1. *Second Church of Christ Scientist v. Dods* (1920), 18 O.W.N. 409 (H.C.) (no principle of law entitling covenantor to escape from one covenant by breaking another).

§373 If there has been a general change in the character of the neighbourhood, the court will not enforce a restriction which in the course of time has become obsolete and meaningless and the enforcement of which could be due only to motives of spite or caprice or a desire to make money out of the enforcement of technical but obsolete restrictions.[1] This doctrine of change in the character of the locality is not confined to a situation where the change has been brought about by the person seeking to enforce the covenant, or where the change has been acquiesced in by that person.[2]

1. *Cowan v. Ferguson* (1919), 45 O.L.R. 161 (C.A.); *Sobey v. Sainsbury*, [1913] 2 Ch. 513; *Knight v. Simmonds*, [1896] 2 Ch. 294.

2. *Cowan v. Ferguson* (1919), 45 O.L.R. 161 (C.A.).

6. APPLICATION OF RULE AGAINST PERPETUITIES

§374 The rule against perpetuities has no application to restrictive covenants.[1]

1. *Mackenzie v. Childers* (1889), 43 Ch. D. 265; *London & South Western Railway v. Gomm* (1882), 20 Ch. D. 562; *Albay Realty Ltd. v. Dufferin-Lawrence Developments Ltd.*, [1956] O.W.N. 302.

7. WORDS AND PHRASES USED IN BUILDING RESTRICTIONS

§375 A church building cannot be considered "a private dwelling house" within the meaning of a restriction.[1] Neither is a church building a "detached residence."[2]

1. *Second Church of Christ Scientist v. Dods* (1920), 18 O.W.N. 409 (H.C.).

2. *Re Eglinton & Bedford Park Presbyterian Church* (1927), 61 O.L.R. 430 (C.A.).

§376   "Physician" used in a restrictive covenant ordinarily means a duly qualified physician under the law of the province.[1]

1. *Second Church of Christ Scientist v. Dods* (1920), 18 O.W.N. 409 (H.C.).

§377   A "sun-room" constructed of brick with several windows in it is not a porch or verandah within the meaning of a restrictive covenant.[1] A "verandah" is an integral part of the building.[2]

1. *Campbell v. Cowdy* (1928), 61 O.L.R. 545 (C.A.).

2. *Fisher v. Goldoff*, [1942] O.W.N. 490 (H.C.); *Williams v. Cornwall (Municipality)* (1900), 32 O.R. 255 (restriction violated if verandah closer to street than distance prescribed for building).

§378   A modern apartment house is not a "detached dwelling house" within the meaning of a restrictive covenant.[1] A duplex house is not a "detached residence" within the meaning of a restrictive covenant.[2]

1. *Pearson v. Adams* (1914), 50 S.C.R. 204; *Robertson v. Defoe* (1911), 25 O.L.R. 286; **see also** *Kimber v. Admans*, [1900] 1 Ch. 412 (meaning of "house"); *Toronto (City) v. King* (1923), 54 O.L.R. 100 (C.A.) (row of six separate dwellings, each designed to house two families, with party walls but no openings from one dwelling to another, not constituting apartment house within meaning of municipal by-law defining apartment house as building "for the purpose of providing three or more separate suites or sets of rooms for separate occupation by one or more persons").

2. *Toronto General Trusts Corp. v. Crowley* (1928), 62 O.L.R. 593 (courts concerned with truth and actuality; facts not changed by architectural hypocrisy by which actuality disguised and house made to appear to be something it is not; question whether building constituting two dwellings or one being question of fact in each case); see *Hoidge v. Davidson* (1923), 25 O.W.N. 430 (H.C.) ("detached house" meaning house which to all appearances being single house, although might be arranged or adapted internally for two families); **see also** *James v. Cutts* (1922), 52 O.L.R. 453 (H.C.) (question of intent); *Ilford Park Estates Ltd. v. Jacobs*, [1903] 2 Ch. 522 (duplex violating covenant that not more than one house to be erected on any lot); *Pepall v. MacPherson* (1922), 23 O.W.N. 71 (H.C.); reversed (1922), 23 O.W.N. 382 (C.A.).

§379   A "store" is "a place where goods are kept for sale"; hence a gasoline station is a store.[1] But a place where "work and labour" predominate, and the sale of goods is only incidental, is not a store.[2]

1. *Re Longley* (1928), 34 O.W.N. 181 (C.A.) (erection of gas station not violating restrictive covenant permitting erection of stores); *Dennis v. Hutchinson*, [1922] 1 K.B. 693 ("shop" defined as "place where goods are sold by retail and stored for sale").

2. *Toronto (City) v. Foss* (1912), 27 O.L.R. 264 (Div. Ct.); affirmed (1913), 27 O.L.R. 612 (C.A.) (house used for dressmaking by owner not store or factory within meaning of municipal by-law); *McCormick v. Toronto (City)* (1923), 54 O.L.R. 603 (H.C.) (restaurant not "store or manufactory" within meaning of municipal by-law).

8. STATUTORY RESTRICTIONS

§380   Restrictive covenants imposed by agreement between vendor and purchaser create an equitable interest in the property; but legislative restrictions or restrictions imposed by local authority pursuant to statute do not create such interests. The obligation to observe statutory restrictions applies to all property owners alike; such statutory restrictions are not subject to waiver by an owner, and they may be modified at any time by statute without reference to the owners of property affected by them.[1]

1. *Miller v. R.,*, [1927] Ex. C.R. 52; affirmed [1928] S.C.R. 318; *Orpen v. Roberts*, [1925] S.C.R. 364 at 369; **see also** Federal Real Property Act, S.C. 1991, c. 50, s. 12 (restrictive covenants); *Bagg v. Savoia* (1989), 67 O.R. (2d) 320 (Dist. Ct.) (Committee of Adjustment imposing condition upon granting of severance application; condition restricting owner from selling property for five years; owner subsequently entering into agreement of purchase and sale; on application by purchaser, condition held to be valid; condition only partial restraint on alienation); *Toronto (City) Roman Catholic Separate School Board v. Toronto (City)*, [1924] S.C.R. 368; reversed [1925] 3 D.L.R. 880 (P.C.); *Hartley v. Toronto (City)* (1924), 55 O.L.R. 275 (H.C.); affirmed (1925), 56 O.L.R. 433 (C.A.); *Toronto (City) v. King* (1923), 54 O.L.R. 100 (C.A.); *McCormick v. Toronto (City)* (1923), 54 O.L.R. 603 (H.C.); **see also** Municipal Corporations; Planning and Zoning.

XIII   Registry Act

1. DEFINITIONS

(a) Instrument

§381   "Instrument" includes every instrument whereby title to land in Ontario may be transferred, disposed of, charged, encumbered or otherwise affected, and includes any general registration and a Crown grant of Canada and of Ontario, a deed, conveyance, mortgage, assignment of mortgage, certificate of discharge of mortgage, assurance, lease, release, discharge, agreement for the sale or purchase of land, caution under the Estates Administration Act[1] or renewal or withdrawal thereof, municipal by-law, certificate of proceedings in any court, judgment or order of foreclosure and every other certificate of judgment or order of any court affecting any interest in or title to land, and a certificate of payment of taxes granted under the corporate seal of any municipality by the treasurer, a sheriff's and treasurer's deed of land sold by virtue of his or her office, a contract in writing, every order and proceeding in bankruptcy and insolvency, a plan of a survey or subdivision of land, and every notice, caution and other instrument registered in compliance with an Act of Canada or Ontario.[2]

1. Estates Administration Act, R.S.O. 1990, c. E.22.

2. Registry Act, R.S.O. 1990, c. R.20, ss. 1("instrument"), 18(6) [am. 1993, c. 27, Sched.; 1998, c. 18, Schedule E, s. 216(1), (2); 1999, c. 12, Schedule F, s. 35; 2000, c. 26, Schedule B, s. 17(2)]; *Henderson v. Toronto (City)* (1898), 29 O.R. 669 (H.C.) (municipal by-law opening road being"instrument" under Act); *Canadian Imperial Bank of Commerce v. Rockway Holdings Ltd.* (1996), 29 O.R. (3d) 350 (Gen. Div.); additional reasons (1996), 29 O.R. (3d) 350 at 357 (Gen. Div.) (licence agreement to extract and remove gravel a profit à prendre constituting instrument); **see also** *Grimshaw v. Toronto (City)* (1913), 28 O.L.R. 512 (Ch.); *Robson v. Carpenter* (1865), 11 Gr. 293 ("Act and Warrant" under Imperial Act, 19-20 Vict., c. 79, whereby sheriff of Lanarkshire, Scotland, transferring all property of debtor, in both Scotland and Canada, to trustee in bankruptcy; document being instruction capable of registration, even though not witnessed and not specifying any lands in Upper Canada); *Willoughby v. Knight* (1973), 1 O.R. (2d) 184 (H.C.) (whether assignment to oneself of interest under unregistered agreement of purchase and sale prohibiting registration).

§382   "Instrument" as defined by the Registry Act[1] includes every instrument which may affect lands either at law or in equity.[2] But an instrument does not"affect" land unless it has some bearing on the title, in professing to convey, charge or affect the title by its own operation; a mere assertion that someone else claims to have an interest or that the registered title of some other person is defective does not come within the statute.[3]

1. Registry Act, R.S.O. 1990, c. R.20, s. 1("instrument").

2. *McMaster v. Phipps* (1885), 5 Gr. 253.

3. *Ontario Industrial Loan & Investment Co. v. Lindsey* (1883), 3 O.R. 66 at 75 (C.A.).

§383   Since a claim of a mechanic's lien is an instrument encumbering or affecting land, it is an "instrument" as defined by the Registry Act.[1]

1. *Charters v. McCracken* (1916), 36 O.L.R. 260 (C.A.).

§384   A will is an instrument within the meaning of the Registry Act.[1]

1. *Dennis v. Lindsay* (1927), 61 O.L.R. 228 (H.C.).

§385   "Instrument" includes, among other things, a municipal by-law. Expropriation by-laws should be registered, because under such a by-law the municipality acquires some right, and failure to register such a by-law would enable the owner of the land to convey to a bona fide purchaser pending the arbitration and thus defraud the purchaser.[1]

1. *Grimshaw v. Toronto (City)* (1913), 28 O.L.R. 512 (Ch.) (nothing preventing registration or rendering it unlawful; nothing improper in registration; but failure to record by-law would be objectionable and likely lead to serious consequences).

§386   A certificate of a declaratory judgment may be registered, to preserve rights against purchasers for value who would otherwise not have notice of those rights.[1]

1. *Hubbs v. Black* (1918), 44 O.L.R. 545 (C.A.).

§387   An agreement for the sale and purchase of land is an "instrument" as defined by the Act.[1] "Land" includes not merely realty but "any estate or interest therein", and therefore a leasehold interest is covered by the term.[2]

1. *Rosenberg v. Bochler* (1913), 4 O.W.N. 757 (H.C.); **see also** *Re Sutherland*, [1967] 1 O.R. 611 (C.A.) (assignment of agreement for sale being "instrument"; person can "convey" to self; "dealing" not confined to transactions between different parties).

2. Registry Act, R.S.O. 1990, c. R.20, s. 1("land") (meaning land, tenements, hereditaments and appurtenances and any estate or interest therein); *Re Risk* (1924), 56 O.L.R. 134 (H.C.).

(b) Land Registrar

§388   "Land registrar" means a land registrar appointed under the Registry Act.[1] A land registrar must be appointed for every registry division and for every land titles division.[2]

1. Registry Act, R.S.O. 1990, c. R.20, ss. 1("land registrar"), 9 [re-en 1998, c. 18, Schedule E, s. 211].

2. Registry Act, R.S.O. 1990, c. R.20, s. 9(1) [re-en 1998, c. 18, Schedule E, s. 211].

2. DUTIES OF REGISTRAR

(a) Production of Books and Registered Instruments

§389   Upon receipt of the required fees, a land registrar must produce for inspection in his or her office during office hours any instrument or document registered in the office or produce any book or public record of the office relating to any such instrument, and must supply a certified copy of the whole or a part of any instrument, document, book or public record registered in the office.[1]

> 1. Registry Act, R.S.O. 1990, c. R.20, s. 15(4) [am. 1994, c. 27, s. 99(1); 1998, c. 18, Schedule E, s. 214(2), (3); 1999, c. 12, Schedule F, s. 34].

§390   The land registrar must keep a by-law index and a general register index. The registrar may also be required to prepare and maintain a separate alphabetical index for any class of general registrations[1]

> 1. Registry Act, R.S.O. 1990, c. R.20, s. 18 [am. 1993, c. 27, Sched.; 1998, c. 18, Schedule E, s. 216; 1999, c. 12, Schedule F, s. 35].

§391   The registrar must enter in the "abstract index", under a separate and distinct head, each separate lot or part of a lot as originally patented by the Crown or that appears on any registered plan of subdivision, judge's plan or municipal plan under the Registry Act.[1] This does not apply, however, to land designated under the Land Registration Reform Act to be recorded automatically.[2]

> 1. Registry Act, R.S.O. 1990, c. R.20, s. 20(1) [am. 1998, c. 18, Schedule E, s. 217(1)].
>
> 2. Registry Act, R.S.O. 1990, c. R.20, s. 20(4); Land Registration Reform Act, R.S.O. 1990, c. L.4, ss. 15 [re-en. 1998, c. 18, Schedule E, s. 98], 16 [am. 1998, c. 18, Schedule E, s. 99; 2000, c. 26, Schedule B, s. 11].

§392   An original copy of an instrument or document may be ordered by a judge of an Ontario court where a certified copy is not sufficient.[1]

> 1. Registry Act, R.S.O. 1990, c. R.20, s. 17(3).

(b) Making Searches and Preparing Abstracts of Title

§393   Mandamus will lie to compel a registrar to give a proper abstract, with a certificate that all the registrations on record in the office upon the lot appear on the abstract.[1]

> 1. *Re Registrar of Carlton (County)* (1862), 12 U.C.C.P. 225.

§394   The duty cast upon the registrar as to making searches and preparing abstracts is purely ministerial in its nature, and it is no part of the registrar's duty to construe a document or give an opinion on its contents.[1]

    1. *Macnamara v. McLay* (1882), 8 O.A.R. 319 at 337.

§395   The registrar must examine and compare the instrument on which the certificate is endorsed with the duplicate or other part registered at length on the books, and must take care to make a correct certificate. Moreover, the registrar must certify without any qualification the facts required to be stated.[1]

    1. *Bradshaw v. Ontario (Registrar of Simcoe)* (1867), 26 U.C.Q.B. 464 (memorandum endorsed on duplicate mortgage not complying with statute).

(c) Numbering and Dating of Instruments

§396   All instruments recorded are to be consecutively numbered, and the year, month, day, hour and minute of registration are to be endorsed thereon.[1] Where two or more instruments are received at the same time, they are, if registrable, to be numbered in the order requested by the person from whom they are received.[2] Priorities are to be determined in accordance with the respective registration numbers.[3]

    1. Registry Act, R.S.O. 1990, c. R.20, s. 49(1), (3).

    2. Registry Act, R.S.O. 1990, c. R.20, s. 49(2)

    3. Registry Act, R.S.O. 1990, c. R.20, s. 49(4); *Forestell v. Robinson* (1920), 19 O.W.N. 128 (C.A.).

3. LIABILITY OF REGISTRAR

§397   A land registrar is a public officer, and any action against a registrar for an act done in pursuance of a statutory duty or in respect of any alleged neglect or default in the execution of any such duty must be brought within six months of the act, neglect or default complained of.[1]

    1. Public Authorities Protection Act, R.S.O. 1990, c. P.38, s. 6; Registry Act, R.S.O. 1990, c. R.20, s. 9 [re-en. 1998, c. 18, Schedule E, s. 211]; **see also** *Harrison v. Brega* (1861), 20 U.C.Q.B. 324 (action against registrar for failure to set out mortgage in abstract of title); *Ross v. McLay* (1876), 40 U.C.Q.B. 83 (action against registrar for neglecting to furnish statement of fees as required by statute); *Ross v. McLay* (1876), 40 U.C.Q.B. 87 (action against registrar to recover back fees charged in excess of those allowed by statute); *Bruce (County) v. McLay* (1884), 11 O.A.R. 477; *MacFarlane v. R.* (1974), 5 O.R. (2d) 665 (C.A.) (order in council containing plan of intent registered against plaintiff's land by Minister of Highways; Act not permitting such registration; registration tortious act being actionable clouding of title; plaintiff not showing unmarketability of title because of registration; proposed highway common knowledge); Public Authorities and Public Officers.

§398   No action or other proceeding for damages may be instituted against an officer or employee of the ministry for any act done in good faith in the execution or intended execution of duty under the Act, or for any alleged neglect or default in the execution in good faith of such duty.[1]

    1.   Registry Act, R.S.O. 1990, c. R.20, s. 118 [am. 2001, c. 9, Schedule D, s. 13].

4.   INVESTIGATIONS OF TITLES

§399   The Registry Act provides that no person dealing with land is required to show lawful entitlement as owner through a good and sufficient chain of title during a period greater than 40 years immediately preceding the date of such dealing.[1]

    1.   Registry Act, R.S.O. 1990, c. R.20, s. 112(1); *Algoma Ore Properties Ltd. v. Smith*, [1953] O.R. 634 (C.A.) (failure of four devisees under devise of mining rights, or their descendants, to register notice required by Act; claim extinguished); **see also** Registry Act, R.S.O. 1990, c. R.20, ss. 111, 112(2), 113, 114 [am. 1998, c. 15, Schedule E, s. 43]; *Finnegan v. Dzus*, [1956] O.R. 69 (H.C.); *Armstrong v. Van der Weyden* (1956), [1965] 1 O.R. 68 (H.C.) (creation of new root of title by conveyance by Director of Veterans Land Act); *Ontario Hydro v. Tkach* (1992), 28 R.P.R. (2d) 1 (Ont. C.A.) (defendant able to claim good title by reason of 40-year limit on search of title imposed first in 1929 and currently incorporated in Registry Act; defendant's title having to be viewed as at moment coming under attack, either when plaintiff issuing proceedings or at date of trial; in either case, date considerably more than 40 years after conveyance to defendant's predecessor in title in 1934, and relevant statute being Act; plaintiff not able to argue that claim coming within exception in s. 106(5), since claim not being "claim arising under any Act"; claim arising from conveyance of 1906); *Camrich Developments Inc. v. Ontario Hydro* (1990), 72 O.R. (2d) 225 (H.C.) (claim no longer maintainable simply by being acknowledged or referred to in instrument; definition of "claim" in statute pertaining to instrument creating interest; therefore respondent's claim not referred to or acknowledged in 1954 by-laws registered against lands; claim not preserved by notice of claim filed pursuant to predecessor legislation prior to 1981, at which time right to assert claim ending; accordingly, respondent's claim expiring in 1984 and not able to be renewed by virtue of s. 106(7); *Lakhani v. Weinstein* (1980), 31 O.R. (2d) 65 (H.C.) (covenants not affecting land unless acknowledged in instrument registered within 40-year period; s. 105 deeming deposit on title not to be registration); *Fire v. Longtin* (1994), 17 O.R. (3d) 418 (C.A.); affirmed (1995), 48 R.P.R. (2d) 1 (S.C.C.) (Act validating title to land conveyed beyond search period).

§400   The Registry Act requires a search only to the first root of title prior to the 40-year period. The purchaser is entitled to rely on the form of the instruments registered and is not bound to inquire into their substance, and if the instrument relied upon as the root of title prior to the 40-year period is on its face sufficient to convey the fee, including mineral rights, the purchaser is entitled to rely upon it. The effect of these provisions[1] is that the person dealing with land must show lawful entitlement as owner through a good chain of title during the statutory period, and no claim in existence before the

40-year period will affect the land unless it has been acknowledged or referred to in an instrument registered against the land within the period, or unless a notice has been registered. This section does not extinguish rights except in favour of a person who acquires land from one who is shown to be owner through a good and sufficient chain of title for the 40-year period prior to the grant to that person.[2]

1. Registry Act, R.S.O. 1990, c. R.20, s. 112.

2. *Headrick v. Calabogie Mining Co.*, [1953] O.W.N. 761 (C.A.).

5. PURPOSE AND EFFECT OF REGISTRATION

(a) Right of Purchaser to Demand Conveyance Capable of Registration

§**401**   Under the Ontario land system, with its method of statutory surveying and statutory registration, it is, in the absence of a contrary provision, an implied term of a contract of sale that the sale be completed and perfected by a proper conveyance capable of registration.[1]

1. Vendors and Purchasers Act, R.S.O. 1990, c. V.2; *Owen v. Mercier* (1906), 12 O.L.R. 529 at 532 (Ch.); reversed on other grounds (1907), 14 O.L.R. 491 (C.A.); *Julien v. Labelle* (1923), 25 O.W.N. 388 (H.C.); **see** Sale of Land (as to implied terms in contracts for sale and purchase of land).

(b) What Constitutes Registration

§**402**   A registration which is defective on its face does not constitute a registration within the meaning of the Registry Act.[1] But if the instrument is received by the registrar, entered in the register book and filed in the office, it is deemed to be registered, even though there may be some defect in the affidavit or other proof for registry which would have been a ground for refusing registration.[2]

1. *Robson v. Waddell* (1865), 24 U.C.Q.B. 574; **see also** *Floyd v. Heska* (1974), 5 O.R. (2d) 273 (H.C.); reversed (1977), 16 O.R. (2d) 12 (C.A.); leave to appeal to S.C.C. refused (1977), 16 O.R. (2d) 12n (S.C.C.) (right of way claimed under Conveyancing and Law of Property Act, R.S.O. 1990, c. C.34, s. 15; right of way unknown to defendants; whether defendants affected by right of way); *Zygocki v. Hillwood* (1975), 12 O.R. (2d) 103 (H.C.) (mortgage deposited pursuant to Railway Act; mortgage not registered under Registry Act).

2. *Magrath v. Todd* (1866), 26 U.C.Q.B. 87; *Jones v. Cowden* (1874), 34 U.C.Q.B. 345; affirmed (1874), 36 U.C.Q.B. 495; *R. v. Middlesex Registrar of Deeds* (1850), 15 Q.B. 976; *1224948 Ontario Ltd. v. 448332 Ontario Ltd.* (1998), 22 R.P.R. (3d) 200 (Ont. Gen. Div.); additional reasons, 1999 CarswellOnt 685 (Ont. Gen. Div.); affirmed (2000), 38 R.P.R. (3d) 1 (Ont. C.A.); additional reasons (2000), 141 O.A.C. 100 (Ont. C.A.) (registrar justified in accepting and registering agreement of purchase and sale even though corporate seal of corporate purchaser not attached; court finding defects in execution were mere irregularities, cured by evidence at trial).

§403 An instrument is deemed to be registered even though the registrar or deputy omits to index it in the alphabetical index afterward.[1] A mere clerical error does not vitiate a registration.[2]

1. *Lawrie v. Rathbun* (1876), 38 U.C.Q.B. 255 (deed registered but registrar failing to enter it in alphabetical index; person searching informed no deed registered; registration valid).

2. *Harty v. Appleby* (1872), 19 Gr. 205 (mortgage and memorial thereof executed 1855; by clerical error, date in mortgage written as 1851; error not rendering registration void).

(c) Registration of Instruments

§404 Except where otherwise provided, and subject to the Registry Act and the Land Registration Reform Act[1], any instrument within the meaning of the latter Act and any instrument specifically permitted to be registered under Pt. I of the Registry Act may be registered.[2]

1. Land Registration Reform Act, R.S.O. 1990, c. L.4.

2. Registry Act, R.S.O. 1990, c. R.20, s. 22(1) [am. 1998, c. 18, Schedule E, s. 219(1)], (2.1) [en. 1994, c. 27, s. 99(3)] (delivery by direct electronic transmission), Pt. I (ss. 3-104); **see also** Registry Act, R.S.O. 1990, c. R.20, ss. 22(2), (3), (4) [am. 1998, c. 18, Schedule E, s. 219(2)], (5), (6), (7) [am. 1998, c. 18, Schedule E, s. 219(3)], (8)-(10), (11) [am. 1998, c. 18, Schedule E, s. 219(4)] (notice of unregistered interests), 66 [am. 1998, c. 18, Schedule E, s. 246], 67 [am. 1993, c. 27, Sched.; 1999, c. 12, Schedule F, s. 38] (discharge of registration); Land Registration Reform Act, R.S.O. 1990, c. L.4, Pt. III (ss. 17-32) [en. 1994, c. 27, s. 85(3)] (electronic registration); *Mazzeo v. Ontario*, 1996 CarswellOnt 1181 (Ont. Gen. Div.); affirmed, 1997 CarswellOnt 3873 (Ont. C.A.); leave to appeal refused (1998), 235 N.R. 196 (note) (S.C.C.) (fact that provisions of Land Titles Act not extending to all counties and districts in Ontario such that some counties or portions thereof governed by Registry Act not constituting discrimination).

§405 An instrument may not be registered unless it contains: a reference to the lot, part lot or other unit on the plan of concession it affects; a registrable description of the land it affects, unless a registrable description of the same land is already recorded in the abstract index; and the property identifier, if any, assigned to the property it affects.[1]

1. Registry Act, R.S.O. 1990, c. R.20, s. 25(2); **see also** Registry Act, R.S.O. 1990, c. R.20, ss. 21(2) [am. 1998, c. 18, Schedule E, s. 218(1)], (4) [am. 1998, c. 18, Schedule E, s. 218(3); 2000, c. 26, Schedule B, s. 17(2)], 49, 50 [am. 1998, c. 18, Schedule E, s. 236; 2000, c. 26, Schedule B, s. 17(6)], 76 [am. 1998, c. 18, Schedule E, s. 250; 1999, c. 12, Schedule F, s. 39; 2000, c. 26, Schedule B, s. 17(10)] (corrections respecting instruments).

§406 [Deleted].

§407 An instrument capable of and properly proven for registration is deemed to be registered as soon as it is accepted for registration by the land registrar in accordance with the regulations. No alterations to the instrument may be made after deemed registration.[1]

1. Registry Act, R.S.O. 1990, c. R.20, s. 77 [re-en. 1998, c. 18, Schedule E, s. 251].

§408 The land registrar may refuse to accept for registration an instrument that is either wholly or partly illegible or unsuitable for microfilming, or that contains or has attached to it material that does not, in the registrar's opinion, affect or relate to an interest in land. The registrar may also refrain from recording a part of a registered instrument where such part, in his or her opinion, does not affect or relate to an interest in land.[1]

1. Registry Act, R.S.O. 1990, c. R.20, s. 23 [am. 1998, c. 18, Schedule E, s. 220]; **see also** Land Registration Reform Act, R.S.O. 1990, c. L.4, Pt. I (ss. 1-14).

(d) Registration of Instruments Not Containing Required Descriptions

§409 An instrument that does not contain a reference to the lot, part lot or other unit on the plan of concession, a registrable description of the land, and the property identifier of the land it affects may be registered where the instrument is presented for registration together with a statement in the pre-scribed form made by a party to the instrument or by the party's solicitor, attorney under a registered power of attorney or registered notarial copy of a power of attorney, or heirs, executors, administrators or estate trustees, or, where the party is a corporation, by an officer of the corporation, stating that the instrument affects land within the registry division, and containing the reference, description property identifier.[1]

1. Registry Act, R.S.O. 1990, c. R.20, s. 25(3) [am. 1993, c. 27, Schedule; 1998, c. 18, Schedule E, s. 222(2), (3)].

§410 The statement required by the Act is only a piece of machinery incidental to the registration of the instrument, and is intended to assist the registrar, by identifying the lands affected by the general terms of the instru-ment, in making entries in the respective abstract indexes in the registrar's office. The declaration does not affect the instrument itself.[1] Thus, if there is any uncertainty in the instrument itself as to the lands it covers, this decla-ration, except for registration purposes, cannot remove that uncertainty; and the rights of the parties affected by the instrument must be determined in-dependently of such declaration.[2]

1. *Aston v. White* (1920), 48 O.L.R. 168 at 171 (H.C.).

2. *Aston v. White* (1920), 48 O.L.R. 168 at 171 (H.C.) (registered instrument not describing lands, but referring to property as described in unregistered instrument; not sufficient to pass property, because of uncertainty in description; very great difference between description by reference to conveyance already registered and description by reference to unregistered agreement; in former case, no difficulty identifying conveyance and therefore land, but in latter case, no real certainty as to what instrument referred to); **see also** *Treleven v. Horner* (1881), 28 Gr. 624 (description of certain land in marriage settlement by reference to certain other registered conveyances sufficient).

(e) Registration of Judgments and Certificates of Lis Pendens

§411   A court judgment affecting land may be registered in the office of the registry division in which the land is situate, on a certificate signed by the proper officer of the court setting forth the substance and effect of the judgment or order.[1] Moreover, unless the judgment is so registered, it is deemed fraudulent and void as against any subsequent purchaser or mortgagee for valuable consideration without actual notice of the judgment.[2]

1. Registry Act, R.S.O. 1990, c. R.20, s. 38(1)(a); **see also** *Mactan Holdings Ltd. v. 431736 Ontario Ltd.* (1980), 31 O.R. (2d) 37 (H.C.) (third party commencing action against vendor and registering caution and lis pendens; prospective purchasers' application to vacate lis pendens dismissed; third party having prima facie case giving rise to equitable interest in lands); *White Holdings Ltd. v. Bolus-Revelas-Bolus Ltd.* (1980), 14 R.P.R. 145 (Ont. H.C.) (claim not supporting lis pendens where parties having defined movable property as chattels and not fixtures or where claimant alleging"fixtures" removable; lis pendens standing in respect of leasehold claim); *Gelakis v. Giouroukos* (1989), 34 C.P.C. (2d) 223 (Ont. H.C.); affirmed (1989), 39 C.P.C. (2d) 96 (H.C.) (certificate subsequently discharged for plaintiff's failure to make full and fair disclosure on ex parte motion pursuant to R. 39.01(6); plaintiff's reapplication for certificate allowed; matter not res judicata; no prejudice resulting to defendants).

2. Registry Act, R.S.O. 1990, c. R.20, s. 70(1); *1224948 Ontario Ltd. v. 448332 Ontario Ltd.* (1998), 22 R.P.R. (3d) 200 (Ont. Gen. Div.); additional reaons, 1999 CarswellOnt 685 (Ont. Gen. Div.); affirmed (2000), 38 R.P.R. (3d) 1 (Ont. C.A.); additional reasons (2000), 141 O.A.C. 100 (Ont. C.A.) (second mortgagee failing to register judgment for immediate foreclosure; mortgagor entering into registered agreement of purchase and sale with company; judge finding agreement registered to take advantage of window of opportunity created by second mortgagee's failure to register judgment; no intention that company would enter into enforceable agreement with mortgagor; agreement not prevailing against unregistered judgment).

§412   The equitable doctrine of lis pendens was that a pending lawsuit afforded implied notice of the existence of the suit to purchasers, on the theory that it was a transaction in a sovereign court of justice and that all people were attentive to what transpired there.[1] Now, however, the Courts of Justice Act provides that the institution of an action or the taking of a proceeding in which any title to or interest in land is brought into question is

not deemed to be notice of the action or proceeding to any person not a party
to it until a certificate, signed by the proper officer of the court, has been
registered in the registry office of the registry division in which the land is
situate.[2]

1. *Worsley v. Scarborough (Earl)* (1746), 26 E.R. 1025, quoted in *Brock v. Crawford*
(1908), 11 O.W.R. 143 (K.B.), and in *Leftley v. Moffatt* (1925), 57 O.L.R. 260 at 263
(H.C.).

2. Courts of Justice Act, R.S.O. 1990, c. C.43, s. 103; Rules of Civil Procedure,
R.R.O. 1990, Reg. 194, R. 42; *Nuforest Watson Bancorp Ltd. v. Prenor Trust Co. of
Canada* (1994), 21 O.R. (3d) 328 (Gen. Div.) (certificate of pending litigation
allowable against mortgage); *Katana v. Wilson* (June 3, 1996), Doc Brampton 92-
CQ-12373 (Ont. Gen. Div.) (plaintiffs liable for damages after their improper registration of certificate causing failure of two subsequent transactions to close); **see also**
Reicher v. Reicher (1980), 20 R.F.L. (2d) 213 (Ont. Div. Ct.) (corporation added as
respondent in divorce petition; allegation in petition construed to mean that intention
to defraud being that of corporation as well as transferor; petition disclosing reasonable cause of action against corporate respondent; appeal from order issuing certificate
of lis pendens for registration dismissed); *Jones v. Jones* (1982), 32 C.P.C. 105 (Ont.
Master) (petitioner alleging fraudulent conveyance by respondent spouse to company
of which spouse sole shareholder; certificate properly registered); *Namasco Ltd. v.
Globe Equipment Sales & Rentals (1983) Ltd.* (1985), 2 C.P.C. (2d) 242 (Ont. H.C.)
(plaintiff alleging that crane having been dismantled by one defendant and that part of
crane becoming affixed to land of other defendant; plaintiff claiming equitable lien
with respect to crane; motion for leave to issue certificate of lis pendens against land
owned by other defendant dismissed; claim not disclosing interest in land of other
defendant); *Davidson v. Hyundai Auto Canada Inc.* (1987), 59 O.R. (2d) 789 (Master)
(plaintiffs arranging with defendants to purchase, build on and develop property for
defendant H. Inc.; transaction not closing; plaintiffs alleging breach of fiduciary duty
and claiming certificate of lis pendens against defendants' second property; certificate
granted); *Keeton v. Cain* (1986), 57 O.R. (2d) 380 (H.C.) (pleading of plaintiff
bringing title to land in question; plaintiff not required to assert interest in land for
self; allegations of fraudulent conveyance not merely bare allegations of fraud;
plaintiff having sufficiently reasonable claim to interest in land to warrant certificate
of lis pendens); *Homebuilder Inc. v. Man-Sonic Industries Inc.* (1987), 22 C.P.C. (2d)
39 (Ont. Master) (builder bringing action alleging competitors having appropriated
builder's sketches and house plans for own use; builder's motion for certificate of lis
pendens dismissed; although not possible to say no triable issues raised, plaintiff
would have difficulty proving claim); *Kakeway v. Canada* (January 12, 1988), Doc.
Kenora SCO 27/85 (Ont. H.C.); affirmed (1988), 64 O.R. (2d) 52 (H.C.) (action for
declaration of ownership of lands as part of Indian reserve; registered owner not party
to action and no relief claimed against owner in statement of claim; plaintiffs serving
notice of motion for certificate of lis pendens on registered owner and on federal and
provincial governments; motion dismissed); *McMurdo v. McMurdo Estate* (1988), 26
C.P.C. (2d) 20 (Ont. Master) (marriage contract providing that wife purchasing half
interest in matrimonial home owned by husband; husband dying; wife wishing to
claim rights under Family Law Act rather than under marriage contract; wife applying
to set aside marriage contract; wife's motion for leave to issue certificate of lis
pendens dismissed); *Royal Bank v. Muzzi* (1987), 22 C.P.C. (2d) 66 (Ont. Master);
additional reasons (1987), 22 C.P.C. (2d) 66 at 71 (Master) (plaintiff claiming
beneficial interest in land in which proceeds of sale of fraudulently conveyed property
invested; plaintiff registering certificate of lis pendens); *358426 Ontario Ltd. v.*

Liappas (1991), 1 C.P.C. (3d) 95 (Ont. Master) (trend to offer in evidence affidavit deposing to truth of contents of statement of claim and then annex statement of claim as exhibit to affidavit should be discontinued; preferred practice being to tender in evidence one or more affidavits relating both to entitlement to certificate and to obligation of disclosure; issued statement of claim need only be shown to Master to ensure compliance with R. 42.01(2)).

§413   The effect of registering a certificate of lis pendens in the registry office is to place the whole world in the same position as if the legislation, now contained in the Courts of Justice Act, had not been passed.[1] But neither the issuing of a writ nor the registration of a lis pendens has any effect upon preceding and executed transactions.[2]

1. *Brock v. Crawford* (1908), 11 O.W.R. 143 (K.B.); *Corsi v. di Cecco* (1988), 25 C.P.C. (2d) 1 (Ont. Master); reversed (1988), 32 C.P.C. (2d) 310 (H.C.) (plaintiff not ready, willing and able to close transaction; plaintiff commencing action and obtaining certificate of lis pendens; plaintiff having reasonable interest in land; certificate not discharged on motion by defendant); *Russell v. Burke* (1989), 33 C.P.C. (2d) 52 (Ont. Master) (plaintiff claiming declaration of entitlement to property ownership six years after cessation of cohabitation; on cross-examination, plaintiff admitting to not knowing purchase price; defendant unsuccessfully moving to discharge lis pendens; no intent to mislead court); *Oliver v. Oliver* (1990), 72 O.R. (2d) 275 (Master) (husband claiming interest in matrimonial home in name of wife by virtue of express trust or resulting or constructive trust; husband entitled to certificate of lis pendens; Courts of Justice Act, S.O. 1984, c. 11, s. 116(1)); *Mosher v. Ontario*, 1999 CarswellOnt 4286 (Ont. S.C.J.); affirmed (2001), 139 O.A.C. 340 (Ont. C.A.) (registration of caution and certificate of pending litigation not giving appellant interest in property, but merely providing notice to public of potential claim).

2. *Sanderson v. Burdett* (1869), 16 Gr. 119; affirmed on another point, 18 Gr. 417; *Leftley v. Moffatt* (1925), 57 O.L.R. 260 at 263 (H.C.) (purchaser seeking specific performance of contract of sale; vendor having conveyed lands subsequently to third party, who had no notice of contract; certificate of lis pendens filed by plaintiff after execution of deed in favour of third party having no effect on that completed transaction).

§413.1   A certificate of lis pendens is designed to protect unregistered interests in land. A subsequent mortgagee's claim for priority cannot support the issuance of a certificate. Claimants of unregistered interests in land, the substantiation of which adversely affects the interest of registrants, are the only ones to property claim a certificate of lis pendens.[1]

1. *1355185 Ontario Inc. v. Jesin* (1999), 28 R.P.R. (3d) 60 (Ont. S.C.J.); additional reasons, 1999 CarswellOnt 4747 (Ont. S.C.J.).

§414   A certificate of lis pendens rests upon the implication of an interest in land, and the existence of the certificate is the shadow of the matter, not the substance of it. If it is clear beyond controversy that there is no arguable or triable point with respect to the substance, an order vacating the lis pendens may be granted. However, where a real issue on fact and in law exists as to the construction of an unconstrued and unregistered document, and where it is arguable whether specific performance of an agreement of sale would be granted, a summary application is not an appropriate method for removing a lis pendens. Rather, the status quo ought to be maintained until the facts appear at trial.[1]

1. *Willoughby v. Knight* (1973), 1 O.R. (2d) 184 (H.C.) (certificate of lis pendens not to be removed on summary application when questionable whether person filing certificate having interest in land); *Bank of Montreal v. Ewing* (1982), 35 O.R. (2d) 225 (Div. Ct.) (motions court judge erring in finding plaintiff needing interest in land; action to set aside fraudulent conveyance constituting action in which title to or interest in land brought into question); *Toronto Dominion Bank v. Zukerman* (1982), 40 O.R. (2d) 724 (H.C.) (court having equitable jurisdiction to vacate lis pendens even if action not frivolous or vexatious; no fraud involved); *McEwen v. 341595 Ontario Ltd.* (1984), 34 R.P.R. 258 (Ont. H.C.) (due to settlement negotiations, purchaser not commencing action for specific performance for several months after transaction falling through; purchaser obtaining certificate of lis pendens on ex parte application; vendor's application to vacate dismissed; no unreasonable delay by purchaser in issuing writ); *Bernhard v. United Merchandising Enterprises Ltd.* (1984), 47 O.R. (2d) 520 (H.C.) (defendant's application to vacate caution registered by plaintiff allowed; plaintiff not having made offer to redeem; success impossible); *Davidson v. Horvat* (1984), 45 C.P.C. 203 (Ont. H.C.) (court refusing to pierce corporate veil in order to give individual defendants interest in land which they did not have directly); *Hess v. Mandzuk* (1984), 44 C.P.C. 179 (Ont. H.C.) (purchaser obtaining certificate of lis pendens on ex parte motion when vendor refusing to complete transaction; purchaser's real estate having title problems; vendor bringing motion to vacate certificate; application allowed); *Toronto Board of Education Staff Credit Union Ltd. v. Skinner* (1984), 47 O.R. (2d) 70 (H.C.) (application to vacate lis pendens being proceeding in nature of review of ex parte order granting lis pendens; accordingly being continuation of original proceeding); *Pete & Marty's (Front) Ltd. v. Market Block Toronto Properties Ltd.* (1985), 5 C.P.C. (2d) 97 (Ont. H.C.) (court having broad discretion under Act to discharge certificate where damages claimed as alternative remedy; defendant need not prove absence of triable issue); *Rocovitis v. Argerys Estate* (1986), 9 C.P.C. (2d) 62 (Ont. Master); affirmed (1988), 26 C.P.C. (2d) 302 (Div. Ct.) (s. 17(8)(a) of Estates Administration Act providing that"debts" of deceased binding real property of deceased for three-year period even though real property conveyed to innocent purchaser for value; creditor then applying for and obtaining leave to register certificate of lis pendens against real property; motion to discharge certificate allowed; claim for unliquidated damages not"debt"; *Tru-Style Designs Inc. v. Greymac Properties Inc.* (1986), 9 C.P.C. (2d) 202 (Ont. Master); affirmed (1986), 56 O.R. (2d) 462 (H.C.) (plaintiff registering cautions against two parcels, alleging oral agreement to convey lands in return for services performed; plaintiff delaying for lengthy time before commencing action; motion to discharge certificate allowed); *Graywood Developments Ltd. v. Campeau Corp.* (1985), 8 C.P.C. (2d) 58 (Ont. Master) (Courts of Justice Act providing that certificate be vacated where plaintiff not having "reasonable claim" to land; predecessor Act providing certificate be vacated where plaintiff not having "claim" to land; test developed under former wording continuing to apply); *Greenbaum v. 619908 Ontario Ltd.* (1986), 11 C.P.C. (2d) 26 (Ont. H.C.) (builder applying for order vacating certificate filed by purchaser in action against builder; application allowed in part; words used in agreement not sufficient to oust purchaser's right to file certificate; continuation of certificate jeopardizing financing agreements based on security of lands; equities favouring conditional discharge of certificate);

Holden Corp. v. Gingerfield Properties Ltd. (1987), 25 C.P.C. (2d) 225 (H.C.); leave to appeal to Div. Ct. refused (1987), 25 C.P.C. (2d) 225n (H.C.) (plaintiff obtaining certificate of lis pendens against entire parcel; defendant agreeing with third parties to develop balance of parcel; certificate discharged upon motion by defendant; plaintiff's appeal allowed; certificate remaining, provided plaintiff agreeing to postpone interest in balance of parcel to third party); *Allen v. Hennessey* (1988), 29 C.P.C. (2d) 209 (Ont. Master); leave to appeal to H.C. refused (1988), 30 C.P.C. (2d) lv (H.C.); leave to appeal to Div. Ct. refused (1988), 30 C.P.C. (2d) lv (Div. Ct.) (Ontario defendant conveying real estate owned by her to husband at time British Columbia action brought; judgment against defendant; husband selling property; portion of proceeds used to purchase second property; action brought in Ontario; certificate of lis pendens obtained; defendants successfully moving to vacate certificate); *Aztec Investments Ltd. v. Wynston* (1988), 27 C.P.C. (2d) 238 (Ont. Master) (defendants moving to discharge certificate on grounds of non-disclosure on motion; plaintiffs adequately protected by another form of security; motion allowed; certificate discharged; land not unique; other security to be posted in lieu of certificate); *Cimaroli v. Pugliese* (1987), 25 C.P.C. (2d) 10 at 11 (Ont. Master); (1988), 25 C.P.C. (2d) 10 (H.C.); leave to appeal to Div. Ct. refused (April 29, 1988), 1615/87 (H.C.) (agreement of purchase and sale containing clause prohibiting registration of certificate of lis pendens until transaction closing; on without-notice motion for certificate of lis pendens, plaintiffs failing to highlight clause in affidavit filed in support of motion; defendant successfully moving for discharge of certificate; failure to highlight clause being material non-disclosure); *Reuel v. Thomas* (1988), 27 C.P.C. (2d) 101 (Ont. Dist. Ct.) (defendants obtaining certificate of lis pendens; plaintiff's motion to discharge certificate allowed on terms; discharge order being discretionary order; possibility that plaintiff able to obtain clear title; plaintiff given 90 days to clear title); *Royal Bank v. Muzzi* (1987), 22 C.P.C. (2d) 66 (Ont. Master); additional reasons (1987), 22 C.P.C. (2d) 66 at 71 (Master) (defendants moving to discharge certificate of lis pendens in substitution for security; motion allowed; defendants entitled to discharge of certificate upon payment of $90,000 into court); *St. Thomas Subdividers v. 639373 Ontario Ltd.* (1988), 29 C.P.C. (2d) 1 (Ont. H.C.); leave to appeal to Div. Ct. refused (1988), 29 C.P.C. (2d) xlv (H.C.) (agreement of purchase and sale personal to purchaser and not creating any interest in land to entitle purchaser to certificate of lis pendens; Courts of Justice Act, S.O. 1984, c. 11, s. 116(6)); *777829 Ontario Ltd. v. 616070 Ontario Inc.* (1988), 65 O.R. (2d) 621 (Master); reversed (1988), 67 O.R. (2d) 72 (H.C.) (former owner registering certificate of lis pendens; plaintiff requisitioning removal of certificate; defendant not complying, and purporting to terminate agreement; plaintiff registering certificate and defendant discharging it; plaintiff's appeal of master's discharge allowed on terms; triable issues arising concerning interpretation of words in agreement and whether defendant making bona fide efforts to complete transaction; certificate to be restored and to remain on title until sale completed); *Memphis Holdings Ltd. v. Plastics Land Partnership* (1989), 35 C.P.C. (2d) 177 (Ont. H.C.) (plaintiffs failing to establish interest in land; agreement not providing for creation of equitable lien; interests created in agreement running not with land but with individual owners; certificate discharged); *Queen's Court Developments Ltd. v. Duquette* (1989), 36 C.P.C. (2d) 297 (Ont. H.C.) (purchaser failing to prove having any reasonable claim to interest in vendor's lands; certificate discharged under s. 116(6)(a)(ii)); *Gelakis v. Giouroukos* (1989), 34 C.P.C. (2d) 223 (Ont. H.C.); affirmed (1989), 39 C.P.C. (2d) 96 (H.C.) (certificate; right to register; subsequent certificates grantable notwithstanding that previous certificate vacated); *Mirrow Homes Ltd. v. Filice* (1989), 44 C.P.C. (2d) 204 (Ont. H.C.); reversing, 44 C.P.C. (2d) 198 (Master) (discharge of certificate reversed on appeal; delay in moving to obtain certificate satisfactorily explained, as parties being brothers and plaintiff reluctant to sue brother; plaintiff showing strong prima facie case; master erring in law in determining credibility on affidavit evidence regarding issues going to root of triable issue); *Orangeville Raceway (Ontario) Inc. v. Frieberg* (1990), 40 O.A.C. 73 (Div. Ct.); affirming, 34 C.P.C. (2d) 75 (H.C.) (refusal to grant purchaser certificate of lis pendens affirmed where balance of convenience weighing against finding that purchaser having interest in land and where registration of certificate causing owner financial hardship); *Metropolitan Toronto Condominium Corp. No. 1006 v. Hollywood Plaza Developments Inc.* (1995), 48 R.P.R. (2d) 269 (Ont. Gen. Div.) (condominium corporations having only tenuous claim to title to residential parking spaces; certificates of pending litigation removed); *Jacobson v. Hakimzadeh* (1996), 11 O.T.C. 122 (Ont. Master) (no failure to make full and fair disclosure on ex parte motion for certificate of pending litigation); *Maletta v. Thiessen* (1996), 1 R.P.R. (3d) 145 (Ont. Div. Ct.); leave to appeal to C.A. refused (1996), 28 O.R. (3d) 251n (C.A.) (certificate of pending litigation not issued where mortgagor alleging fraud but not making offer to redeem mortgage); *Fernicola v. Mod-Aire Homes Ltd.* (1996), 6 R.P.R. (3d) 138 (Ont. C.A.) (plaintiff obtaining certificate against 50-acre parcel but claiming interest in only 10 acres; minutes of settlement providing that registration of certificate of pending litigation continuing against "all" lands until execution agreement; defendant unsuccessfully moving for order removing certificate against 40 acres); *962690 Ontario Inc. v. Ernst & Young Inc.* (1997), 28 O.T.C. 363 (Ont. Gen. Div.) (discharge not mandatory in circumstances where claim for money alternative to interest in property); *West v. West* (1997), 33 O.R. (3d) 472 (Gen. Div.) (defendant's alleged beneficial interest in property sufficient to ground certificate of pending litigation); *Aldap Investments Ltd. v. All-Borough Properties Ltd.*, 1997 CarswellOnt 124 (Ont. Gen. Div.) (plaintiffs bringing action respecting default under partnership agreement and failure of option agreement intended to give plaintiffs opportunity to rectify default; no basis in equity for ordering certificate of pending litigation); *Peate v. Elmsmere Ltd. Partnership* (1997), 14 C.P.C. (5th) 312 (Ont. Master) ("interest in land" broad enough to encompass alleged right to share of partnership in retirement home).

§415   The Courts of Justice Act[1] grants jurisdiction "to the court" to discharge a certificate of lis pendens, and the Rules of Civil Procedure[2] stipulate that an order discharging a certificate may be obtained on motion "to the court". Since the definition of "court" in the Rules includes a master having jurisdiction to hear motions under R. 37,[3] and since a master is given jurisdiction subject to certain exceptions,[4] none of which are applicable to R. 42, therefore, under the new Rules, a master has jurisdiction to hear motions under R. 42.02.[5]

1. Courts of Justice Act, R.S.O. 1990, c. C.43, s. 103(6).

2. Rules of Civil Procedure, R.R.O. 1990, R. 42.02 [am. O. Reg. 171/98, s. 20].

3. Rules of Civil Procedure, R.R.O. 1990, R. 1.03("court") [re-en. O. Reg. 570/98, s. 1; am. O. Reg. 292/99, s. 1(2)].

4. Rules of Civil Procedure, R.R.O. 1990, R. 37.02(2).

5. *Young v. 503708 Ontario Ltd.* (1986), 12 C.P.C. (2d) 245 (Ont. H.C.); *Tru-Style Designs Inc. v. Greymac Properties Inc.* (1986), 9 C.P.C. (2d) 202 (Ont. Master); affirmed (1986), 56 O.R. (2d) 462 (H.C.); *Whitelaw v. Van Donkersgoed* (1986), 11 C.P.C. (2d) 263 (Ont. H.C.); leave to appeal granted (1986), 11 C.P.C. (2d) 263n (H.C.) (order of local judge dismissing defendants' motion for discharge of certificate

of lis pendens; defendants' appeal to H.C. dismissed; appeal to be brought in Div. Ct., with leave; order of local judge being interlocutory order of kind not within jurisdiction of master); **but see** *Holden Corp. v. Gingerfield Properties Ltd.* (1988), 26 C.P.C. (2d) 221 (Ont. Master); appeal quashed (1988), 30 C.P.C. (2d) 302 (H.C.) (motion to discharge certificate dismissed; master not having jurisdiction to review, vary, change, reverse or affirm order of High Court Judge; recourse being to bring motion before judge having made order or any other High Court Judge; test under s. 116(6)(a)(ii) same as on motion for summary judgment under R. 20.01(3) or R. 21.01(3)(d)); *Getz v. Barnes* (1989), 71 O.R. (2d) 450 (H.C.) (transaction not closing, as vendor becoming mentally incompetent; purchasers registering certificate of lis pendens; vendor's committee, unable to sell property, having certificate vacated by master's order; appeal dismissed; pursuant to s. 116(6), purchasers not proceeding with reasonable diligence with action, and being adequately protected by Master's order).

§416   The Courts of Justice Act does not limit the court's discretion to vacate a certificate of lis pendens to situations where there is no triable issue. On such applications, the court is required to examine all relevant matters and to make the order requested where the interest of the party at whose instance the certificate was issued could be adequately protected by another form of security.[1]

1.   *Sandhu v. Braebury Homes Corp.* (1986), 39 R.P.R. 10 (Ont. H.C.); *Cougs Investments (Pickering) Ltd. v. Forbes* (1996), 1 O.T.C. 279 (Gen. Div.) (certificate of pending litigation not to be vacated in view of all surrounding circumstances); *Pring v. Thompson* (1996), 15 O.T.C. 397 (Ont. Gen. Div.) (certificate of pending litigation unnecessarily tying up land beyond temporarily freezing mortgage); *Woodheath Developments Inc. v. Singh* (1996), 15 O.T.C. 212 (Ont. Gen. Div.) (notice to discharge dismissed even though plaintiff taking no further steps; no actual harm to defendants); *Chiu v. Pacific Mall Developments Inc.* (1998), 19 R.P.R. (3d) 236 (Ont. Gen. Div.); *876761 Ontario Inc. v. Maplewood Ravines Ltd.* (2001), 41 R.P.R. (3d) 288 (Ont. S.C.J.); *1376273 Ontario Inc. v. Woods Property Development Inc.* (2001), 43 R.P.R. (3d) 19 (Ont. Master); affirmed (2001), 46 R.P.R. (3d) 210 (Ont. S.C.J.); *Woodburn v. National Capital Commission*, 1999 CarswellOnt 3696 (Ont. S.C.J.) (test to be applied on application to vacate based on plaintiff's failure to make full and fair disclosure of all material facts on ex parte application being whether omitted fact might have had impact on original granting of order); *Toll v. Marjanovic* (2001), 39 R.P.R. (3d) 146 (Ont. S.C.J.); additional reasons, 2001 CarswellOnt 1357 (Ont. S.C.J.) (claim for return or deposit money not amounting to interest in land such as to sustain right to obtain certificate of lis pendens; certificate not intended to be used as means of obtaining security for unproven claim for damages; elderly vendor; equities favouring vacating certificate); *G.P.I. Greenfield Pioneer Inc. v. Moore* (2002), 47 R.P.R. (3d) 169 (Ont. C.A.) (role of court on motion to discharge certificate of lis pendens limited to deciding whether registrant has reasonable claim to interest in land; since no actual adjudication of registrant's interest in land is required on motion, finding on motion was not decision in rem and could not support plea of res judicata at trial of claim for damages).

§417   An entitlement to a certificate of lis pendens does not necessarily require that the interest in the land in question be claimed directly by a plaintiff.[1]

1. *Chilian v. Augdome Corp.* (1991), 2 O.R. (3d) 696 (C.A.); *Vettese v. Fleming* (1992), 8 C.P.C. (3d) 237 (Ont. Gen. Div.) (possible to grant certificate of lis pendens in action to set aside fraudulent conveyance even if plaintiff having no interest in land and not yet being judgment creditor; plaintiff establishing reasonable claim to interest in property and establishing prima facie case; sufficient evidence to justify granting certificate).

§417.1   Statements in a certificate of pending litigation are issued in and part of the court's process and are absolutely privileged; therefore, an allegation of slander of title based on statements in a certificate of pending litigation are not valid.[1]

1. *Geo. Cluthe Manufacturing Co. v. ZTW Properties Inc.* (1995), 23 O.R. (3d) 370 (Div. Ct.); leave to appeal to C.A. refused (1995), 39 C.P.C. (3d) 322n (Ont. C.A.) (registered declaration wrongly claiming that certain lots included in order granting leave to issue certificate of pending litigation not privileged as it was not in certificate and not part of court's process).

(f) Statements as Proof for Registration Purposes

§418   The Registry Act may require, as a condition for registration of an instrument, proof in the form of a statement, prescribed by the Act or regulations, or approved by the director of titles.[1] This condition applies to registrations of a licence of occupation affecting unpatented Crown land for the purpose of a pipeline;[2] a notice of agreement of purchase and sale or an option to purchase, and any renewals thereof;[3] an instrument not containing the required descriptions and property identifier of the land affected;[4] an instrument executed by a corporation;[5] a judgment or order of a court, other than an order or certificate endorsed on an instrument;[6] an assignment or discharge of a mortgage made by the trustee or trustees of a registered pension plan;[7] a will;[8] a change of name of a mortgagee where the change is consequential to a marriage, annulment or dissolution of marriage, or an adoption;[9] and an instrument, duly executed, that does not refer to the proper plan, where any party thereto has died, or where it would be impossible or inconvenient to obtain a new instrument containing the proper description.[10]

1. Registry Act, R.S.O. 1990, c. R.20, s. 32 [re-en. 1998, c. 18, Schedule E, s. 225; am. 2000, c. 26, Schedule B, s. 17(2)].

2. Registry Act, R.S.O. 1990, c. R.20, s. 22(4)(f) [am. 1998, c. 18, Schedule E, s. 219(2)].

3. Registry Act, R.S.O. 1990, c. R.20, s. 22(11) [re-en. 1998, c. 18, Schedule E, s. 219(4)].

4. Registry Act, R.S.O. 1990, c. R.20, s. 25(3) [am. 1993, c. 27, Schedule; 1998, c. 18, Schedule E, s. 222(2), (3)].

5. Registry Act, R.S.O. 1990, c. R.20, s. 37(3).

6. Registry Act, R.S.O. 1990, c. R.20, s. 38(1.1) [en. 1999, c. 12, Schedule F, s. 36].

7. Registry Act, R.S.O. 1990, c. R.20, s. 48(5) [am. 1998, c. 18, Schedule E, s. 234(2)].

8. Registry Act, R.S.O. 1990, c. R.20, s. 53(1)(a) [re-en. 1998, c. 18, Schedule E, s. 237(1); 1999, c. 12, Schedule F, s. 37; am. 2000, c. 26, Schedule B, s. 17(7), (8)].

9. Registry Act, R.S.O. 1990, c. R.20, s. 57 [am. 1993, c. 27, Schedule; 1998, c. 18, Schedule E, s. 241].

10. Registry Act, R.S.O. 1990, c. R.20, s. 86 [am. 1998, c. 18, Schedule E, s. 253].

§419 Where an instrument that is otherwise capable of registration is not accompanied by a statement required by the Act or is accompanied by an incomplete or defective statement, a person who is or claims to be interested in the registration of the instrument may apply to a judge of the Superior Court of Justice for an order dispensing with the statement. The judge may grant the order if the applicant proves that the required statement cannot be obtained conveniently and the facts were as are required to be stated by the statement. On granting the order, the judge must endorse on the instrument or securely attach to it a certificate, in the prescribed form, stating the facts that have been proven, and the certificate must be received in lieu of the required statement.[1]

1. Registry Act, R.S.O. 1990, c. R.20, s. 47 [re-en. 1998, c. 18, Schedule E, s. 233; am. 2000, c. 26, Schedule B, s. 17(5)].

§420 If a document is actually upon the register, a subsequent purchaser has notice thereof by which he or she is bound, notwithstanding an informality in the proof of execution, which does not make the registration a nullity.[1]

1. *Rooker v. Hoofstetter* (1896), 26 S.C.R. 41.

§421 Every subscribing witness is compellable by order of a judge of the Superior Court of Justice to make an affidavit or proof of execution of an instrument for the purpose of registration, and to do all other acts necessary for that purpose, upon being paid or tendered his or her reasonable expenses therefor.[1]

1. Registry Act, R.S.O. 1990, c. R.20, s. 34 [am. 2000, c. 26, Schedule B, s. 17(3)]; *Davis v. Winn* (1910), 22 O.L.R. 111 at 120 (C.A.); **see also** *R. v. O'Meara* (1857), 15 U.C.Q.B. 201 (mandamus lying to compel witness to prove execution of deed for registration purposes).

§422 An instrument otherwise capable of registration but not duly executed may be proved before a judge of the Superior Court of Justice by any person who is or claims to be interested in the registration of the instrument. The instrument may be registered where a certificate in the prescribed form is endorsed on the instrument and signed by the judge.[1]

1. Registry Act, R.S.O. 1990, c. R.20, s. 35 [re-en. 2000, c. 26, Schedule B, s. 17(4)]; *Rooker v. Hoofstetter* (1896), 26 S.C.R. 41 (S.C.C.).

§423   The registration of a mortgage is not invalidated by the mere fact that the mortgagee subscribes his or her name to the instrument after registration.[1] Where a witness to a registered conveyance is ignorant as to the contents of the conveyance, he or she is not estopped by anything it might contain.[2]

1. *Muir v. Dunnett* (1864), 11 Gr. 85.

2. *Western Canada Loan Co. v. Garrison* (1888), 16 O.R. 81 (C.A.).

(g) Priorities

(i) NOTICE DEPRIVING REGISTERED INSTRUMENT OF PRIORITY

§424   Actual notice of a prior executed conveyance is necessary in order to deprive a subsequently registered conveyance of its priority under the Registry Act. Such actual notice renders the subsequent purchaser's act of registering his or her conveyance fraudulent.[1]

1. *New Brunswick Railway v. Kelly* (1896), 26 S.C.R. 341; *Ross v. Hunter* (1882), 7 S.C.R. 289 [N.S.]; *Peterkin v. McFarlane* (1885), 13 S.C.R. 677; *Hollywood v. Waters* (1857), 6 Gr. 329; *Maclennan v. Foucault* (1908), 11 O.W.R. 659 (C.A.).

(ii) NOTICE GENERALLY

§425   Actual notice is knowledge: not presumed knowledge as in the case of constructive notice,[1] but knowledge shown to have been actually brought home to the party to be charged with it, either by proof of his or her own admission or by the evidence of witnesses who are able to establish that the very fact of which notice is to be established, and not merely something which would have led to discovery of the fact upon inquiry, was brought to the party's knowledge.[2] The burden of proving the absence of notice is on the person alleging that he or she is a purchaser for valuable consideration without notice.[3]

1. *Winchester v. N. Rattenbury Ltd.* (1953), 31 M.P.R. 69 (P.E.I.C.A.) (discussion of actual and constructive notice, with particular reference to Registry Act).

2. *Harrington v. Spring Creek Cheese Manufacturing Co.* (1904), 7 O.L.R. 319 (purchaser not having actual notice of agreement permitting neighbouring owner to run pipes under property purchased, although purchaser knowing of presence of pipes and of use being made of them); *Ferguson v. Zinn*, [1933] O.R. 9 at 17 (H.C.).

3. *Toronto (City) v. Rudd*, [1952] O.R. 84 (H.C.).

§426 Possession of land by a grantee or a grantee's successors under an unregistered conveyance does not confer actual notice of that conveyance on persons claiming under a subsequent registered conveyance.[1] A person who is entitled to an easement by virtue of an unregistered instrument, and who wishes to enforce that easement against a purchaser of the servient tenement who claims under a registered instrument, must establish that the purchaser had notice of the legal right of the person claiming the easement; it is not enough to prove that the purchaser knew of the user of the easement.[2] Although in such a situation it is essential to prove the purchaser had actual notice of the legal right, it is not essential to prove he or she had actual notice of the instrument creating the right.[3] Where a purchaser is informed of the existence of an unregistered agreement but is told that the agreement does not affect the lands he or she is purchasing, he or she does not have actual notice of the agreement, which in fact affects such lands.[4]

1. *New Brunswick Railway v. Kelly* (1896), 26 S.C.R. 341; *Grey v. Ball* (1876), 23 Gr. 390; *Cooley v. Smith* (1877), 40 U.C.Q.B. 543; *Ihde v. Starr* (1909), 19 O.L.R. 471 at 478 (Div. Ct.); affirmed (1910), 21 O.L.R. 407 (C.A.) (appellant having notice that respondent being in possession and making valuable improvements on land over which appellant claiming right; such notice not sufficient to entitle respondent's equitable interest to prevail against appellant's registered title); *Roe v. Braden* (1877), 24 Gr. 589; *McVity v. Tranouth* (1905), 9 O.L.R. 105 at 110 per Osler J.A. (C.A.); affirmed (1905), 36 S.C.R. 455; which was reversed [1908] A.C. 60 (P.C.).

2. *Smith v. Thornton* (1922), 52 O.L.R. 492 (C.A.).

3. *Smith v. Thornton* (1922), 52 O.L.R. 492 (C.A.); *Peath v. Tucker*, [1954] O.W.N. 252 (Dist. Ct.).

4. *Coolidge v. Nelson* (1900), 31 O.R. 646 (C.A.); *McMaster v. Phipps* (1855), 5 Gr. 253 at 257; *Ferras v. McDonald* (1855), 5 Gr. 310.

§427 Priority of registration does not avail if the person claiming under the prior registration has actual notice of the earlier claim. Actual notice of an earlier claim which has not ripened into an interest in land as at the date of registration deprives the registered instrument of its priority over that interest.[1] Recitals of a prior unregistered mortgage, contained in a registered conveyance, do not afford actual notice of the unregistered mortgage to a subsequent purchaser or mortgagee.[2]

1. *Morse v. Kizer* (1919), 59 S.C.R. 1 (under Nova Scotia Registry Act, which permits registration of judgments, mortgagee who registered mortgage with notice of judgment against mortgagor, which was subsequently registered, not obtaining priority over judgment creditor); *Millar v. Smith* (1873), 23 U.C.C.P. 47.

2. *Foster v. Beall* (1868), 15 Gr. 244 (expressions have been used by appeal justices during argument which indicated that this decision might not be followed); **but see** *Haynes v. Gillen* (1874), 21 Gr. 15.

§428 If a purchaser claiming under a registered conveyance has actual notice of the existence of an unregistered conveyance affecting the lands purchased, the unregistered conveyance has priority, even though the purchaser is mistaken as to the extent of land conveyed by it, and even though the purchaser does not know the names of all the parties interested under the unregistered conveyance.[1]

> 1. *Severn v. McLellan* (1872), 19 Gr. 220.

§429 A person claiming under a registered conveyance is not entitled to priority if, at the date the conveyance was taken, the claimant knew that the vendor had conveyed his or her interest by an unregistered deed to someone, even though the claimant does not know the name of the person entitled under the unregistered deed.[1] Priority conferred by the Registry Act upon a grantee claiming under a registered instrument is not lost by the grantee's knowledge of circumstances sufficient to put him or her on inquiry as to the existence of prior unregistered instruments.[2]

> 1. *McLellan v. McDonald* (1871), 18 Gr. 502.
>
> 2. *Soden v. Stevens* (1850), 1 Gr. 346; *Ferras v. McDonald* (1855), 5 Gr. 310; *Foster v. Beall* (1868), 15 Gr. 244.

§430 Thus, where the owner of two lots sells a portion of lot 1 to P, but by mistake the description in the deed passes the whole of lot 1, the registration of a subsequent deed to the plaintiff of lot 2 and all that part of lot 1 not contained in the conveyance to P affects subsequent purchasers from P of all of lot 1, with notice of the equitable right of the plaintiff.[1]

> 1. *Haynes v. Gillen* (1874), 21 Gr. 15.

(iii) NOTICE TO SOLICITOR OF PURCHASER OR MORTGAGEE

§431 Notice to the purchaser's solicitor of a prior agreement for sale affecting the land constitutes notice to the solicitor's client.[1] However, a solicitor's knowledge of the right of a prior owner to have a transaction set aside for fraud does not constitute notice to the client of the former owner's equity where the solicitor is a party to the fraud.[2]

> 1. *Green v. Stevenson* (1905), 9 O.L.R. 671 (C.A.); *Fidelity Trust Co. v. Purdom*, [1930] S.C.R. 119 (mortgagee's solicitor having notice of prior encumbrance); **see also** *Toronto (City) v. Rudd*, [1952] O.R. 84 (H.C.) (some evidence that purchasers' solicitor having knowledge of restrictive by-law; such knowledge to be taken to be knowledge of purchasers themselves; purchasers not satisfying onus of proving lack of actual notice).
>
> 2. *Smith v. Hunt* (1901), 2 O.L.R. 134 (C.P.); varied on another point (1902), 4 O.L.R. 653 (C.A.) (doctrine of notice to principal proceeding on presumption that knowledge will be communicated because of duty of solicitor or agent to communicate

such; presumption rebutted where solicitor or agent having motives sufficient with ordinary men to withhold information; this statement of law confined to case of knowledge existing in agent or solicitor; case of notice expressly given to one who is agent to receive such notice excluded); *Cameron v. Hutchinson* (1869), 16 Gr. 526; **see also** *Durbin v. Monserat Investments Ltd.* (1978), 20 O.R. (2d) 181 (C.A.) (notice to defeat priority; notice to solicitor; knowledge in dishonest solicitor not imputed to principal); *Young v. 253819 Developments Ltd.* (1979), 24 O.R. (2d) 73 (H.C.) (defendant exercising power of sale in mortgage registered prior to plaintiff's interest; plaintiff occupying property under agreement to purchase as condominium unit; defendant having no actual notice of plaintiff's interest; constructive notice not sufficient to defeat defendant's priority).

(iv) NOTICE OF TRUST

§432 A purchaser who has agreed to buy property from a"trustee" for certain unnamed individuals is entitled to proof that the sale by the trustee is authorized under the terms of the trust.[1] But where lands conveyed years earlier to a person"as trustee" are sold and conveyed by that person to a purchaser, and there is no evidence on the register of the trustee's authority to sell, then, as between subsequent purchasers, it should be presumed, having regard to the age of the previous conveyance, that the sale was properly made by the trustee.[2] A statement in a land transfer tax affidavit to the effect that "I am trustee" has been held not to constitute actual notice under a previous statute.[3]

1. *Thompson v. Jenkins* (1928), 63 O.L.R. 33 (H.C.).

2. *McKinley v. McCullough* (1919), 46 O.L.R. 535 (Div. Ct.); *Gidley v. Frost* (1922), 23 O.W.N. 217 at 218 (H.C.) (held that *McKinley v. McCullough* decided that words "in trust" and nothing more constituted constructive, not actual, notice of trust, and that thus, under Registry Act, R.S.O. 1990, c. R.20, subsequent purchaser taking unaffected by trust); **see also** *Thompson v. Beer* (1919), 17 O.W.N. 4 (H.C.) (conveyance to one "as trustee" constituting express notice of trust to subsequent purchasers); *Hoback Investment Ltd. v. Loblaws Ltd.* (1981), 32 O.R. (2d) 95 (H.C.) (conveyance to or from party "in trust" not constituting actual notice of terms of trust; no obligation to make or answer inquiries into trust provisions; purchaser without actual notice of provisions not bound thereby); *Ignjatic v. McLennan* (1981), 32 O.R. (2d) 104 (C.A.) (client conveying property to solicitor in trust to obtain financing for building construction; solicitor mortgaging property for own as well as client's benefit; client commencing action to set aside mortgages; mortgagees under no obligation to inquire into terms of trust; mortgages valid in absence of actual notice of trust provisions).

3. *Seperich v. Madill*, [1946] O.R. 864 (H.C.) (dealing with R.S.O. 1937, c. 170).

6. NOTICE OF INSTRUMENT BY ITS REGISTRATION

§433 Registration of an instrument constitutes notice of the instrument to all persons subsequently claiming any interest in the land, notwithstanding any defect in the proof for registration. However, it is the duty of a registrar not to register any instrument except on such proof as is required by the Act.[1]

1. Registry Act, R.S.O. 1990, c. R.20, s. 74(1); *Orsi v. Morning*, [1971] 3 O.R. 185 (C.A.) (registration of assignment of agreement to purchase not constituting actual

notice of unregistered agreement); *Pierce v. Canada Permanent Loan & Savings Co.* (1896), 23 O.A.R. 516; *Gilleland v. Wadsworth* (1877), 1 O.A.R. 82 (effect of registration of assignment of mortgage on rights of owner of equity of redemption paying mortgage money to original mortgagee when unaware of existence of assignment); *Watson v. Grant* (1907), 9 O.W.R. 53 (H.C.); *Trust & Loan Co. v. Shaw* (1869), 16 Gr. 446; *McLeod v. Curry* (1921), 51 O.L.R. 68 (H.C.); reversed (1923), 54 O.L.R. 205 (C.A.); *Beck v. Moffatt* (1870), 17 Gr. 601; **see also** *Fries v. Fries*, [1949] O.W.N. 482 (H.C.); reversed on procedural grounds [1949] O.W.N. 654 (C.A.) (deeds made out to husband as grantee; deeds altered after delivery; subsequent mortgage for value and without notice; wife's dower rights); *Bing v. May*, [1946] O.W.N. 247 (H.C.); *Brisebois v. Chamberland* (1990), 1 O.R. (3d) 417 (C.A.) (company's awareness, through trustee, of previous rights over strip of land rendering subsequent deed of sale non-opposable, even registered); *Garont Investments Ltd. v. Dodds* (1990), 13 R.P.R. (2d) 27 (Ont. Gen. Div.) (right reserved in favour of applicant being option to purchase and being equitable interest in land which was enforceable against all subsequent purchasers with notice; respondents deemed to have notice of right as initially contained in deed from applicant to Z by virtue of operation of s. 69(1) of Registry Act, R.S.O. 1980, c. 445); *Chugal Properties Ltd. v. Levine*, [1971] 2 O.R. 331 (H.C.); reversed on other grounds [1972] 1 O.R. 158 (C.A.); affirmed (1973), 33 D.L.R. (3d) 512 (S.C.C.) (agreement to purchase land registered after vendor conveying land to third party but before registration of conveyance by third party; registration not being constructive notice of existence of agreement, and not effective to postpone rights of subsequent purchaser under registered instrument); *Edwards v. Gilboe*, [1959] O.R. 119 (C.A.) (registration of tax certificate as notice that someone other than municipality having interest in land which redeemable within year); *King v. McMillan* (1982), 24 R.P.R. 207 (Ont. H.C.) (subsequent mortgagee relying on discharge of prior mortgage; prior mortgagee subsequently obtaining declaration that discharge void on ground of mental incompetence; subsequent mortgagee without notice having priority); **see** Mortgages.

§434   If an instrument actually appears on the register, notice of it is thereby afforded to all persons subsequently claiming an interest in the land, even though there might be some defect in the formal proofs of execution for registration purposes.[1] The statute provides that registration of an instrument constitutes notice thereof to all persons subsequently claiming an interest in the land, notwithstanding any defect in the proof for registration, and this clause is wide enough to cover a case where the registered instrument, although received by the registrar, has no proof of execution at all.[2]

1. *Rooker v. Hoofstetter* (1896), 26 S.C.R. 41; *Armstrong v. Lye* (1897), 24 O.A.R. 543.

2. *Armstrong v. Lye* (1897), 24 O.A.R. 543; **see also** *Winberg v. Kettle* (1917), 12 O.W.N. 327 (C.A.) (subsequent purchaser having notice of prior agreement which in fact appearing on register, even though no proof of execution as required by Act attached to agreement).

§435   The registration of an assignment of an equitable interest gives notice of the equitable interest of the assignee to subsequent purchasers or mortgagees.[1]

1. *Cope v. Crichton* (1899), 30 O.R. 603 (Ch.).

§436   The definition of "instrument" in the Registry Act includes a co-tenancy agreement in writing which purports to create joint ownership and contains a buy-sell option.[1]

1. Registry Act, R.S.O. 1990, c. R.20, s. 1("instrument"); *Finlay v. Weren Brothers Co.* (1979), 22 O.R. (2d) 667 (H.C.).

§437   Registration of a prior mortgage against a parcel acquired by a purchaser is notice to the purchaser of the right of other persons who may have purchased other parcels covered by the mortgage before the purchaser acquired his or her parcel, so as to throw the burden of the mortgage onto the purchaser's lot under the doctrine of marshalling.[1]

1. *Clark v. Bogart* (1880), 27 Gr. 450.

§438   Registration of a conveyance creating a life estate with a remainder to another in fee simple is notice to all persons subsequently claiming an interest in the lands, of the title of the remainderman.[1] If an agreement for sale is registered, it operates as notice to a subsequent purchaser of the full rights of the purchaser under the agreement.[2]

1. *Bell v. Walker* (1873), 20 Gr. 558.

2. *Strathy v. Stephens* (1913), 29 O.L.R. 383 (H.C.); *Croll v. Greenhow* (1930), 38 O.W.N. 101 (H.C.); affirmed (1930), 39 O.W.N. 105 (C.A.); **but see** *Whiteley v. Richards* (1920), 48 O.L.R. 537 (H.C.).

§439   A deed, conveyance, transfer, agreement for sale, or mortgage in favour of a bona fide purchaser or a mortgage for adequate valuable consideration and covering real property affected by a receiving order or an assignment is valid and effectual as if no receiving order or assignment had been made, unless the receiving order or assignment or notice thereof has been registered against the property prior to registration of the deed, conveyance, transfer, agreement for sale or mortgage.[1]

1. Bankruptcy and Insolvency Act, R.S.C. 1985, c. B-3, s. 75.

§440   Although by the Registry Act the registration of an instrument is notice thereof to subsequent purchasers, the Act does not preclude the court from making an investigation as to whether a purchaser in fact knew of the existence of previous encumbrances, in a case where the purchaser claims the right to be subrogated to the position of an encumbrancer whom he or she has paid off.[1]

1. *Abel v. Morrison* (1890), 19 O.R. 669 (C.A.).

7. REGISTERED PLAN OF SUBDIVISION

§441   A composite plan under the Registry Act[1] is not a"registered plan of subdivision" under the Planning Act.[2] A composite plan merely locates land, while a plan of subdivision provides for the subdividing of land which was previously a single parcel.[3]

> 1. Registry Act, R.S.O. 1990, c. R.20, ss. 78-81, 82 [re-en. 1998, c. 18, Schedule E, s. 252], 83-85, 86 [am. 1998, c. 18, Schedule E, s. 253], 87, 88 [am. 1999, c. 12, Schedule M, s. 32], 89-91, 93.
>
> 2. Planning Act, R.S.O. 1990, c. P.13, s. 50 [am. 1994, c. 23, s. 29; 1996, c. 4, s. 27; 1997, c. 26, Schedule; 1998, c. 15, Schedule E, s. 27(4)-(10); 1999, c. 12, Schedule M, s. 27].
>
> 3. *Elrick v. Hespeler*, [1967] 2 O.R. 448 (C.A.); **see also** *Pattison v. Sceviour* (1983), 43 O.R. (2d) 229 (H.C.) (effect of trust arrangement being that grantor "retained the fee" in southerly part of parcel while appearing to convey entire parcel; conveyance to grantees void as contravening s. 29(4) of Planning Act).

8. FAILURE TO REGISTER

(a) General

§442   The Registry Act provides that after a grant of land by the Crown, and the issue of letters patent therefor, every instrument affecting the land[1] or any part thereof, except a lease for a term not exceeding seven years where actual possession goes along with the lease, is to be adjudged fraudulent and void as against any subsequent purchaser or mortgagee for valuable consideration, unless such instrument is registered before the registration of the instrument under which the subsequent purchaser or mortgagee claims.[2]

> 1. *Harding v. Cardiff* (1882), 2 O.R. 329 (Ch.) (opening and closing of highways); *Henderson v. Toronto (City)* (1898), 29 O.R. 669 (H.C.); *Chinara v. Oshawa (City)* (1928), 35 O.W.N. 30 (H.C.); *Girardot v. Curry* (1917), 38 O.L.R. 350 (C.A.) (registration of notices of exercise of power of sale contained in mortgages); Mortgages (as to questions of tacking, consolidation, priorities between mortgagees and lienholders; operation of discharges; and exercise of power of sale and notice thereof generally); Mechanics' and Construction Liens; Crown (as to effect of Registry Act on dealings with land before issue of patent from Crown); Highways and Streets.
>
> 2. Registry Act, R.S.O. 1990, c. R.20, s. 70; *Thomson v. Harrison* (1927), 60 O.L.R. 484 (H.C.) (plaintiff agreeing to sell land to defendant H; conveyance executed; H giving mortgage back for part of purchase price; mortgage left with H to be registered; H negotiating loan on property, and giving mortgage to S; H registering deed from plaintiff and then mortgage to S, but not registering mortgage to plaintiff; plaintiff and S acting in good faith; result of transaction between plaintiff and H being that H acquiring fee simple subject to plaintiff's lien for unpaid balance of purchase price; apart from Registry Act, plaintiff clearly entitled to priority over S; but by s. 74, mortgage from H to S taking priority over mortgage from H to plaintiff); **see also** *Toronto Suburban Railway v. Rogers* (1920), 48 O.L.R. 72 (C.A.); *Metropolitan Trust Co. of Canada v. Henneberry (Trustee of)* (1995), 44 R.P.R. (2d) 161 (Ont. C.A.);

affirming (1992), 1 D.R.P.L. 182 (Gen. Div.) (first mortgagee orally agreeing to postponement but not signing written agreement until after transferring mortgage to officer; equity not permitting officer to take advantage of unexpected priority in registration to change substance of agreement officer party to; postponement agreement valid against officer under s. 70(1) of Registry Act because officer not mortgagee without notice of agreement).

§443 Priority of registration prevails unless before the prior registration there has been actual notice of the prior instrument by the person claiming under the prior registration.[1]

1. Registry Act, R.S.O. 1990, c. R.20, s. 71; *Besinnett v. White* (1925), 58 O.L.R. 125 (C.A.) (Act affording no protection to person claiming under registered instrument if claimant having actual notice of unregistered instrument when purchasing); *Watt Milling Co. (Trustee of) v. Jackson*, [1951] O.W.N. 841 (H.C.); *Donaldson v. Lapp*, [1953] O.R. 178 (H.C.); *Wise v. Axford*, [1954] O.W.N. 822 (C.A.); *Harrell v. Mosier,*, [1956] O.R. 152 (C.A.); *Weeks v. Rogalski*, [1956] O.R. 109 (C.A.); *Canadian Imperial Bank of Commerce v. Rockway Holdings Ltd.* (1996), 29 O.R. (3d) 350 (Gen. Div.); additional reasons (1996), 29 O.R. (3d) 350 at 357 (Gen. Div.) (test of whether one had actual notice was whether registered instrument holder in receipt of such information as would cause a reasonable person to make enquiries as to terms and legal implications of prior instrument); **see also** *Willoughby v. Knight* (1973), 1 O.R. (2d) 184 (H.C.) (defeat of prior registration of subsequent purchaser requiring actual notice; registration of assignment of interest under agreement of sale by person to self not constituting actual notice of agreement).

§444 Although the Registry Act makes every unregistered conveyance fraudulent and void as against purchasers or mortgagees without notice, failure to register the instrument does not affect its validity as between the parties thereto.[1]

1. *McVity v. Tranouth*, [1908] A.C. 60 (P.C.).

§445 The Registry Act does not require that the creation of legal rights or their transfer be evidenced by any new form of words; it requires only that instruments creating or transferring rights to land be registered.[1] The court has power to make a declaratory judgment, upon such terms as may seem just, declaring that a grantee in a subsequent conveyance, registered before the registration of a previous conveyance of which the grantee had no actual notice, is entitled to priority over the previous conveyance.[2]

1. *Israel v. Leith* (1890), 20 O.R. 361 (C.A.) (plaintiff's conveyance, prior in time to defendant's, passing to plaintiff certain legal rights in land which defendant subsequently purchasing; instrument under which rights passed being first in time and first in registration; nothing in Act to take away rights acquired by plaintiff under conveyance).

2. *Weir v. Niagara Grape Co.* (1886), 11 O.R. 700 (C.A.); *Truesdell v. Cook* (1871), 18 Gr. 532; *Dynes v. Bales* (1878), 25 Gr. 593; see Judgments and Orders (as to power of court to make declaratory judgments).

§446   The principle behind the Registry Act is that a party acquiring land ought to be able to see whether there is anything registered against the property which he or she is about to acquire; but this does not apply to one who is parting with, not acquiring, an interest in property.[1]

   1. *Trust & Loan Co. v. Shaw* (1869), 16 Gr. 446 at 448.

§447   A defendant who relies on the Registry Act should plead the Act, although in some circumstances an amendment to the pleadings may be allowed so as to permit a defendant to rely on the Act.[1]

   1. *Smith v. Thornton* (1922), 51 O.L.R. 492 (C.A.).

(b) Purchaser for Value

§448   Since the Registry Act only avoids unregistered instruments against purchasers for value without notice, if priority is sought to be established for a registered conveyance over an unregistered, earlier conveyance, it is essential to give proof that valuable consideration was given for the subsequent registered conveyance.[1]

   1. *Barber v. McKay* (1890), 19 O.R. 46 (Ch.); *Doe d. Cronk v. Smith* (1850), 7 U.C.Q.B. 376; *McKenny v. Arner* (1858), 8 U.C.C.P. 46; *Leech v. Leech* (1865), 24 U.C.Q.B. 321; *Blackburn v. Gummerson* (1860), 8 Gr. 331; *Dunlop v. King* (1924), 25 O.W.N. 533 (C.A.); **see also** *Stackhouse v. Morin*, [1948] O.R. 864 (H.C.); *King v. McMillan* (1982), 24 R.P.R. 207 (Ont. H.C.) (mortgage registered subsequent to registration of discharge of prior mortgage and before registration of declaration of invalidity of discharge on ground of mental incompetence; subsequent mortgage having priority over prior one).

§449   In order to prove the payment of valuable consideration, as against a stranger to the deed, production of the deed with a receipt or recital as to payment endorsed thereon is not enough.[1] It is necessary in such a situation to prove the giving of valuable consideration, but such consideration need not be money.[2] The giving of additional time to a debtor is sufficient consideration to support a claim for priority.[3] A mortgage to creditors for the purpose of securing their debts involves a sufficient consideration to give such a registered mortgage priority over a conveyance made before but registered after the mortgage.[4]

   1. *Barber v. McKay* (1890), 19 O.R. 46 (Ch.).

   2. *Bondy v. Fox* (1869), 29 U.C.Q.B. 64; *Wilkinson v. Conklin* (1860), 10 U.C.C.P. 211; *Patulo v. Boyington* (1854), 4 U.C.C.P. 125.

   3. *Johnston v. Reid* (1881), 29 Gr. 293.

   4. *Fraser v. Sutherland* (1851), 2 Gr. 442.

(c) Assignment for Benefit of Creditors

§450 An assignee for the benefit of creditors takes no greater title to land than the assignor has; hence, an unregistered mortgage or conveyance, made by the assignor before the assignment for the benefit of creditors, takes priority over the assignment, even though the assignee has no notice of the mortgage or conveyance at the time he or she registers the assignment to him or herself.[1]

> 1. *Re Wilson* (1915), 33 O.L.R. 500 (H.C.); *Craig v. McKay* (1906), 12 O.L.R. 121 (C.A.); *Thibaudeau v. Paul* (1895), 26 O.R. 385 (C.A.); *Steele v. Murphy* (1841), 13 E.R. 181.

(d) Forgery

§451 It has been held by the Court of Appeal in England that the registration of a forged conveyance, the conveyance itself being absolutely void, does not operate to convey any title, even in favour of purchasers for value.[1]

> 1. *Re Cooper* (1880), 20 Ch. D. 611 (registration under Middlesex Registry Act, 7 Anne, c. 20); **see also** *Toderan v. Bacchus* (1979), 13 R.P.R. 122 (Ont. H.C.) (forged mortgages amounting to nullities); *Comay Planning Consultants Ltd. v. Starkman* (1986), 57 O.R. (2d) 223 (H.C.) (solicitor registering forged discharge of mortgage; bona fide purchaser taking title; discharge being nullity; purchaser taking title subject to mortgage).

9. LEGAL RIGHTS NOT ARISING UNDER INSTRUMENT

(a) General

§452 Legal rights which do not arise by virtue of an express grant do not fall within the scope of the Registry Act, and such legal rights are enforceable even against purchasers for value without notice of such legal right.[1] The Act deals with the registration of documents and with the rights arising through such registered documents. The Act does not in any way affect a legal claim which arises by operation of law and not from a deed or other instrument.

> 1. *Israel v. Leith* (1890), 20 O.R. 361 (C.A.); *Harrison v. Armour* (1865), 11 Gr. 303; **see also** *Floyd v. Heska* (1974), 5 O.R. (2d) 273 (H.C.); reversed (1977), 16 O.R. (2d) 12 (C.A.); leave to appeal to S.C.C. refused (1977), 16 O.R. (2d) 12n (S.C.C.).

(b) Easements

§453 An easement arising by implied grant and not by express grant is binding upon subsequent purchasers of the land, even though such purchasers have no notice of the existence of the easement.[1] However, an easement created by an express grant is void as against subsequent purchasers without notice unless the instrument creating the easement is registered.[2]

1. *Israel v. Leith* (1890), 20 O.R. 361 (C.A.); *Duchman v. Oakland Dairy Co.* (1928), 63 O.L.R. 111 at 125 (C.A.); **see also** Easements.

2. *Ross v. Hunter* (1882), 7 S.C.R. 289; *Israel v. Leith* (1890), 20 O.R. 361 (C.A.).

§**454** An easement acquired by prescription under the Limitations Act[1] does not come within the Registry Act, and may be enforced against purchasers of the land burdened with the easement, even though the purchasers have no notice thereof.[2] However, if the right asserted is not an easement but is an equitable right arising out of an agreement, such as a licence, that equitable right, even though not derived from a written instrument, is not valid as against purchasers for value without notice of the equitable right.[3]

1. Limitations Act, R.S.O. 1990, c. L.15.

2. *Myers v. Johnston* (1922), 52 O.L.R. 658 (C.A.); **see also** Federal Real Property Act, S.C. 1991, c. 50, ss. 2("federal real property"), ("interest"), ("real property") (real property including interest in land), 14 (no person acquiring any federal real property by prescription); *Adrian v. McVannel* (1992), 28 R.P.R. (2d) 109 (Ont. Gen. Div.) (possible to establish prescriptive easement despite origin on consent, so long as 20-year period under s. 31 of Limitations Act for establishing adverse possession having passed; respondent deemed to have had constructive knowledge of potentially adverse use of property; respondent not taking any steps which reasonable owner would have taken to ascertain true extent of property); Limitation of Actions.

3. *Andoniadis v. Bell*, [1947] O.W.N. 509 (H.C.) (oral contract to buy house for future wife; house subsequently registered in husband's name only; purchase from husband protected, as claim of vendor's wife not arising under instrument but being equitable lien); **see also** *Toronto (City) v. Jarvis* (1894), 25 S.C.R. 237; *Myers v. Johnston* (1922), 52 O.L.R. 658 (C.A.).

§**455** An agreement entered into by an owner permitting a neighbour to run pipes under the owner's land, whether it be considered as creating a quasi-easement or a mere licence, comes within the scope of the Registry Act and cannot be enforced against a purchaser for value without notice who claims under a registered instrument.[1]

1. *Harrington v. Spring Creek Cheese Manufacturing Co.* (1904), 7 O.L.R. 319.

§**456** The Registry Act does not afford any protection to a purchaser for value who claims under a registered conveyance from the owner of the paper title where in fact some other person has acquired title to the land in question by length of possession under the Limitations Act.[1]

1. *Canada Permanent Loan & Savings Co. v. McKay* (1881), 32 U.C.C.P. 51; *Bishop v. Cox*, [1928] 2 D.L.R. 441 (Ont. H.C.); affirmed [1928] 2 D.L.R. 990 (C.A.).

10. EQUITABLE INTERESTS

§457   A purchaser for value without notice of an existing equitable interest is protected against the equitable interest by the Registry Act.[1] A claim for rectification of a deed in respect of the land conveyed thereby is an assertion of an equitable interest which cannot, in view of the Act, prevail against a prior registered deed covering the land in question.[2]

> 1. Registry Act, R.S.O. 1990, c. R.20, s. 72; *Canada Permanent Loan & Savings Co. v. McKay* (1881), 32 U.C.C.P. 51; *Roe v. Braden* (1877), 24 Gr. 589; *Cooley v. Smith* (1877), 40 U.C.Q.B. 543; *Bridges v. Real Estate Loan & Debenture Co.* (1884), 8 O.R. 493 (C.A.); *Core v. Ontario Loan & Debenture Co.* (1885), 9 O.R. 236 (C.A.).
>
> 2. *Wise v. Axford*, [1954] O.W.N. 822 (C.A.); *Bouris v. Button* (1975), 9 O.R. (2d) 305 (H.C.) (deed not including part of property intended to be conveyed; equitable right to rectification).

§458   A trust which is not mentioned or set out in a registered instrument cannot be enforced against a subsequent purchaser or mortgagee who claims under an instrument registered without notice of the trust[1]

> 1. *Bank of Montreal v. Stewart* (1887), 14 O.R. 482 (C.P.); *Building & Loan Assn. v. Poaps* (1896), 27 O.R. 470 (H.C.); *Bell v. Walker* (1873), 20 Gr. 558; *Grey v. Ball* (1876), 23 Gr. 390.

§459   The Registry Act provision that no equitable lien, charge or interest affecting land is valid as against a registered instrument executed by the same person or his or her heirs or assigns,[1] does not apply to a case in which the party registering such instrument has notice of the equitable lien, charge or interest, even though the same has been created by parol.[2] This section is not confined in its operation to equitable interests originating under instruments capable of registration, but applies to all equitable interests.[3]

> 1. Registry Act, R.S.O. 1990, c. R.20, s. 72.
>
> 2. *Peterkin v. McFarlane* (1885), 13 S.C.R. 677; *Forrester v. Campbell* (1870), 17 Gr. 379; *Trinidad Asphalte Co. v. Coryat*, [1896] A.C. 587; *McMaster v. Phipps* (1885), 5 Gr. 253; *Wigle v. Setterington* (1872), 19 Gr. 512.
>
> 3. *Toronto (City) v. Jarvis* (1894), 25 S.C.R. 237; *Peterkin v. McFarlane* (1885), 13 S.C.R. 677; *Thomson v. Harrison* (1927), 60 O.L.R. 484 (H.C.) (equitable interest or claim not valid as against one having no notice of claim and claiming under registered instrument executed by person against whom equity originally arising).

§460   As between equitable encumbrancers, priority may be gained by priority of registration unless there has been actual notice of the equitable encumbrance that is prior in time.[1]

> 1. *Bethune v. Caulcutt* (1849), 1 Gr. 81.

§461   The right of a person entitled to relief in equity on the ground of mistake is an equitable lien, charge or interest which is void as against a purchaser without notice claiming under a registered instrument.[1]

> 1. *Haynes v. Gillen* (1874), 21 Gr. 15.

§462   An unregistered agreement for the sale of land is void as against a purchaser who pays the purchase moneys and takes a conveyance without notice of the agreement, even though the purchaser receives notice of the unregistered agreement.[1]

> 1. *Peebles v. Hyslop* (1914), 30 O.L.R. 511 (C.A.); **see also** *Paramount Theatres Ltd. v. Brandenberger* (1928), 62 O.L.R. 579 (H.C.).

11. WILLS

§463   A will may be registered by registering: the original will or a notarial copy thereof together with the required statements; the letters probate, letters of administration with the will annexed, the certificate of appointment of estate trustee with or without a will or any grant based on a will given by a court outside Ontario or a notarial copy thereof; or an exemplification or certified copy of such letters, certificate of appointment or grant under the seal of the granting court or a notarial copy of such exemplification or certified copy.[1]

> 1. Registry Act, R.S.O. 1990, c. R.20, s. 53 [am. 1998, c. 18, Schedule E, s. 237; 1999, c. 12, Schedule F, s. 37; 2000, c. 26, Schedule B, s. 17(7), (8), (9)].

§464   The conveyancing effect of a will disposing of real property, quite independently of the grant of probate, is recognized. Such a will may be registered under the Registry Act, without probate, if accompanied by due proof of its execution, of the death of the testator, and of the payment of succession duties, and is effective without probate to convey the testator's real estate to the devisee, subject to the Estates Administration Act as to temporary vesting in the executor.[1]

> 1. Estates Administration Act, R.S.O. 1990, c. E.22; *Re Howard* (1923), 54 O.L.R. 109 at 120 (H.C.); **see also** *Kinross Mortgage Corp. v. Central Mortgage & Housing Corp.* (1979), 22 O.R. (2d) 713 (H.C.) (effect of Registry Act on wills; limitation period; claim to freehold estate by beneficiaries shown on will appearing on abstract of title not extinguished).

12. EXECUTIONS AND SALES MADE BY SHERIFF

§465   A purchaser of land at a sheriff's sale,[1] on registration of his or her conveyance, takes free from an unregistered mortgage made by the execution debtor, even though the execution creditor could not claim priority over the unregistered mortgage.[2]

1. Execution Act, R.S.O. 1990, c. E.24; *McDonald v. Royal Bank*, [1933] O.R. 418 (C.A.) (rights of execution creditors against assignee of registered mortgage claiming under unregistered assignment from debtor; Registry Act concerned with protecting rights of actual purchasers or mortgagees under registered instruments as against claims under unregistered documents; Act not in any way dealing with rights of creditors); Execution.

2. *Jellett v. Wilkie* (1896), 26 S.C.R. 282; *Dickenson v. Gegg* (1921), 19 O.W.N. 492 (H.C.).

13. LIENS

§466   By the combined effect of the Registry Act and the Construction Lien Act, a purchaser for value claiming under a registered conveyance has priority over lienholders whose claims of lien are not registered and of which the purchaser has no notice, even though the liens arise before the making of the conveyance.[1]

1. Construction Lien Act, R.S.O. 1990, c. C.30, s. 14(1) [see 1997, c. 23, s. 4(2) for Transition note]; *Charters v. McCracken* (1916), 36 O.L.R. 260 (C.A.); *Re Pridham*, [1934] O.W.N. 560 (unregistered mechanic's lien void as against registered title); *Coupland Acceptance Ltd. v. Walsh*, [1954] S.C.R. 90; **see also** *Del Chute & Son Ltd. v. Padlock Warehouses Ltd.* (1980), 13 R.P.R. 205 (Ont. H.C.) (mortgagee registering mortgage to secure loan previously advanced with actual notice of lien claim; registration occurring prior to giving written notice of lien and prior to registration of claim for lien; lien claimant having priority).

14. LEASEHOLD INTERESTS

§467   Leases for less than seven years do not lose their priority where actual possession goes along with the lease; but the possession must be under the lease for which priority is claimed.[1]

1. Registry Act, R.S.O. 1990, c. R.20, s. 70(2); *Howe v. 635362 Ontario Ltd.* (1997), 23 O.T.C. 1 (Ont. Gen. Div.) (lessee not in possession of property at time agreement of purchase and sale entered into; lease not constituting bar to completion of agreement); **see also** *Davidson v. McKay* (1867), 26 U.C.Q.B. 306; *Canada Permanent Building & Savings Society v. Rowell* (1860), 19 U.C.Q.B. 124.

15. REGISTRATION OF UNAUTHORIZED INSTRUMENTS

§468   A charge created and registered against property by a person who has no interest in the property constitutes a cloud upon the title of the owner, and the court will order the instrument removed from the register.[1] The registration of an instrument not authorized by the Registry Act also constitutes such a cloud, and the court will order the instrument removed.[2] Thus, a mortgage subsequently registered takes priority.[3]

1. *Fee v. Macdonald Manufacturing Co.* (1912), 22 O.W.R. 314 (H.C.); varied (1912), 23 O.W.R. 189 (Div. Ct.) (company with no interest in plaintiff's lands

registering agreement purporting to charge lands with price of machine ordered from company; registered agreement constituting cloud on title; removal ordered; plaintiff also awarded damages for loss and inconvenience resulting from company's refusal to vacate charge).

2. *Ontario Industrial Loan & Investment Co. v. Lindsey* (1883), 3 O.R. 66 (C.A.).

3. *Anton v. Erich Maaser Construction Ltd.* (1978), 19 O.R. (2d) 537 (C.A.).

16. FEES OF REGISTRARS

§469   In cases where the registrar is required to perform services but no fees therefor are provided[1] by the Registry Act or regulations or by any other Act of Ontario, the registrar, in the absence of any express provision requiring gratuitous performance of such services, is entitled to such reasonable fees therefor as the director may fix, to be paid by the person requiring the services.[2]

1. *Lindsey v. Toronto* (1875), 25 U.C.C.P. 335; *Ross v. McLay* (1876), 26 U.C.C.P. 190; *Ross v. McLay* (1876), 40 U.C.Q.B. 87; *Macnamara v. McLay* (1882), 8 O.A.R. 319; *Bruce v. McLay* (1884), 11 O.A.R. 477; *Gray v. Ingersoll* (1888), 16 O.R. 194 (Ch.).

2. Registry Act, R.S.O. 1990, c. R.20, s. 94(1); **see also** *Simcoe (County) v. Sanderson* (1921), 51 O.L.R. 239 (C.A.) (salary paid after retirement to former deputy registrar for services rendered as advisory clerk to registrar being warranted disbursement by registrar and not reviewable by court).

17. ASSURANCE FUND

§470   A person wrongfully deprived of land registered under the Registry Act, by reason of the deletion of an entry or by reason of any error or omission in recording a registered instrument, may be entitled to compensation out of the Land Titles Assurance Fund formed under the Land Titles Act.[1]

1. Registry Act, R.S.O. 1990, c. R.20, Pt. IV (ss. 116-118); Land Titles Act, R.S.O. 1990, c. L.5, s. 54; *Kerr v. Ontario (Land Titles Assurance Fund)* (1999), 28 R.P.R. (3d) 266 (Ont. S.C.J.) (mortgagees entitled to recover from fund legal costs incurred in attempting to restore mortgages to register, but not to principal amounts under mortgages where mortgagees' failure to protect interest could not be attributed to absence of interest from register); **see also** *Ontario Hydro v. Tkach* (1992), 28 R.P.R. (2d) 1 (Ont. C.A.) (defendant able to claim good title by reason of 40-year limit on search of title imposed first in 1929 and currently incorporated in Registry Act; defendant's title having to be viewed as at moment coming under attack, either when plaintiff issuing proceedings or at date of trial; in either case, date considerably more than 40 years after conveyance to defendant's predecessor in title in 1934, and relevant statute being Act; plaintiff not able to argue that claim coming within exception in s. 106(5), since claim not being "claim arising under any Act"; claim arising from 1906 conveyance); *Camrich Developments Inc. v. Ontario Hydro* (1990), 72 O.R. (2d) 225 (H.C.); affirmed (1993), 14 O.R. (3d) 410 (C.A.) (claim no longer maintainable simply by being acknowledged or referred to in instrument; definition of "claim" in statute

pertaining to instrument creating interest; therefore respondent's claim not referred to or acknowledged in 1954 by-laws registered against lands; claim not preserved by notice of claim filed pursuant to predecessor legislation prior to 1981, at which time right to assert claim ending; accordingly, respondent's claim expiring in 1984 and not able to be renewed by virtue of s. 106(7)); *Lakhani v. Weinstein* (1980), 31 O.R. (2d) 65 (H.C.) (covenants not affecting land unless acknowledged in instrument registered within 40-year period; s. 105 deeming deposit on title not to be registration).

XIV   Land Titles Act

1. PURPOSE OF ACT AND DUTIES OF LAND REGISTRAR

(a) General

§471   The Land Titles Act[1] deals simply with the question of registration; it does not interfere with any common law or other rights of an owner of land to mortgage the same by an instrument not capable of registration under the Land Titles Act.[2] While the land titles system might be said to be one for the registration of title rather than of deeds, execution and delivery in the prescribed form of the instrument of transfer, particularly when accompanied by the affidavits required for registration, confer a title in equity for all purposes except as against some other title that may obtain priority by being recorded. Upon registration and completion of the transfer on the register, the transferee becomes fully protected against any other transfer.[3]

> 1. Land Titles Act, R.S.O. 1990, c. L.5.
>
> 2. *John Macdonald & Co. v. Tew* (1914), 32 O.L.R. 262 (C.A.); see also *Skill v. Thompson* (1908), 17 O.L.R. 186 (C.A.); *Re Shier* (1922), 52 O.L.R. 464 (H.C.) (Act being essentially paternal; underlying theory being that title must at all times be carefully investigated, and then certificate of registration gives indefeasible title).
>
> 3. *Abigail v. Lapin*, [1934] A.C. 491 (P.C.) [Aus.]; *Macedo v. Stroud*, [1922] 2 A.C. 330 (P.C.); *Hooper v. Hooper*, [1953] O.R. 753 (C.A.).

§472   It is one of the terms of a contract for the sale of lands which are registered under the land titles system that the sale should be completed and perfected by a proper transfer susceptible of registration under the Act.[1] An agreement to sell in fee simple carries with it the right of the purchaser to proper covenants, and a transferee under the Land Titles Act must be considered to be in at least as high a position with respect to his or her transferor as if he or she were the holder of a contract of sale and entitled to the usual covenants.[2]

> 1. *Owen v. Mercier* (1906), 12 O.L.R. 529 (Ch.); reversed on other grounds (1907), 14 O.L.R. 491 (C.A.).
>
> 2. *Guest v. Cochlin* (1929), 64 O.L.R. 165 (C.A.).

§473   A land registrar (formerly master of titles) is not a mere administrative officer, and having regard to the effect of registration under the Act, it is the registrar's duty to pass upon the legality of any document submitted to him or her.[1]

> 1. *Re Mutual Investments Ltd.* (1924), 56 O.L.R. 29 (H.C.); **see also** *Brooks v. Pavlick*, [1964] S.C.R. 108 (jurisdiction of master not contrary to s. 96 of British North America Act).

§474   Where a hearing has been held under the Land Titles Act, the decision or order of the director of land registration, director of titles or land registrar may be appealed to the Superior Court of Justice, and the appeal is to be by way of a new trial.[1] Any person affected by an order made under the Act by a judge of the Superior Court of Justice may appeal to the Divisional Court within the prescribed time and, subject to the rules, in like manner as in the case of other appeals to the latter court.[2] A matter which rests in the sound discretion of the registrar should not be reviewed on appeal.[3]

> 1. Land Titles Act, R.S.O. 1990, c. L.5, s. 26 [re-en. 1998, c. 18, Schedule E, s. 117]; *683728 Ontario Ltd. v. North Barrie Developments Ltd.* (1995), 26 O.R. (3d) 91 (Gen. Div.) (appeal governed by R. 61; time limit for appeal 30 days).
>
> 2. Land Titles Act, R.S.O. 1990, c. L.5, s. 27 [am. 1998, c. 18, Schedule E, s. 118].
>
> 3. *Re Gund* (1923), 53 O.L.R. 371 (H.C.).

§475   If, upon examination of a title or upon an application with respect to registered land, the land registrar entertains a doubt as to any matter of law, he or she may state a case for the opinion of the court and may name the parties to it; and if the registrar entertains a doubt as to any matter of fact, he or she may direct an issue to be tried for the purpose of determining such fact.[1]

> 1. Land Titles Act, R.S.O. 1990, c. L.5, s. 21(1); **see also** *Boyle v. McCabe* (1911), 24 O.L.R. 313 (C.A.) (land registrar directing issue to ascertain identity of person claiming interest in registered land; since person being beyond court's jurisdiction and being real, not merely nominal, actor in issue directed, person required to post security for costs); *Re Hewitt* (1912), 3 O.W.N. 902 (H.C.); **but see** Land Titles Act, R.S.O. 1990, c. L.5, s. 21(2) (power conferred by s. 21 cannot be exercised by land registrar except with approval of director of titles.

§476   Any jurisdiction of the court under the Land Titles Act, except an appeal to which the Courts of Justice Act applies, may be exercised by a judge of the court.[1]

> 1. Land Titles Act, R.S.O. 1990, c. L.5, s. 27(1); Courts of Justice Act, R.S.O. 1990, c. C43, s. 19 [am. 1994, c. 12, s. 6; 1996, c. 25, s. 1(2); 1996, c. 25, s. 9(17), (18)]; **see also** *Re Woodhouse* (1913), 5 O.W.N. 148 (C.A.) ("action" as used in Rules of Practice not including proceeding under Land Titles Act).

(b) Director of Titles

§477   The deputy minister has the authority to appoint a public servant[1] who is a barrister and solicitor to be director of titles.[2] The director may then appoint public servants as representatives of the director, to whom the director has the authority to delegate any of the director's powers and duties.[3]

1. Public Service Act, R.S.O. 1990, c. P.47.

2. Land Titles Act, R.S.O. 1990, c. L.5, s. 9(1) [re-en. 1998, c. 18, Schedule E, s. 107; am. 2000, c. 26, Schedule B, s. 12(2)].

3. Land Titles Act, R.S.O. 1990, c. L.5, s. 9(2) [re-en. 1998, c. 18, Schedule E, s. 107]; **see also** *Fetterer v. Dyment* (1974), 5 O.R. (2d) 770 (Div. Ct.) (whether assistant deputy director having jurisdiction to extend time for appeals); *Bayliss v. Wren Lake Estates Ltd.* (1991), 49 C.P.C. (2d) 274 (Ont. Gen. Div.) (30-day time for appealing provided in R. 61.04 applying unless statute or Rules of Civil Procedure providing otherwise; where Land Titles Act silent on time for appealing decision of deputy director, by analogy rule, R. 1.04(2), provisions of R. 61.04 applying).

(c) Director of Land Registration

§478 The director of land registration appointed under the Registry Act has general supervision over land titles offices and the system for registration therein, and has powers and duties similar to those described in the Registry Act.[1]

1. Land Titles Act, R.S.O. 1990, c. L.5, s. 8 [am. 1998, c. 18, Schedule E, s. 106]; **see also** Registry Act, R.S.O. 1990, c. R.20, s. 97 [am. 1998, c. 18, Schedule E, s. 254; 2000, c. 26, Schedule B, s. 17(2), (13), (14)].

2. REGISTRATION OF LAND UNDER ACT

§479 In conducting the examination of a title offered for registration, the land registrar may receive and act upon any evidence that is received in court on a question of title, or any evidence that the practice of conveyancers authorizes to be received on an investigation of title out of court, or any other evidence, whether the same is or is not receivable or sufficient in point of strict law or according to the practice of conveyancers, if it satisfies the registrar of the truth of the facts intended to be made out thereby.[1]

1. Land Titles Act, R.S.O. 1990, c. L.5, s. 41¶5; **see also** Land Registration Reform Act, R.S.O. 1990, c. L.4; *Re G.* (1891), 21 O.R. 109 (Q.B.) (land devised to petitioner for life, with remainder in fee to her children surviving her; petitioner, at age 56, and one child to whom all other surviving children had conveyed their interests applying to be registered as owners with absolute title; evidence of physician that petitioner exhibiting senile atrophy of uterus and ovaries so far advanced that pregnancy impossible; held that land registrar should have accepted evidence as sufficient proof that petitioner physically incapable of bearing more children, and should have granted certificate of absolute title); compare decision in *Re G.* to cases involving rule against perpetuities, for purposes of which courts always conclusively presume that any person capable of having children, no matter their age and regardless of such physiological facts as menopause, impotency, etc.; *Jee v. Audley* (1787), 1 Cox 324; *Ivor v. Emery* (1980), 27 O.R. (2d) 579 (Co. Ct.); affirmed (1982), 37 O.R. (2d) 272 (Div. Ct.) (jurisdiction of court on appeal from first registration; court refusing to make order preserving right of way or claim for improvements with regard to dispute over option agreement); *Ennisclare on the Lake Ltd. v. Preston Glen Corp.* (1982), 139 D.L.R. (3d) 344 (Ont. Co. Ct.) (s. 42 of Land Titles Act giving standing to any

person wishing to object to first registration; wording of statute indicating that objection must relate to title of applicant; no further limitations); *Mazzeo v. Ontario*, 1996 CarswellOnt 1181 (Ont. Gen. Div.); affirmed, 1997 CarswellOnt 3873 (Ont. C.A.); leave to appeal refused (1998), 235 N.R. 196 (note) (S.C.C.) (fact that provisions of Land Titles Act not extending to all counties and districts in Ontario such that some counties or portions thereof governed by Registry Act not constituting discrimination); Morris and Leach, The Rule Against Perpetuities, p. 74.

3. INTEREST TO WHICH REGISTERED LANDS ARE SUBJECT

§480   All land registered under the Land Titles Act is, unless the contrary is expressed on the register, subject to such easements as for the time being may be subsisting in reference thereto, and such easements are not deemed encumbrances within the meaning of the Act.[1] Unity of title to the dominant and servient tenements extinguishes an easement, and there is nothing in the Land Titles Act which affects this general principle.[2]

> 1. Land Titles Act, R.S.O. 1990, c. L.5, s. 44(1)¶2; *Stodgill v. Ostrander* (1921), 21 O.W.N. 95 (H.C.) (easement for access of light, on doctrine of implied grant); *Aluminum Goods Ltd. v. Federal Machinery Ltd.*, [1970] 2 O.R. 235 (H.C.) (if right of way already crystallized before land going under Act, then title subject to right of way not only at time of first registration but on all subsequent transfers).
>
> 2. *McClellan v. Powassan Lumber Co.* (1908), 17 O.L.R. 32 (C.A.).

§481   All land registered under the Land Titles Act is, unless the contrary is expressed on the register, subject to any title or lien which, by possession or improvements, the owner or any person interested in any adjoining land has acquired to or in respect of the registered land.[1] But this provision is not intended to apply to a case of an adverse claim to the title, founded upon rights alleged to have arisen before the land is registered; what is preserved is any right the owner of a property adjoining another property, which is registered land under the Land Titles Act, may have acquired to or in respect of the registered land by reason of possession or improvements or otherwise.[2]

> 1. Land Titles Act, R.S.O. 1990, c. L.5, s. 44(1)¶3.
>
> 2. *Farah v. Glen Lake Mining Co.* (1908), 17 O.L.R. 1 at 21, per Moss C.J.O (C.A.); *Gatz v. Kiziw*, [1959] S.C.R. 10.

§482   In addition, all land registered under the Land Titles Act is, unless the contrary is expressed on the register, subject to: any public highway;[1] the unexpired period of an existing lease, which period does not exceed three years where there is actual occupation under it;[2] construction liens;[3] rights of expropriation, access or user, or any other right by the Crown under the authority of any statute of Canada or Ontario;[4] provincial taxes and succession duties, as well as municipal taxes and charges;[5] liabilities, rights and interests under the Public Transportation and Highway Improvement Act;[6]

by-laws under the Planning Act and municipal by-laws which do not directly affect title;[7] the subdivision provisions of the Planning Act;[8] and to certain interests with respect to railway companies created by deposit of an instrument in the office of the Secretary of State of Canada.[9] .

1. Land Titles Act, R.S.O. 1990, c. L.5, s. 44(1)¶8; *Larcher v. Sudbury* (1913), 4 O.W.N. 1289 (H.C.).

2. Land Titles Act, R.S.O. 1990, c. L.5, s. 44(1)¶4.

3. Land Titles Act, R.S.O. 1990, c. L.5, s. 44(1)¶6.

4. Land Titles Act, R.S.O. 1990, c. L.5, s. 44(1)¶7.

5. Land Titles Act, R.S.O. 1990, c. L.5, s. 44(1)¶1.

6. Land Titles Act, R.S.O. 1990, c. L.5, s. 44(1)¶9; Public Transportation and Highway Improvement Act, R.S.O. 1990, c. P.50, s. 38.

7. Land Titles Act, R.S.O. 1990, c. L.5, s. 44(1)¶10; Planning Act, R.S.O. 1990, c. P.13, s. 34 [am. 1994, c. 23, s. 21; 1996, c. 4, s. 20; 1999, c. 12, Schedule M, s. 25; 2000, c. 26, Schedule K, s. 5].

8. Land Titles Act, R.S.O. 1990, c. L.5, s. 44(1)¶11 [re-en. 1991, vol. 2, c. 9, s. 2; am. 1993, c. 27, Sched.]; Ontario Planning Act, ss. 50 [am. 1994, c. 23, s. 29; 1996, c. 4, s. 27; 1997, c. 26, Schedule; 1998, c. 15, Schedule E, s. 27(4)-(10); 1999, c. 12, Schedule M, s. 27], 50.1 [en. 1991, vol. 2, c. 9, s. 1].

9. Land Titles Act, R.S.O. 1990, c. L.5, s. 44(1)¶12.

4. REGISTRATION OF EASEMENTS

§483 The land registrar may register the owner of any easement in the same manner and with the same incidents as the registrar is empowered to register the owner of land, or as near thereto as circumstances permit.[1]

1. Land Titles Act, R.S.O. 1990, c. L.5, s. 39(1).

§484 An easement in or over unregistered land granted as appurtenant to registered land may be registered in the register of the dominant land with a declaration that the title thereto is absolute, qualified or possessory, or otherwise as the case requires.[1]

1. Land Titles Act, R.S.O. 1990, c. L.5, s. 39(2)

§485 The land registrar may issue a certificate of easement when the dominant land is unregistered, which certificate may be registered in the registry division in which the land is situate, and in such a case the registrar must note on the register that such certificate has been issued.[1]

1. Land Titles Act, R.S.O. 1990, c. L.5, s. 39(3).

§486 Where the existence of an easement is proved, the land registrar may, if he or she thinks fit, enter notice thereof on the register.[1]

1. Land Titles Act, R.S.O. 1990, c. L.5, s. 39(4).

5. EFFECT OF ACT ON POSSESSORY TITLES

§487 A title to or any right or interest in land registered under the Land Titles Act that is adverse to or in derogation of the title of the registered owner cannot be acquired by any length of possession.[1]

1. *Smith v. National Trust Co.* (1912), 45 S.C.R. 618 (registered titles of mortgagors under Manitoba Real Property Act protected by provisions of that statute denying acquisition of title adverse to or in derogation of title of registered owner by length of possession only; Limitations Act limitation in favour of mortgagees having no application to lands after lands brought under Real Property Act, corresponding to Ontario Land Titles Act); **see also** Federal Real Property Act, S.C. 1991, c. 50, s.C. 1991, c. 50, s. 14 (no person acquiring any federal real property by prescription); *Scott v. Pickell* (1984), 45 O.R. (2d) 158 (C.A.) (s. 23(1) of Limitations Act not barring sale proceedings brought ten years after right of action accruing; s. 23(1) applying to action for recovery of money out of land, not action for recovery of land; immediate object of action being to sell land so as to create fund of money).

§488 The Land Titles Act protects only possessory titles in existence at the date of first registration and expressly prevents their subsequent acquisition, thus excluding the operation of the Limitations Act.[1]

1. Land Titles Act, R.S.O. 1990, c. L.5, s. 51; Limitations Act, R.S.O. 1990, c. L.15, s. 4; *Gatz v. Kiziw*, [1959] S.C.R. 10; **but see** *Hurren v. Hurren* (1995), 11 R.F.L. (4th) 12 (Ont. Gen. Div.) (under s. 11 of Limitations Act, R.S.O. 1990, c. L.15, separate possessions occurring when wife leaving home; husband having continuous exclusive possession for 17 years thereafter; husband having possession for sufficient time to extinguish wife's interest under s. 4 of Limitations Act; registration of home under Land Titles system not preventing husband from acquiring wife's interest by adverse possession).

§489 This provision of the Land Titles Act does not mean that a claim of an adjoining owner to possessory title acquired prior to first registration cannot be asserted under the Act on an application for first registration by someone else. However, the failure of the possessory claimant to file any notice of objection upon the application for first registration is fatal to the possessory claim.[1]

1. *Mills v. Star Quality Homes Ltd.* (1978), 21 O.R. (2d) 39 (C.A.); see Land Titles Act, R.S.O. 1990, c. L.5, ss. 44(3), 51(1); **see also** *Bovey v. Gananoque (Town)*, [1992] 2 S.C.R. 5; affirming (1990), 38 O.A.C. 276 (C.A.) (plaintiff failing to meet onus to prove possessory title to leased water lot; nothing causing limitation period to start to run after plaintiff taking possession of boathouse under bill of sale; bill of sale simply conveying boathouse; whatever interest plaintiff's father previously having in water lot being that of tenant at will; no adverse possession); *Keil v. 762098 Ontario*

Inc. (1992), 24 R.P.R. (2d) 244 (C.A.) (neighbour's long usage of driveway extinguishing owner's title to overlapping land; owner appealing on basis that neighbour not demonstrating that use by neighbour inconsistent with use owner intending to make of land, and that eventual development of sidelot not interfered with by laying of gravel and passage of vehicles; appeal dismissed; owner's argument overlooking rule that use by neighbour having to conflict with use being made by owner during limitation period; owner's decision to develop land coming long after possessory title vesting in neighbour); *Sherrah v. Serkeyn*, 1992 CarswellOnt 3124 (Ont. C.A.); reversing, 1990 CarswellOnt 1463 (Ont. Gen. Div.) (plaintiff failing to discharge onus of proving that acts sufficient to establish adverse possession being performed on disputed piece of land for longer than ten years; *Sawyer v. North York (City)* (1992), 27 O.M.B.R. 464 (certain surplus hydro lands, zoned as semi-public open space, offered to city; city refusing to purchase; lands sold to private developer seeking to construct houses; applicant requiring zoning by-law amendment to permit residential use; city's approval of amendment appealed on ground that neighbours having acquired prescriptive right to use "public"lands; hydro company having leased part of lands for garden plots; appeal dismissed; lands not having acquired public use by prescription; opponents failing to establish that public use carried on for over 60 years, and in fact hydro company's use of lands specifically permitted by lease during past 60 years).

6. CHARGES UNDER ACT

§490   Every registered owner may in the manner prescribed by the Land Titles Act charge[1] his or her land with the payment of money; and the charge, when registered, confers upon the chargee a charge upon the interest of the chargor as appearing in the register, subject to the encumbrances and qualifications to which such interest is subject, but free from any unregistered interests in the land.[2] Only the registered owner can charge lands that are registered under the Land Titles Act.[3]

1. **See** Mortgages (as to rights of chargees and assignees of charges, powers of sale, foreclosures, etc.).

2. Land Titles Act, R.S.O. 1990, c. L.5, s. 93 [am. 1998, c. 18, Schedule E, s. 135]; **see also** Land Registration Reform Act, R.S.O. 1990, c. L.4, ss. 2 [re-en. 1998, c. 18, Schedule E, s. 93], 6, 7 [am. 1998, c. 18, Schedule E, s. 94], 8 [am. 1994, c. 27, s. 85(1), (2);; 1998, c. 18, Schedule E, s. 95], 9-13; *G. Grossi Plumbing & Heating Inc. v. North American Life Assurance Co.* (1983), 3 P.P.S.A.C. 94 (Ont. H.C.) (s. 96 giving chargee right to take rents and profits of charged property in event of default of payment; mortgagee entitled to employ notices of attornment to that end; "profits" clearly applying to rental supplements owing by Ontario Housing Corp.).

3. Land Titles Act, R.S.O. 1990, c. L.5, s. 68.

§491   The Land Titles Act speaks of a charge, not of a mortgage, and it is clear from the whole scheme of the Act that legal title does not pass to a chargee.[1]

1. *Kennedy v. Agricultural Development Board* (1926), 59 O.L.R. 374 (H.C.) (although chargee not obtaining legal title, relationship of landlord and tenant may be created between chargee and chargor by attornment clause in charge so as to create right of distress); **see also** Land Registration Reform Act, R.S.O. 1990, c. L.4, s. 6.

§492   As a matter of conveying, a charge under the Land Titles Act cannot be regarded as a mortgage; but the Act provides that a charge may be enforced in the same manner and under the same circumstances by foreclosure or sale as if the land had been transferred by mortgage.[1] Any final judgment or order of a court of record, so long as it stands, is conclusive as to the matters determined by it; and a land registrar must give full effect to an order of foreclosure made by the court. The land registrar is not entitled to demand proof that the order was properly made and that the proper parties were served with notice, but is entitled to proof that there has been no appeal or application to reopen the foreclosure.[2]

> 1. Land Titles Act, R.S.O. 1990, c. L.5, s. 99 [am. 1998, c. 18, Schedule E, s. 137]; **see also** *Re West* (1928), 61 O.L.R. 540 at 544 (C.A.); *Canadian Financial Co. v. First Federal Construction Ltd.* (1982), 22 R.P.R. 38 (Ont. C.A.); leave to appeal to S.C.C. refused (1982), 41 N.R. 353n (S.C.C.) (chargee not obliged to go behind register to obtain guarantors' names; guarantors also lacking any interest in land; chargee not required to serve guarantors with notice of sale).
>
> 2. *Re West* (1928), 61 O.L.R. 540 at 544 (C.A.).

§493   Where a charge purports to authorize the chargee to furnish or assist in furnishing an apartment building upon the lands charged, and in connection therewith to pay any unpaid purchase money owing for any of the chattels and to add any such sums to the principal sum secured by the charge, such sums to form a charge upon the lands and to bear interest, the charge cannot be entered on the register, as it is impossible to state the amount of the principal sum which the charge secures in respect of possible payments for chattels.[1]

> 1. *London Life Insurance Co. v. Maloney* (1932), 41 O.W.N. 314 (H.C.).

§494   The Land Titles Act does not prohibit a trust; it only prohibits entering the trust upon the register. So long as the parties to a charge enter into an agreement which is embodied in the charge and the agreement discloses no trust, the land registrar is not concerned and must register the agreement no matter what the facts may be.[1]

> 1. *Canadian Credit Men's Assn. v. Dunfield*, [1933] O.W.N. 659 (H.C.); *Randvest Inc. v. 741298 Ontario Ltd.* (1996), 5 R.P.R. (3d) 198 (Ont. Gen. Div.) (inclusion of terms of trust as adjunct to deed not deemed notice of trust); **see also** Land Titles Act, R.S.O. 1990, c. L.5, s. 62.

7. TRANSFER OF CHARGES UNDER ACT

§495   The registered owner of a charge may, in the manner prescribed by the Act, transfer the charge, and the transfer when registered confers on the transferee the ownership of the charge free from any unregistered interests therein.[1]

1. Land Titles Act, R.S.O. 1990, c. L.5, ss. 101(1)-(3); **see also** *Ovington Investments Ltd. v. Rexdale Holding (Toronto) Ltd.* (1974), 5 O.R. (2d) 320 (Co. Ct.); *Roboak Developments Ltd. v. Lehndorff Corp.* (1987), 47 R.P.R. 275 (Ont. Div. Ct.); affirming (1986), 39 R.P.R. 194 (H.C.) (doctrine of actual notice applicable under Land Titles Act; defendant as assignee of first charge taking subject to any interest of plaintiff of which defendant having actual notice at time of assignment of charge).

§496 Although the Land Titles Act provides that every transfer of a charge is subject to the state of account upon the charge between the chargor and the chargee, this provision must be read in conjunction with the Conveyancing and Law of Property Act,[1] which in effect provides that a receipt for consideration money endorsed on a mortgage is to be, in favour of a subsequent purchaser not having notice that the money acknowledged to be received was not in fact paid, sufficient evidence of the payment of the consideration.[2] Thus, where a registered transferee of a charge has no notice that the consideration acknowledged by the chargor to have been paid has not in fact been paid, the registered transferee is not affected by the fact of non-payment and is entitled to foreclose the charge.[3]

1. Conveyancing and Law of Property Act, R.S.O. 1990, c. C.34, s. 7.

2. Land Titles Act, R.S.O. 1990, c. L.5, s. 101(4); **see also** *Dodds v. Harper* (1916), 37 O.L.R. 37 (H.C.).

3. *Dodds v. Harper* (1916), 37 O.L.R. 37 (H.C.).

8. EFFECT OF ACT ON UNREGISTERED INTERESTS

§497 Until a transfer is actually registered, a transferor is deemed to be the owner of the land.[1] While the system might be said to be one for the registration of title rather than of deeds, execution and delivery of the instrument of transfer in the prescribed form, particularly when accompanied by the affidavits required for registration, confers a title in equity until registration, and that title is good for all purposes except as against some other title that might obtain priority by being recorded.[2]

1. Land Titles Act, R.S.O. 1990, c. L.5, s. 86.

2. *Hooper v. Hooper*, [1953] O.R. 753 (C.A.).

§498 The Land Titles Act recognizes the existence of unregistered estates, and although a transferor retains the legal estate until the transfer is registered, the transferee pending registration is in equity the real owner for whose benefit the transferor holds the legal estate on trust.[1]

1. *Guest v. Cochlin* (1929), 64 O.L.R. 165 (C.A.).

9. PROTECTION UNDER ACT FOR TRANSFEREES FOR VALUABLE CONSIDERATION

§499 A transfer for valuable consideration of land registered with an absolute title, when registered, confers on the transferee an estate in fee simple in the land transferred, together with all rights, privileges and appurtenances belonging or appurtenant thereto, subject to the encumbrances, if any, noted on the register; and such liabilities, rights and interests, if any, as are declared for the purposes of the Act not to be encumbrances unless the contrary is expressed on the register.[1]

> 1. Land Titles Act, R.S.O. 1990, c. L.5, s. 87; *Bucovetsky v. Cook* (1910), 1 O.W.N. 998 (K.B.); **see also** Land Registration Reform Act, R.S.O. 1990, c. L.4, s. 5 [am. 1992, c. 32, s. 17] (implied covenants on transfer).

§500 Under the Land Titles Act, a registered transferee for valuable consideration has more complete protection than the first registered owner.[1] A transfer for valuable consideration of land registered with a qualified title, when registered, has the same effect as a transfer for valuable consideration of the same land registered with an absolute title, except that such a transfer does not affect the enforcement of any right or interest appearing by the register to be excepted.[2]

> 1. *Farah v. Glen Lake Mining Co.* (1908), 17 O.L.R. 1 (C.A.).
>
> 2. Land Titles Act, R.S.O. 1990, c. L.5, s. 88.

§501 A transfer for valuable consideration of land registered with a possessory title does not affect or prejudice the enforcement of any right or interest adverse to or in derogation of the title of the first registered owner; otherwise, such a transfer, when registered, has the same effect as a transfer for valuable consideration of an absolute title.[1] A transfer of registered land made without valuable consideration is subject, so far as the transferee is concerned, to any unregistered rights subject to which the transferor held it; but otherwise, when registered, in all respects and in particular as respects any registered dealings on the part of the transferee, it will have the same effect as a transfer of the same land for valuable consideration.[2]

> 1. Land Titles Act, R.S.O. 1990, c. L.5, s. 89.
>
> 2. Land Titles Act, R.S.O. 1990, c. L.5, s. 90.

10. EFFECT OF ACT ON TRANSFEREES WHO DO NOT GIVE VALUABLE CONSIDERATION

§502 A transfer of land registered under the Act, if made without valuable consideration, is subject, so far as the transferee is concerned, to any unregistered estates, rights, interests or equities subject to which the transferor held the same.[1]

1. Land Titles Act, R.S.O. 1990, c. L.5, s. 90; **see also** *John Macdonald & Co. v. Tew* (1914), 32 O.L.R. 262 (C.A.) (unregistered mortgage having priority over registered assignment for benefit of creditors); *Marcobalt Mining Syndicate Ltd. v. Gray*, [1955] O.R. 761 (C.A.) (transfer not shown to have been for valuable consideration; held to be subject, so far as transferee concerned, to any unregistered interests or equities subject to which transferor held land).

11. TRANSMISSION OF REGISTERED LANDS ON DEATH OF OWNER

§503 The fact of any person having become entitled to any land or charge in consequence of the death of a registered owner must be proved in the prescribed manner.[1]

1. Land Titles Act, R.S.O. 1990, c. L.5, s. 124 [am. 2000, c. 26, Schedule B, s. 12(8)]; **see also** Federal Real Property Act, S.C. 1991, c. 50, s. 20 (grants to deceased persons not void).

§504 A devisee of land brought under the land titles system cannot require the land registrar to register the will under which the devisee claims, after the expiry of three years from the death of the testator, in a case where the will has not been admitted to probate in Ontario; the land registrar has the right to require such evidence as he or she, in his or her discretion, deems necessary, and ordinarily a registrar should require probate of the will by a Surrogate Court in Ontario before he or she registers the will.[1]

1. *Re Gund* (1923), 53 O.L.R. 371 (H.C.).

§505 Where land has been transferred to a person beneficially entitled thereto within three years after the death of the registered owner, or has become vested in the person beneficially entitled thereto under the Estates Administration Act, the land registrar, upon application and upon production of satisfactory evidence showing that all the debts of the deceased registered owner have been paid and the creditors notified, may either delete the reference to the unpaid debts from the register or register the person beneficially entitled to the land without reference to the unpaid debts of the deceased registered owner.[1]

1. Land Titles Act, R.S.O. 1990, c. L.5, s. 125 [am. 2000, c. 26, Schedule B, s. 12(9)]; Estates Administration Act, R.S.O. 1990, c. E.22.

12. EFFECT OF ACT ON EXECUTIONS

§506 No registered land is bound by any writ of execution until a copy of the writ, delivered by the sheriff, has been received and recorded by the land registrar.[1]

1. Land Titles Act, R.S.O. 1990, c. L.5, s. 136(2) [re-en. 1998, c. 18, Schedule E, s. 152(1)]; *Robinson v. Moffatt* (1916), 37 O.L.R. 52 at 60 (C.A.); *Gibb v. Jiwan*, 1996 CarswellOnt 1222 (Ont. Gen. Div.) (purchaser accidentally failing to register transfer of parcel from vendor; writ of seizure and sale not affecting land transferred to purchaser prior to filing of writ).

§507 No sale or transfer under a writ of execution is valid as against a person purchasing for valuable consideration before entry of the writ is made, although the purchaser may have had notice of the writ.[1]

1. Land Titles Act, R.S.O. 1990, c. L.5, s. 136(3) [re-en. 1998, c. 18, Schedule E, s. 152(1)].

§508 Where a person applies for registration of an instrument and claims that a writ of execution apparently affecting land does not affect the land or charge, the person must produce such evidence thereof as the land registrar considers necessary. The registrar may: require all interested parties to be notified of the application; decide the question him or herself or direct an issue to be tried or a case to be stated; and make such order as to costs as the registrar considers just.[1]

1. Land Titles Act, R.S.O. 1990, c. L.5, s. 137; **see also** *Vilneff v. Waugh* (1926), 31 O.W.N. 79 (H.C.) (on appeal, matter remitted to land registrar to direct trial of issue as required by section).

13. BANKRUPTCY OF REGISTERED OWNER

§509 Although no person other than the registered owner is entitled to transfer registered land, the Act provides that the land registrar may enter as owner of land any person who is entitled to such land by virtue of any power conferred by a statute, whether the person so entitled claims directly under the power or through a succession of transfers or transmissions.[1]

1. Land Titles Act, R.S.O. 1990, c. L.5, s. 80.

14. REGISTRATION OF CAUTIONS

(a) Registered Land

§510 A person claiming to have an interest in registered land or in a registered charge of which that person is not the registered owner may apply to the land registrar for registration of a caution so that the registered owner cannot deal with the land or charge without the consent of the cautioner.[1]

1. Land Titles Act, R.S.O. 1990, c. L.5, s. 128(1); *Ovington Investments Ltd. v. Rexdale Holding (Toronto) Ltd.* (1974), 5 O.R. (2d) 320 (Co. Ct.) (plaintiff starting action for breaches of warranty and guarantee by vendor; caution registered by plaintiff against purchase money charge transferred to vendor; not necessary to obtain

certificate of lis pendens before applying for caution); **see also** *Hawksmoor Investments Ltd. v. Marr Construction Ltd.*, [1973] 1 O.R. 313 (H.C.); affirmed [1973] 1 O.R. 820n (Div. Ct.) (application to remove respondent's caution allowed where respondent having right of first refusal but failing to exercise right in refusing to match offer made for land, thereby defeating interest in land).

§511 Although a person may be entitled to compensation from the owner of registered land, that person cannot register a caution under the Act unless he or she claims to be a person interested in the land.[1] A cautioner must be a person interested in the lands; in what way that person is interested does not matter, so long as the interest is one recognizable by law. Mere relationship to the owner is not enough; but any claim upon or derived from the owner or one who has an estate or interest in the land in respect of which legal or equitable relief could be given is sufficient.[2]

1. *Kay v. White Silver Co.* (1907), 9 O.W.R. 712 (Ch.); affirmed, 10 O.W.R. 10 (C.A.).

2. *Clagstone v. Hammond* (1897), 28 O.R. 409 (Ch.) (Land Titles Act relating mainly to conveyancing; whatever dealing giving valid claim to call for or receive conveyance being "interest" within scope of statute; cautioner, as appointee or nominee of purchaser of one-third interest, having standing under Act); *Singer v. Singer* (1979), 24 O.R. (2d) 14 (H.C.) (claim under Family Law Reform Act, S.O. 1978, c. 2, for interest in property of spouse's corporation; caution vacated, as plaintiff lacking registrable interest in land).

§512 After a caution has been registered, the land registrar cannot, without the consent of the cautioner, register any dealing with the land or charge.[1]

1. Land Titles Act, R.S.O. 1990, c. L.5, s. 129(1); *Diplock v. Richmond*, [1954] O.R. 54 (H.C.).

§513 In assessing the registrability of a claim of a proposed cautioner the master should not try out the rights of the parties or go into the merits respecting any question, but should satisfy him or herself that a bona fide claim has been sworn to for the purpose of registration, and that if an action has been brought, the claim affects the land.[1]

1. *Diplock v. Richmond*, [1954] O.R. 54 (H.C.).

§514 A caution registered before June 16, 1999, ceases to have effect five years from June 16, 1999, if the date that the caution ceases to have effect is not specified in the caution or by the Act, or if there is a date specified in the caution or by the Act, the earlier of that date and five years from the date of registration of the caution.[1] However, the registered owner of the land or any other person having an interest in the land or the charge may, on application to the land registrar, have the land registrar delete the entry of the caution from the register if the applicant has served a notice of the application on the cautioner at least 60 days before making the application.[2]

1. Red Tape Reduction Act, 1998, S.O. 1998, c. 18, Schedule E, s. 151(2).

2. Land Titles Act, R.S.O. 1990, c. L.5, s. 129(3) [re-en. 1998, c. 18, Schedule E, s. 150(1); am. 1998, c. 18, Schedule E, s. 150(2)].

§515   A caution registered under the Land Titles Act on or after June 16, 1999, ceases to have effect 60 days from the date of its registration and may not be renewed.[1]

1. Land Titles Act, R.S.O. 1990, c. L.5, s. 128(4) [re-en. 1998, c. 18, Schedule E, s. 149(1); am. 1998, c. 18, Schedule E, s. 149(2)].

§515.1   The land registrar must delete the entry of a caution from the register as soon as practicable when the caution ceases to have effect or the land registrar receives a withdrawal of the caution in the prescribed form.[1]

1. Land Titles Act, R.S.O. 1990, c. L.5, s. 129(7) [re-en. 1998, c.18, Schedule E, s. 150(3)].

§516   A caution registered under the Land Titles Act amounts to no more than the notice of an adverse claim equivalent to a lis pendens, and expires by lapse of time or otherwise as may be directed by the court in an action.[1]

1. *Ontario (Attorney General) v. Hargrave* (1906), 11 O.L.R. 530 (Master); **see also** *Bowgray Investments Ltd. v. Fournier* (1988), 67 O.R. (2d) 173 (H.C.); affirmed (1991), 3 O.R. (3d) 384 (C.A.) (plaintiff selling property to purchaser in 1975; parties entering into agreement whereby purchaser holding rear parcel in trust for plaintiff; caution registered; property subsequently sold to third party and then to fourth party, subject to agreement; in 1985, fourth party selling entire property to fifth party without notice of agreement; plaintiff's action for declaration that fifth party having no interest in rear parcel dismissed; caution expiring in 1981; amendments to Land Titles Act necessitating such result; fifth party under no obligation to obtain actual notice).

§517   To register a caution, a party need not apply for and issue a certificate of lis pendens; it is sufficient that an action claiming an interest in the lands be commenced.[1] A caution may be vacated if due diligence is not used in the prosecution of the action, or if it is shown that the action was a mere frivolous proceeding, or if the cautioner is not a person interested in the lands within the meaning of the Land Titles Act.[2]

1. *Aldo v. Dellelce* (1977), 2 R.P.R. 41 (Ont. H.C.); **see also** *Ovington Investments Ltd. v. Rexdale Holding (Toronto) Ltd.* (1974), 5 O.R. (2d) 320 (Co. Ct.).

2. *Skill v. Thompson* (1908), 17 O.L.R. 186 (C.A.); *Diplock v. Richmond*, [1954] O.R. 54 (H.C.); **see also** *Lucky v. Cancelliere* (1981), 19 R.P.R. 24 (Dist. Ct.) (circumstances under which order to vacate caution refused); *Bank of Montreal v. James Main Holdings Ltd.* (1982), 23 R.P.R. 180 (Ont. H.C.); affirmed on other grounds (1982), 28 C.P.C. 157 (Div. Ct.) (affidavit in support of application for caution not fully and completely disclosing bank's position; bank having no possible interest in land; caution removed).

§518 After notice has been served on the cautioner it is not the duty of the land registrar to try the rights of the parties, but merely to satisfy him or herself that a bona fide claim had been sworn to for the purpose of registration;[1] or the caution may be vacated upon the giving of satisfactory security.[2] But nothing in the Land Titles Act requires the land registrar to try the rights of the parties in a summary way, the jurisdiction of the courts in this respect not being ousted.[3]

1. *Kay v. White Silver Co.* (1907), 9 O.W.R. 712 (Ch.); affirmed (1907), 10 O.W.R. 10 (C.A.); see *Yemen v. Mackenzie* (1906), 7 O.W.R. 866 (C.A.); *Diplock v. Richmond*, [1954] O.R. 54 (H.C.).

2. *Diplock v. Richmond*, [1954] O.R. 54 (H.C.).

3. *Skill v. Thompson* (1908), 17 O.L.R. 186 (C.A.) (overruling opinion of Clute J. in *Hebert v. O'Brien* (1907), 9 O.W.R. 172; **see also** *Davmark Developments Ltd. v. White* (1974), 5 O.R. (2d) 269 (H.C.) (lack of jurisdiction in Supreme Court Judge in chambers with respect to application to remove caution).

§519 Where a caution has been registered by a person claiming under an agreement to purchase, and an action for specific performance of the agreement has already been commenced, the land registrar is justified in refusing to vacate the caution, and it is proper that the caution be allowed to stand, pending diligent prosecution of the action, without requiring security.[1]

1. *Skill v. Thompson* (1908), 17 O.L.R. 186 (C.A.); *Brown v. Clendennan* (1911), 2 O.W.N. 1013 (H.C.).

§520 The filing of a counterclaim in an action in which the title to lands is brought into question does not constitute notice of the claim to a transferee who at the time of the transfer was not a party to the action.[1]

1. *Farah v. Glen Lake Mining Co.* (1908), 17 O.L.R. 1 (C.A.).

§521 The Land Titles Act provides that any person who registers a caution without reasonable cause is liable to make to any person who might sustain damage by its registration such compensation as may be just.[1]

1. Land Titles Act, R.S.O. 1990, c. L.5, s. 132; *Ontario (Attorney General) v. Hargrave* (1906), 11 O.L.R. 530 (Master) (claim against Crown because of wrongful registration of caution).

(b) Unregistered Land

§522 A person having or claiming an interest in unregistered land which entitles that person to object to any disposition thereof without his or her consent may apply to the land registrar for the registration of a caution entitling him or her to notice of any application that may be made for the registration of the land.[1]

1. Land Titles Act, R.S.O. 1990, c. L.5, s. 43(1)

15. COSTS OF APPLICATIONS UNDER ACT

§523   An applicant under the Land Titles Act is prima facie liable to pay all costs, charges and expenses incurred by or in consequence of the application, except where parties whose rights are sufficiently secured without their appearance object, or where any costs, charges or expenses are incurred unnecessarily or improperly.[1]

> 1. Land Titles Act, R.S.O. 1990, c. L.5, s. 170(1) [am. 1993, c. 27, Sched.].

§524   The land registrar may order costs, either party and party or solicitor and client, to be paid by or to any person who is a party to a proceeding under the Act, and may give directions as to the fund out of which the costs shall be paid.[1] If any person disobeys an order of the land registrar as to costs, the registrar may certify the disobedience to the court, whereupon, subject to appeal, the order may be enforced as if it were an order of the court.[2]

> 1. Land Titles Act, R.S.O. 1990, c. L.5, s. 170(2); **see also** *Ross v. Stobie* (1891), 14 P.R. 241 (Ont. Ch.) (when ordering caution vacated, local land registrar having power to order payment of solicitor and client costs and to give special direction that costs be taxed).
>
> 2. Land Titles Act, R.S.O. 1990, c. L.5, s. 170(4); **see also** *Craig v. Leslie* (1898), 18 P.R. 270 (Ch.) (Land Titles Act as it then read not contemplating enforcement of costs order of master of titles by appointment of receiver; present-day statute broader and, semble, permitting enforcement of such an order by appointment of receiver).

16. DISCHARGE OR MODIFICATION OF RESTRICTIVE COVENANTS

§525   Any restrictive condition or covenant attached to land may be modified or discharged by an order of the Superior Court of Justice.[1]

> 1. Conveyancing and Law of Property Act, R.S.O. 1990, c. C.34, s. 61 [am. 1994, c. 27, s. 6], 61(3), (4) [en. 1994, c. 27, s. 6] (exceptions); Land Titles Act, R.S.O. 1990, c. L.5, s. 119(5).

17. REGISTRATION OF PART OWNERS

§526   Two or more persons entitled to estates, rights or interests in land which if vested in one person would entitle that person to be registered as owner may apply to the land registrar to be registered as joint owners in the same manner and with the same incidents, as far as circumstances admit, in and with which an individual owner may be registered under the Act.[1]

> 1. Land Titles Act, R.S.O. 1990, c. L.5, s. 60.

§527   No person can be registered as owner of an undivided share in freehold or leasehold or of a charge apart from the other share or shares.[1]

Where the extent of a co-owner's interest is not shown on the register, the co-owner may: (a) transfer or charge a specified share in the land, or transfer a share in the charge, as the case may be, if the land registrar is satisfied, by an affidavit of all co-owners setting out the percentage or fractional interest that belongs to the transferor or chargor, that the transferor or chargor has a sufficient interest to transfer or charge such share; or (b) transfer or charge all of his or her unspecified share.[2]

1. Land Titles Act, R.S.O. 1990, c. L.5, s. 61(1).
2. Land Titles Act, R.S.O. 1990, c. L.5, s. 61(2).

§528   Where a joint tenant of land delivers a transfer of his or her interest to a third party without the concurrence of the other joint tenant, and a question arises as to whether such transfer ought to be accepted for registration having regard to the part ownership provisions, a joint tenant will be found to have a right to terminate the joint tenancy by transfer of the undivided share.[1]

1. Land Titles Act, R.S.O. 1990, c. L.5, s. 61; *Re Cameron*, [1957] O.R. 581 (H.C.).

18.   [Deleted].

§529 [Deleted].
§530 [Deleted].

19.   NOTICES UNDER ACT

§531   A purchaser for valuable consideration, when the instrument under which he or she claims is registered, is not affected by the omission to send any notice the Act directs to be given, or by the non-receipt of any such notice.[1]

1. Land Titles Act, R.S.O. 1990, c. L.5, s. 91; **see also** *Lord v. Ellis* (1914), 30 O.L.R. 582 (C.A.).

20.   RECTIFICATION OF REGISTER

§532   Subject to any estates or rights acquired by registration pursuant to the Land Titles Act, where any court of competent jurisdiction decides that any person is entitled to any estate, right or interest in or to any registered land or charge, and as a consequence of such decision the court is of the opinion that a rectification of the register is required, the court may direct that the register be rectified in such manner as may be considered just.[1]

1. Land Titles Act, R.S.O. 1990, c. L.5, s. 159; **see also** *John Macdonald & Co. v. Tew* (1914), 32 O.L.R. 262 (C.A.) (unregistered mortgage made by owner of land registered under Act having priority over registered assignment for benefit of creditors; court divided as to whether register should be rectified); *Perry v. Vise* (1919), 45 O.L.R. 117 (C.A.) (wrong lot named in transfer, charge and second transfer; rectification ordered so as to correct error and remedy wrong done to true owner).

21. EFFECT OF FRAUD ON TITLE OF REGISTERED OWNER

(a) General

§533   Subject to the provisions of the Land Titles Act with respect to registered dispositions for valuable consideration, any disposition of land or of a charge on land that would be fraudulent and void if unregistered is fraudulent and void in like manner despite registration.[1] This provision is, of course, of no avail as against purchasers in good faith without notice of the fraud who rely on the register.[2]

> 1. Land Titles Act, R.S.O. 1990, c. L.5, s. 155.
>
> 2. *Fawkes v. Ontario (Attorney General)* (1903), 6 O.L.R. 490 (Ch.) (plaintiff registered owner of lands induced by fraud of two persons to transfer lands to D; purported subsequent transfer from D forged; pretended transferee transferring in turn to two persons having been parties to original fraud on plaintiff; ultimately, transfer made to innocent purchaser for value without notice; parties to fraud being financially worthless; plaintiff not entitled to recover amount of which she had been "wrongfully deprived").

§534   The main purpose of the Land Titles Act is to assure the title of a purchaser from a registered owner, not to protect a registered owner against his or her own fraud.[1] However, the Act provides that any person who fraudulently procures, attempts to fraudulently procure, or is privy to the fraudulent procurement of any entry, erasure or alteration on the register is guilty of an offence and, on conviction, liable to imprisonment for not more than two years or to a fine of up to $1,000.[2]

> 1. *Skill v. Thompson* (1908), 17 O.L.R. 186 (C.A.), per Meredith J.A.
>
> 2. Land Titles Act, R.S.O. 1990, c. L.5, s. 156.

(b) Forgery

§535   Any forgery, erasure or alteration is void as between all parties or privies to the fraud.[1]

> 1. Land Titles Act, R.S.O. 1990, c. L.5, s. 156; Criminal Code, R.S.C. 1985, c. C-46, s. 134 [re-en. 1985, c. 27 (1st Supp.), s. 17].

22. ASSURANCE FUND

§536   The Land Titles Act provides for the formation of an assurance fund[1] for the indemnity of persons who may be wrongfully deprived of land or some estate or interest therein by reason of the land being brought under the provisions of the Act, or by reason of some other person being registered as owner through fraud, or by reason of any misdescription, omission or other error in a certificate of ownership of land or of a charge or in any entry on the register.[2]

1. Land Titles Act, R.S.O. 1990, c. L.5, s. 54.

2. Land Titles Act, R.S.O. 1990, c. L.5, s. 57(1).

§537   A person is not entitled to any compensation from the assurance fund on the ground of wrongful deprivation of land by reason of some other person having been fraudulently registered as owner, unless there has been an actual "deprivation", in its true meaning of an involuntary taking away.[1]

1. *Fawkes v. Ontario (Attorney General)* (1903), 6 O.L.R. 490 (Ch.).

23. REGULATIONS

§538   The Minister has the power to make regulations under the Land Titles Act.[1]

1. Land Titles Act, R.S.O. 1990, c. L.5, s. 163 [re-en. 1998, c. 18, Schedule E, s. 157 (1); am. 2000, c. 26, Schedule B, s. 12 (12)].

§538.1   The Director of Titles may make regulations prescribing forms and providing for their use.[1]

1. Land Titles Act, R.S.O. 1990, c. L.5, s. 163(2) [re-en. 1998, c. 18, Schedule E, s. 157 (1); am. 2000, c. 26, Schedule B, s. 12 (12)].

XV   Certification of Titles Act

1. POLICY AND INTENT OF ACT

§539 The Certification of Titles Act[1] provides the means whereby titles to land registered under the Registry Act may be certified and guaranteed by the Province of Ontario, and new roots of title created, thereby eliminating protracted delays in the investigation of titles. The Minister of Consumer and Business Services is responsible for the administration of the Act.[2]

    1.   Certification of Titles Act, R.S.O. 1990, c. C.6.

    2.   Certification of Titles Act, R.S.O. 1990, c. C.6, s. 2 [am. 1993, c. 27, Sched.; 2001, c. 9, Schedule D, s. 13].

2. APPLICATION UNDER ACT

§540 Anyone claiming a fee simple estate in land, including a person claiming on the basis of adverse possession, may apply to the director to have title certified. Such an application is deemed to be an action for recovery of land within the meaning of the Limitations Act.[1] A notice of application must be served on every person of a class designated by regulation.[2]

    1.   Certification of Titles Act, R.S.O. 1990, c. C.6, s. 4; Limitations Act, R.S.O. 1990, c. L.15; **see also** Federal Real Property Act, S.C. 1991, c. 50, s. 14 (no person acquiring any federal real property by prescription).

    2.   Certification of Titles Act, R.S.O. 1990, c. C.6, s. 5.

§541 Any person having a claim that is adverse to or inconsistent with the claim of the applicant may file a statement of his or her claim with the Director of Titles at any time before the certificate of title is executed. Where a statement of claim is filed, the director must afford an opportunity for a hearing to determine the validity of the claim, or may instead refer the matter to a judge of the Superior Court of Justice for determination.[1]

    1.   Certification of Titles Act, R.S.O. 1990, c. C.6, s. 6 [am. 1993, c. 27, Sched.; 2000, c. 26, Schedule B, s. 4]; **see also** Bovey v. Gananoque (Town), [1992] 2 S.C.R. 5; affirming (1990), 38 O.A.C. 276 (C.A.) (plaintiff failing to meet onus to prove possessory title to leased water lot; nothing triggering limitation period after plaintiff taking possession of boathouse under bill of sale; bill of sale merely conveying boathouse; whatever interest plaintiff's father previously having in water lot being that of tenant at will; no adverse possession); Keil v. 762098 Ontario Inc. (1992), 24 R.P.R. (2d) 244 (C.A.) (court determining that neighbour's long usage of driveway extinguishing owner's title to overlapping land; owner appealing on basis that neighbour not demonstrating that neighbour's use being inconsistent with use owner intending to make of land, and that eventual development of sidelot not being interfered with by laying of gravel and passage of vehicles; appeal dismissed; owner's argument overlooking rule that use by neighbour having to conflict with use by owner during limitation period; owner's decision to develop land coming long after posses-

sory title vesting in neighbour); *Sherrah v. Serkeyn*, 1992 CarswellOnt 3124 (Ont. C.A.); reversing, 1990 CarswellOnt 1463 (Ont. Gen. Div.) (plaintiff failing to discharge onus of proving that acts sufficient to establish adverse possession being performed on disputed land for longer than ten years).

§542   An applicant is prima facie liable for all costs, charges and expenses incurred as a result of the application, except where objection is raised by parties whose rights are sufficiently secured without their appearance or where any costs, charges or expenses are incurred unnecessarily or improperly. The director may order either party and party or solicitor and client costs to be paid to or by any party to a certification proceeding.[1]

1. Certification of Titles Act, R.S.O. 1990, c. C.6, s. 8 [am. 1993, c. 27, Sched.; 1998, c. 18, Schedule 8, s. 43; 2000, c. 26, Schedule B, s. 4].

§543   Any party aggrieved by a decision of the director may appeal to a judge of the Superior Court of Justice for appeal by way of trial de novo. From that judge's decision, a further appeal lies to the Divisional Court.[1]

1. Certification of Titles Act, R.S.O. 1990, c. C.6, s. 7 [am. 1998, c. 18, Schedule E, s. 42; 2000, c. 26, Schedule B, s. 4].

3. EFFECT OF CERTIFICATE OF TITLE

§544   When the director has completed an examination under Pt. I of the Act and any matter referred to a judge has been finally disposed of, or where a hearing has been held and the director has made a decision and any appeal therefrom has been disposed of, or where the time for appeal has elapsed and no appeal has been taken, the director may issue a certificate of title to all or part of the land or may dismiss the application.[1] The certificate of title, once granted, is then registered by the director in the land registry office for the registry division in which the land is situate.[2]

1. Certification of Titles Act, R.S.O. 1990, c. C.6, s. 9, Pt. I (ss. 4-9).

2. Certification of Titles Act, R.S.O. 1990, c. C.6, s. 13.

§545   The director may, of his or her own initiative and without holding a hearing, certify the title of the owner of land included in a plan,[1] as of the date of registration of the plan.[2] Subject to compliance with the Certification of Titles Act, the director may issue a certificate of title to all or part of the land included in the plan.[3]

1. Certification of Titles Act, R.S.O. 1990, c. C.6, s. 10 ("plan" meaning plan of subdivision registered under Registry Act).

2. Certification of Titles Act, R.S.O. 1990, c. C.6, s. 11(1); **see also** Certification of Titles Act, R.S.O. 1990, c. C.6, s. 11(2)-(4), (5) [am. 2000, c. 26, Schedule B, s. 4(1)¶[5], (6), (7).

3. Certification of Titles Act, R.S.O. 1990, c. C.6, s. 12(1); **see also** Certification of Titles Act, R.S.O. 1990, c. C.6, s. 12(2).

§546 Upon registration, a certificate of title is conclusive as of the day, hour and minute stated therein that the title of the person named as owner of the land described therein was absolute and indefeasible as regards the Crown and all persons whomsoever, subject only to the exceptions, limitations, qualifications, reservations and conditions, covenants, restrictions, charges, mortgages, liens and other encumbrances mentioned therein, and is conclusive that every application, notice, publication, proceeding and act that ought to have been made, given or done has been made, given or done in accordance with the Act.[1]

1. Certification of Titles Act, R.S.O. 1990, c. C.6, s. 14; *Moore v. Moore* (1974), 49 D.L.R. (3d) 479 (S.C.C.) (effect where conveyance obtained by fraud).

§547 Where, as a result of the registration of a certificate of title, any person is wrongfully deprived of an interest in land, such person may apply for compensation pursuant to the Land Titles Act.[1]

1. Certification of Titles Act, R.S.O. 1990, c. C.6, ss. 15, 16; **see also** Land Titles Act, R.S.O. 1990, c. L.5, ss. 26 [re-en. 1998, c. 18, Schedule E, s. 117], 57(6)-(9), (10) [am. 1998, c. 18, Schedule E, s. 125], (11)-(13), 58, 162(3).

§548 Where the director becomes aware of a possible error in a certificate of title, he or she may give notice of the possible error by registering a notice in the prescribed form, and the notice gives notice of the possible error to all persons until the notice is deleted from the abstract index by the director.[1]

1. Certification of Titles Act, R.S.O. 1990, c. C.6, s. 17.

§549 Subject to the regulations, the director, on his or her own initiative or upon application by any interested person may, before the receipt of any conflicting instruments or after notifying all persons interested, upon such evidence as appears to the director sufficient, correct errors and omissions in any certificate of title by issuing an amendment to the certificate.[1]

1. Certification of Titles Act, R.S.O. 1990, c. C.6, s. 18(1); **see also** Certification of Titles Act, R.S.O. 1990, c. C.6, s. 18(2)-(7).

§550 Proceedings under the Certification of Titles Act are not to be abated or suspended by any death or change of interest, but in any such event, the director may require notice to be given to persons becoming interested, or may make an order for discontinuing, suspending or carrying on the proceedings or otherwise as the director considers proper.[1]

1. Certification of Titles Act, R.S.O. 1990, c. C.6, s. 19.

XVI   Subdivision Control

1. REGISTRATION OF SUBDIVISION PLANS UNDER REGISTRY ACT

§551   A plan of subdivision cannot be registered unless it has been prepared by a surveyor and complies with the regulations under the Registry Act.[1] An instrument that refers to a plan of subdivision cannot be registered unless the plan is registered.[2]

    1. Registry Act, R.S.O. 1990, c. R.20, s. 78(1); *Boland v. Baker*, [1953] O.R. 239 (H.C.); affirmed [1953] O.W.N. 519 (C.A.); *Windsor (City) v. Canadian Pacific Railway* (1922), 52 O.L.R. 83 (H.C.); affirmed (1923), 54 O.L.R. 222 (C.A.) (effect of registration of plan where question as to dedication of highway); *Morton v. St. Thomas (City)* (1881), 6 O.A.R. 323; **see also** Planning and Zoning.

    2. Registry Act, R.S.O. 1990, c. R.20, s. 78(2).

§552   A plan of subdivision of land within an area to which the Land Titles Act applies may not be registered under the Registry Act.[1]

    1. Registry Act, R.S.O. 1990, c. R.20, s. 78(9); **see also** Registry Act, R.S.O. 1990, c. R.20, s. 78(10) (plan of subdivision within certification area), (11) (Condominium Act descriptions); **but see** Land Titles Act, R.S.O. 1990, c. L.5, s. 144(2), (3) [re-en. 1998, c. 18, Schedule E, s. 155].

§553   The land registrar may not register a plan of subdivision unless every person who appears by the abstracts index to be the owner of the land has endorsed the plan as owner and unless every person who appears by the index to be a mortgagee consents in writing, but nothing in this provision requires the consent to any such plan of the owner of an easement or of a right in the nature of an easement in respect of the land.[1] The consent of a mortgagee is not required unless the plan of subdivision dedicates part of the mortgaged land as a public highway.[2]

    1. Registry Act, R.S.O. 1990, c. R.20, s. 78(5); *Chisholm v. Oakville (Town)* (1885), 12 O.A.R. 225; *Nevitt v. McMurray* (1886), 14 O.A.R. 126.

    2. Registry Act, R.S.O. 1990, c. R.20, s. 78(6); **see also** Registry Act, R.S.O. 1990, c. R.20, s. 78(3).

§554   Where a duly executed instrument does not conform and refer to the proper plan, and where, in the registrar's opinion, it would be impossible or inconvenient to obtain a new instrument containing the proper description, the instrument may be registered if it is accompanied by a statement in proper form.[1]

    1. Registry Act, R.S.O. 1990, c. R.20, s. 86(1) [am. 1998, c. 18, Schedule E, s. 253(1)]; *Thompson v. Webster* (1866), 25 U.C.Q.B. 237; *Re Henderson* (1898), 29 O.R. 669; *Rathbun v. Culbertson* (1875), 22 Gr. 465.

§555   No instrument referring to an unregistered plan may be registered unless an instrument referring to such plan has already been registered in respect of the same land, and if the registrar objects to the registration of an instrument on the ground that it refers to an unregistered plan, he or she may refuse to register it unless the person desiring its registration refers the registrar to the number of an instrument registered in respect of the same land referring to the unregistered plan.[1]

    1.   Registry Act, R.S.O. 1990, c. R.20, s. 85.

§556   No plan of survey or subdivision to which the Planning Act applies can be registered without being approved under that Act.[1]

    1.   Registry Act, R.S.O. 1990, c. R.20, s. 78(7); *Cardinal v. O'Malley*, [1952] O.W.N. 817 (H.C.); affirmed [1952] O.W.N. at 818 (C.A.) (refusal to register plan of subdivision where not approved under Planning Act).

§557   When lands are described by a reference to a plan, either expressly or by implication, the plan is considered as incorporated with the deed, and the contents and boundaries of the land conveyed, as defined by the plan, are to be taken as part of the description, just as though an extended description to that effect were in words contained in the body of the deed itself.[1]

    1.   *Grasett v. Carter* (1884), 10 S.C.R. 105 at 114; *Ferguson v. Winsor* (1884), 11 O.R. 88 (C.A.).

§558   A plot of land left vacant on a plan, and not marked as a lot or a road, may be closed up or utilized in any way by the owner.[1]

    1.   *Scottish Ontario Investment Co. v. Bayley* (1908), 12 O.W.R. 130 (C.A.); *Whitehouse v. Hugh*, [1906] 1 Ch. 253; affirmed [1906] 2 Ch. 283; **see also** *Ihde v. Starr* (1909), 19 O.L.R. 471 (Div. Ct.); affirmed (1910), 21 O.L.R. 407 (C.A.) (effect of sales of lots under plan showing spaces marked "private entrance" and "park" in creating easements in favour of purchasers).

2. REGISTRATION OF SUBDIVISION PLANS UNDER LAND TITLES ACT

§559   Where land is being subdivided for the purpose of being sold or conveyed in lots, the person making the subdivision must register in the proper land titles office a plan prepared by an Ontario land surveyor.[1] The person by whom or on whose behalf a plan is registered must sign the plan.[2] However, it is always to be remembered that no plan of subdivision to which the Planning Act applies can be registered unless approved under that Act.[3]

    1.   Land Titles Act, R.S.O. 1990, c. L.5, s. 161(2).

    2.   Land Titles Act, R.S.O. 1990, c. L.5, s. 161(3).

    3.   Planning Act, R.S.O. 1990, c. P.13; **see** Planning and Zoning.

3. EXTENSION OF LAND TITLES ACT BY JUDGE'S PLAN

§560   The Land Titles Act may be extended in its application by its adoption by a municipal council. Where the application of the Act has been so extended to a county, city or town, the council can pass a by-law ordering any land within the municipality to be registered under the Act.[1]

1. Land Titles Act, R.S.O. 1990, c. L.5, s. 31 [am. 1998, c. 18, Schedule E, s. 120].

XVII   Recovery of Land

1. NATURE OF ACTION

§561   Although the action referred to in the Rules of Civil Procedure as the action for the recovery of land now takes the place of the old action of ejectment, some of the peculiarities of the old action have been preserved, since they were necessary for the purpose of doing justice.[1] The action is brought to recover possession, and where possession is not sought, an action for the establishment of title or for the establishment of title and recovery of rents is not an action for the recovery of land under the Rules of Civil Procedure.[2]

> 1. *Gledhill v. Hunter* (1880), 14 Ch. D. 492; *Ball v. Cathcart* (1888), 16 O.R. 525 at 528 (C.A.); **see also** *Central Trust Co. of New York v. Algoma Steel Co.* (1903), 6 O.L.R. 464 (H.C.) (action by mortgagee for possession of land included in mortgage held to be action "for the recovery of land" within meaning of Unorganized Territory Act, R.S.O. 1897, c. 109, under which district courts having jurisdiction in such actions); *Independent Order of Foresters v. Pegg* (1900), 19 P.R. 80; *Chartered Trust & Executor Co. v. Pinel* (1926), 31 O.W.N. 104 (H.C.); affirmed (1927), 31 O.W.N. 391 (Div. Ct.) (action by mortgagee); *Kendell v. Ernst* (1894), 16 P.R. 167 (action for cancellation of mining lease, and for possession of location if successful in securing cancellation; held not to be action of ejectment).

> 2. *Gledhill v. Hunter* (1880), 14 Ch. D. 492; *Hyde v. Toronto Theatre Co.* (1910), 17 O.W.R. 380 (C.P.) (right to recover damages for being "ejected" from place such as theatre).

§562   Ejectment was a special form of trespass based upon a wrongful dispossession. Originally the remedy for trespass of land was damages only. Gradually the recovery of the land by the dispossessed tenant was added, and ultimately ejectment became the mode by which conflicting claims to title, as well as possession, were adjudicated. Gradually also the claim for substantial damages or mesne profits beyond the nominal damages in the main action came to be severed from the ejectment, and on judgment for the latter the courts treated the unlawful possession as a continuing trespass for which an action lay.[1]

> 1. *Minaker v. Minaker*, [1949] S.C.R. 397; **see also** *Lemesurier v. Macaulay* (1893), 20 O.A.R. 421.

§563   A special endorsement for possession of land as against an alleged trespasser is proper.[1]

> 1. *Phillips v. Kranjcec* (1977), 4 C.P.C. 91 (Ont. H.C.).

2. WHO MAY RECOVER POSSESSION

(a) General

§564   Once it is shown that the plaintiff is entitled to possession, the court will give the plaintiff possession whether his or her right is legal or equitable,[1] and a person who relies only on prior possession is entitled to eject all but a person having a better right.[2] The right to possession is sufficient to support the action even against the person having the legal title.[3] Where a plaintiff in ejectment recovers land of which he or she has been dispossessed for 20 years, and is put into possession by the sheriff, the defendant is not precluded from trying the right again and, in an action brought by him or her, relying upon his or her title acquired by the 20 years' possession.[4]

1. *Thorne v. Williams* (1887), 13 O.R. 577 (C.A.); *Jones v. McGrath* (1888), 16 O.R. 617 (C.A.); *Turley v. Benedict* (1882), 7 O.A.R. 300.

2. *Poulin v. Eberle* (1911), 20 O.W.R. 301 (K.B.); *Vancouver (City) v. Vancouver Lumber Co.*, [1911] A.C. 711; *Dominion Improvement & Development Co. v. Lally* (1911), 24 O.L.R. 115 (C.A.); *Freeman v. Allen* (1866), 6 N.S.R. 293 (C.A.); *Tobin v. McDougall* (1914), 47 N.S.R. 470 (C.A.).

3. *Doe d. Barker v. Crosby* (1850), 7 U.C.Q.B. 202 (purchaser in possession under agreement for sale letting vendor into possession under express condition to restore possession on happening of certain event, which occurring); **see also** *Robinson v. Smith* (1859), 17 U.C.Q.B. 218.

4. *Moran v. Jessup* (1858), 15 U.C.Q.B. 612; *Hirschfield v. Hirschfield* (1933), 7 M.P.R. 423 (N.S.C.A.); *Welland (County) v. Buffalo & Lake Huron Railway* (1870), 30 U.C.Q.B. 147; affirmed (1871), 31 U.C.Q.B. 539 (railway company failing to tender or pay compensation before taking possession of land for railway purposes; failure not entitling owner to maintain ejectment); *McLean v. Great Western Railway* (1873), 33 U.C.Q.B. 198; *McDonald v. McDonald* (1873), 34 U.C.Q.B. 369 (right of one devisee to maintain ejectment against other devisees); **see also** *Ryerse v. Teeter* (1878), 44 U.C.Q.B. 8, *Grant v. McLennan* (1866), 16 U.C.C.P. 395.

§565   Possession is good against all the world except the person who can show a better title than can the person in possession.[1] Where, at the opening of his or her case, a plaintiff relies on a prima facie title by possession, and the defendant proves prior possession, the plaintiff cannot then attempt to defeat the defendant's claim by attempting to show a landlord and tenant relationship between the parties. Rather, the plaintiff should go into his or her case fully at the outset.[2]

1. *Asher v. Whitlock* (1865), L.R. 1 Q.B. 1, quoted in *Cosbey v. Detlor* (1911), 18 O.W.R. 479 (C.A.).

2. *Doe d. Osborne v. McDougall* (1849), 6 U.C.Q.B. 135; **see also** *Kennedy v. Freeth* (1863), 23 U.C.Q.B. 92 (parties claiming by different titles); *McKinley v. Bowbeer* (1853), 11 U.C.Q.B. 86; *Doe d. Lawrence v. Stalker* (1849), 5 U.C.Q.B. 346.

§566 If a person having title can get into possession of land that is in the actual occupation of a person having no title, he or she may continue such possession, and the person who was in actual occupation cannot succeed in ejectment against him or her on the strength merely of his or her own former occupation. The presumption of title which arises from simple occupation or possession is answered and the person who has no title cannot succeed against the person who has both title and possession.[1]

1. *Emmerson v. Maddison*, [1906] A.C. 569 (P.C.) [N.B.].

§567 A plaintiff is not deprived of the right to rely on prior possession where he or she also brings forward documents in an unsuccessful attempt to establish title to the property in question.[1]

1. *Poulin v. Eberle* (1911), 20 O.W.R. 301 (K.B.).

§568 Where neither party has the paper title, and the defendant has shown the same or a better kind of possession extending over many years and shown that his or her claim has been acknowledged by the persons through whom the plaintiff purports to claim, the plaintiff is not entitled to succeed.[1]

1. *Mann v. Fitzgerald* (1912), 3 O.W.N. 488 (Ch.); affirmed (1912), 3 O.W.N. 1529 (C.A.); *Doe d. Eaton v. Thomson* (1860), 9 N.B.R. 461.

§569 A plaintiff cannot found a claim on the weakness of the defendant's title, but must recover on the strength of his or her own title.[1] Consequently, possession is a good defence against anyone who does not prove a better title;[2] but the person in possession is not allowed to deny the title under which he or she went into possession.[3]

1. *Danford v. McAnulty* (1883), 8 App. Cas. 456 (H.L.); *Jones v. Stone*, [1894] A.C. 122; **see also** *Sinclair v. McNeil* (1903), 2 O.W.R. 915; *Brown v. Touks* (1918), 14 O.W.N. 46 (H.C.); *Hartley v. Maycock* (1897), 28 O.R. 508 (Ch.); *Gaudet v. Hayes* (1906), 3 E.L.R. 152 (P.E.I.S.C.); *Donnelly v. Ames* (1896), 27 O.R. 271 (Q.B.) (plaintiff's action failing where another person having title, despite fact that defendant not claiming under or in privity with such other person).

2. *Danford v. McAnulty* (1883), 8 App. Cas. 456 (H.L.); *McLeod v. Austin* (1875), 37 U.C.Q.B. 443; *Tobique Salmon Club v. McDonald* (1904), 36 N.B.R. 589 (C.A.).

3. *Dods v. McDonald* (1905), 36 S.C.R. 231; *White v. Thompson* (1911), 18 O.W.R. 478 (Div. Ct.); *Eccles v. Paterson* (1862), 22 U.C.Q.B. 167; *McLeod v. Welsh* (1859), 4 N.S.R. 85 (C.A.); **but see** *Lyster v. Kirkpatrick* (1866), 26 U.C.Q.B. 217.

§570 A person in possession of land who is acting as owner and exercising the ordinary rights of ownership has good title against everyone but the rightful owner. If the rightful owner does not come forward and assert his or her title by process of law within the applicable limitation period, his or her right is forever extinguished and the possessory owner acquires an absolute title.[1]

1. *Parry v. Clissold*, [1907] A.C. 73; *McAllister v. Defoe* (1915), 8 O.W.N. 175 (Div. Ct.); affirmed (1915), 8 O.W.N. 405 (C.A.) (aboriginal chief proving title by length of possession); *McDiarmid v. Hughes* (1888), 16 O.R. 570 (H.C.) (corporation empowered by statute to hold lands for definite period; no provision as to reverter; corporation holding beyond period; only Crown able to take advantage of situation; not defence to action of ejectment that lands acquired by plaintiff from corporation after period fixed by statute); *Jeffbrett Enterprises Ltd. v. Marsh Bros. Tractors Inc.* (1996), 5 O.T.C. 161 (Ont. Gen. Div.) (defendant in actual, open, notorious, exclusive and visible possession for over 10 years; defendant entitled to order vesting title in disputed lands); *Leichner v. Windy Briars Holdings Ltd.* (1997), 31 O.R. (3d) 700 at 710 (Ont. C.A.); additional reasons to (1996), 6 R.P.R. (3d) 91 (Ont. C.A.); which reversed, 1996 CarswellOnt 1237 (Ont. Gen. Div.) (plaintiffs not establishing that predecessor in title had either actual possession or intention to exclude true owner); *MacArthur v. Pilon*, 1996 CarswellOnt 1594 (Ont. C.A.) (plaintiff having exercised ordinary rights of ownership for period in excess of limitation period; adverse possession established); *Newfoundland v. Collingwood* (1994), 116 Nfld. & P.E.I.R. 194 (Nfld. T.D.); reversed in part on other grounds (1996), 1 R.P.R. (3d) 233 (Nfld. C.A.) (adverse possession; seasonal use; shared use in accordance with custom); *Commission de l'aménagement agricole (N.-B.) c. Côté* (1996), 179 N.B.R. (2d) 378 (N.B.C.A.) (claimant's predecessor acknowledging owner's title and ending occupation period); *Raso v. Lonergan* (1996), 5 R.P.R. (3d) 65 (Ont. Gen. Div.) (statutory declaration of predecessors in title indicating fenced boundary remaining in same location for 17 years; enclosure strongest possible evidence of adverse possession); *Campbell v. Nicholson* (1997), 26 O.T.C. 241 (Ont. Gen. Div.) (plaintiff and his predecessors establishing requisite intent and taking all reasonable steps to exclude true owners from possession by using lands for 14 years as horse corral and large perennial garden).

§571   An equitable defence is allowable in an action for ejectment.[1]

1. *Milner v. Ringwood* (1875), R.E.D. 123 (N.S.C.A.); *Souci v. Ouillette* (1906), 37 N.B.R. 393 (C.A.).

§572   A tenant of a mortgagee has a right to set up the title of the latter as a defence to an action of ejectment brought by the person holding the equity of redemption. Where on a sale of land the purchaser who has paid the purchase price is put into possession by the vendor, neither the vendor nor his or her heirs or assigns with notice can maintain ejectment against the purchaser or his or her successors in title, even though no deed of conveyance was made in pursuance of the sale.[1]

1. *Halifax Power Co. v. Christie* (1914), 48 N.S.R. 264; affirmed (October 12, 1915), (S.C.C.).

§573   Several plaintiffs, each claiming an undivided interest, do not have to prove joint title, or any privity, but may maintain a joint action upon separate titles.[1]

1. *Bradley v. Terry* (1861), 20 U.C.Q.B. 563; *Humphreys v. Hunter* (1870), 20 U.C.C.P. 456 (trustees under Religious Institutions Act, C.S.U.C. 1859, c. 69, main-

taining ejectment in own individual names, with description "as trustee", etc., stating name of congregation or religious body for which they were trustees, according to description in deed of conveyance).

§574   A joint tenant may not maintain an action for possession against a lessee without joining the other joint tenant.[1]

1. *Tepper v. Abramsky*, [1937] O.W.N. 142 (C.A.).

§575   In an action for possession of land against a person who is without title, a tenant in common can recover judgment for the possession of his or her share only.[1]

1. *Barnier v. Barnier* (1892), 23 O.R. 280 (Q.B.); *Tobin v. McDougall* (1914), 47 N.S.R. 470 (C.A.); *McDonald v. McDonald* (1884), 17 N.S.R. 298 (C.A.); **see also** *Adamson v. Adamson* (1889), 17 O.R. 407 (right to possession as between tenants in common).

(b) Effect of Prior Possession

§576   The possession necessary to bar the title of the true owner must be an actual, constant, visible occupation by some person or persons to the exclusion of the true owner for the full statutory period; it must not be equivocal, occasional or for a special or temporary purpose.[1]

1. *Ledyard v. Chase* (1925), 57 O.L.R. 268 (C.A.); *Sherren v. Pearson* (1887), 14 S.C.R. 581; *McConaghy v. Denmark* (1880), 4 S.C.R. 609; *McIntyre v. Thompson* (1901), 1 O.L.R. 163 (C.A.); *Coffin v. North American Land Co.* (1891), 21 O.R. 80 at 87 (C.A.); **see also** *McDonald v. Brown* (1920), 19 O.W.N. 223 (C.A.); **see also** Limitation of Actions.

§577   Possession must be considered having regard to the circumstances. Acts implying possession in one case may be wholly inadequate to prove it in another. Factors such as the character and value of the property, the suitable and natural mode of using it, and the course of conduct the proprietor might reasonably be expected to follow with due regard for his or her own interests vary greatly under various conditions and are to be taken into account in determining the sufficiency of a possession.[1]

1. *Kirby v. Cowderoy*, [1912] A.C. 599 (P.C.); **see also** *Hunter v. Farr* (1864), 23 U.C.Q.B. 324 (sufficiency of evidence of possession); *Covert v. Robinson* (1865), 24 U.C.Q.B. 282; *Shaver v. Jamieson* (1866), 25 U.C.Q.B. 156; *Henderson v. Morrison* (1868), 18 U.C.C.P. 221; *Thompson v. Bennett* (1872), 22 U.C.C.P. 393; *Wallbridge v. Gilmour* (1872), 22 U.C.C.P. 135; *Heck v. Knapp* (1861), 20 U.C.Q.B. 360; *Doe d. Miller v. Tiffany* (1848), 5 U.C.Q.B. 79; *Nelles v. White* (1881), 29 Gr. 338; varied (C.A.); affirmed (1885), 11 S.C.R. 587; *McLeod v. Austin* (1875), 37 U.C.Q.B. 443; *Mulholland v. Conklin* (1872), 22 U.C.C.P. 372; *Mitchell v. Hawkins* (1922), 22 O.W.N. 105 (C.A.) (construction and effect of instrument executed by person in possession).

§578   The existence of a fence does not constitute occupation, but it is evidence, albeit not conclusive, that such occupation as exists is exclusive.[1]

> 1. *Ledyard v. Chase* (1925), 57 O.L.R. 268 (C.A.) (allowing cattle to roam land and using land for shooting and trapping not sufficient acts of possession).

(c) Estoppel

§579   Where possession has been accepted under a certain title, the persons so accepting and those claiming under them are estopped from disputing that title.[1]

> 1. *Dods v. McDonald* (1905), 36 S.C.R. 231; **see also** Estoppel; Landlord and Tenant.

§580   In an action brought by a landlord, if it is shown that the defendant obtained possession of the land from the plaintiff's tenant by representing that he or she had the title to it and by threatening to eject the tenant, the defendant is estopped from disputing the landlord's title and setting up an adverse title.[1]

> 1. *White v. Nelles* (1885), 11 S.C.R. 587; **see also** *Mulholland v. Harman* (1884), 6 O.R. 546 (C.A.); **see also** Landlord and Tenant.

(d) Grantee from Crown

§581   In an ejectment suit brought by a patentee from the Crown, the plaintiff is entitled to succeed where he or she makes out a clear case under the Crown grant and the defendant does not show any grant or conveyance from the Crown or any legal title or equitable interest in the land under any statutory provision.[1]

> 1. *Farmer v. Livingstone* (1880), 5 S.C.R. 221; additional reasons (1882), 8 S.C.R. 140; **see also** Federal Real Property Act, S.C. 1991, c. 50, ss. 21 (correction of defective grants), 22 (relief from inconsistent transactions); *Maddison v. Emmerson* (1904), 34 S.C.R. 533 at 556; affirmed [1906] A.C. 569 (P.C.).

3. COMPENSATION FOR IMPROVEMENTS

§582   Mesne profits may be recovered, though not specifically demanded, at least where the plaintiff is a landlord suing an overholding tenant, and without the plaintiff having obtained possession.[1] Under the head of special damages, a jury may take into consideration the plaintiff's trouble and inconvenience by reason of being kept out of possession, and the costs of ejectment.[2]

> 1. *Montreuil v. Ontario Asphalt Co.* (1922), 63 S.C.R. 401 at 438; **see also** *White v. Thompson* (1911), 2 O.W.N. 667 (Div. Ct.).

> 2. *Montreuil v. Ontario Asphalt Co.* (1922), 63 S.C.R. 401.

§583   Where the dispossessed occupant is held entitled under the Conveyancing and Law of Property Act.[1] to compensation for lasting improvements made by him or her, such compensation is set off against the mesne profits; but in such an action, the right of recovery in respect of improvements, being entertained merely in mitigation of damages, cannot exceed the amount to which plaintiffs may be found entitled under their claim for mesne profits. The purpose of allowing the set-off is to restrict plaintiff's recovery to the actual damages he or she has sustained.[2]

1. Conveyancing and Law of Property Act, R.S.O. 1990, c. C.34, s. 38; *Noel v. Page* (1995), 47 R.P.R. (2d) 116 (Ont. Gen. Div.); additional reasons, 1996 CarswellOnt 1236 (Ont. Gen. Div.) (defendant's residence and well significantly encroaching on plaintiff's property; balance of convenience favouring defendant although defendant's conduct reckless; defendant entitled to conveyance of improved portion of plaintiff's land in exchange for compensation).

2. *Montreuil v. Ontario Asphalt Co.* (1922), 63 S.C.R. 401; *McCarthy v. Arbuckle* (1880), 31 U.C.C.P. 405; *Derrickson v. Ellis* (1904), 3 O.W.R. 828 (K.B.); **see also** *Canada v. Smith*, [1983] 1 S.C.R. 554 [Can.] (province setting aside land for Indian reserve prior to 1867; squatters occupying land sited in reserve since 1838; Indians surrendering lands of federal Crown in 1895; squatter writing letter in 1919 to federal Crown stating desire for grant of Indian land upon which then residing; federal Crown suing on behalf of Indians to recover possession; action dismissed; federal Crown successfully appealing and ordered to compensate for improvements; squatter appealing; appeal allowed).

4. PRACTICE AND PROCEDURE

(a) Joinder

§584   A plaintiff may add claims for an injunction to restrain waste and for an accounting for waste already committed.[1]

1. Rules of Civil Procedure, R.R.O. 1990, Reg. 194, R.R.O. 1990, Reg. 194, RR. 5, 9, 10, 12 [re-en. O. Reg. 770/92, s. 5; am. O. Reg. 288/99, s. 9], 38, 55; **see also** *White v. Nelles* (1885), 11 S.C.R. 587; *French v. Taylor* (1876), 23 Gr. 436; *Fraser v. Robbins* (1857), 2 P.R. 162.

(b) Parties

§585   All persons found in possession of land may be made defendants,[1] without reference to whether their possession is joint or several.[2] Where plaintiff relies on an equitable right, the owner of the legal estate should be made a party.[3]

1. **See also** *Lemesurier v. Macaulay* (1893), 20 O.A.R. 421 (effect of death of plaintiff or defendant; *Irvine v. Macaulay* (1894), 16 P.R. 181; *Johnston v. McKenna* (1863), 3 P.R. 229; *Davy v. Cameron* (1857), 15 U.C.Q.B. 175; *Doe d. Hay v. Hunt* (1855), 12 U.C.Q.B. 625; **see** Parties.

2. *Bannerman v. Dewson* (1866), 17 U.C.C.P. 257.

3. *Cope v. Crichton* (1899), 30 O.R. 603 (Ch.).

§586 Where a defendant is not is possession and claims no right to the land, he or she is entitled to have his or her name struck out.[1] An application by a defendant to have his or her name struck out on the above ground is regularly made before appearance, although the application will be entertained after appearance where the justice of the case requires it.[2] One defendant is not entitled to have his or her name struck out at the trial, on disclaiming all right to possession, in order to be called as witness for his or her co-defendants.[3]

1. *Hall v. Yuill* (1858), 2 P.R. 242.

2. *Anglo-Canadian Mortgage Co. v. Cotter* (1879), 8 P.R. 111; *Kerr v. Waldie* (1867), 4 P.R. 138 (action against landlord, and against tenant in actual possession; held, though with much doubt, that tenant's name might be struck out; practice laid down in *D'Arcy v. White* (1865), 24 U.C.Q.B. 570 questioned).

3. *Grogan v. Adair* (1857), 14 U.C.Q.B. 479; **see also** *Bannerman v. Dewson* (1866), 17 U.C.C.P. 257 (right of defendant to have name struck out); *Weaver v. Burgess* (1871), 5 P.R. 307; *Robinson v. Bell* (1859), 9 U.C.C.P. 21; *D'Arcy v. White* (1865), 24 U.C.Q.B. 570; *Johnston v. Oliver* (1883), 9 P.R. 353; *Henderson v. White* (1873), 23 U.C.C.P. 78 (adding of parties); *Mitchell v. Smellie* (1870), 20 U.C.C.P. 389; *Ogilvie v. McRory* (1865), 15 U.C.C.P. 557; *Peebles v. Lotridge* (1860), 19 U.C.Q.B. 628 (substitution of defendant and insertion, by mistake, of original defendant's name as a co-defendant; effect on verdict).

(c) Enforcement of Orders

§587 An order for the recovery or delivery of the possession of land may be enforced by a writ of possession.[1] A writ of possession requires leave of the court, obtained on motion without notice or at the time an order entitling a party to possession is made. The court may grant leave only where it is satisfied that all persons in actual possession of any part of the land are in receipt of sufficient notice of the proceeding for which the order was obtained to have enabled them to apply to the court for relief.[2]

1. Rules of Civil Procedure, R.R.O. 1990, Reg. 194, R. 60.03; *Rudd v. Frank* (1899), 17 O.R. 758 (C.A.); *Toronto (City) v. Fisken* (1898), 29 O.R. 738 (in action by landlord, subtenants may be put out of possession under writ even though not parties to action).

2. Rules of Civil Procedure, R.R.O. 1990, Reg. 194, R. 60.10(1), (2); **see also** *Community Trust Co. v. Pollock* (1982), 36 C.P.C. 227 (Ont. Master) (spouse in possession of mortgaged lands must be party to proceedings for possession); *Kinross Mortgage Corp. v. Balfour* (1981), 33 O.R. (2d) 213 (H.C.) (leave refused where judgment for possession not obtained against mortgagor); *Jamort Investments Ltd. v. Fitzgerald*, [1968] 1 O.R. 541 (Master) (nature of material to be put before court).

§588   The court will not interpose summarily to deprive a plaintiff in ejectment of the full benefit of his or her writ by restraining him or her from
taking possession of part of the premises recovered, except in a very plain
case.[1]

1. *Hemmingway v. Hemmingway* (1854), 11 U.C.Q.B. 317; **see also** *Campbell v.
Royal Canadian Bank* (1872), 19 Gr. 334 (injunction requiring possession to be
redelivered to defendants pending appeal); *McDermott v. McDermott* (1868), 4 P.R.
252 (Ont. H.C.); *Fisher v. Johnston* (1866), 25 U.C.Q.B. 616.

Index to Fundamentals of Ontario Real Property Law

All references are to paragraph numbers.